ALL THIS AND SAILING, TOO
AN AUTOBIOGRAPHY

For the Kendal Library

[signature] 28 Jan 2000

ALL THIS AND SAILING, TOO

AN AUTOBIOGRAPHY

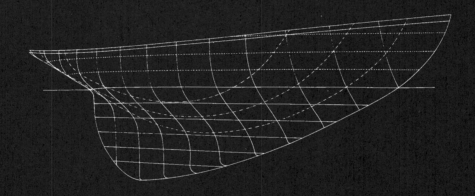

OLIN J. STEPHENS II

MYSTIC SEAPORT
MYSTIC, CONNECTICUT
1999

Cataloging-in-Publication data:

Stephens, Olin.
    All this and sailing, too / Olin J. Stephens II. - 1st ed. - Mystic, Conn.:
Mystic Seaport, 1999.
    p.: ill,. ports.; cm.
    Includes index.

    1. Stephens, Olin. 2. Naval architects-Biography. 3. Yacht designers-
Biography. I. Title.

VM140.S7A3

ISBN 0-913372-89-7

This book was edited by John Rousmaniere and Joseph Gribbins

Design by Clare Cunningham, Essex, CT
Printing by Thomson-Shore, Dexter, MI

The publication of this book was made possible by the generosity of the following friends and admirers of Olin J. Stephens II:

Charles Butt
Dayton T. Carr
Mr. and Mrs. Charles A. Dana III
E. Llwyd Ecclestone
A. Searle Field
Bernard H. Gustin
Anthony P. Halsey
Ted and Susan Hood
Joseph C. Hoopes
Commodore and Mrs. Robert L. James
Robert C. Kyle
Timothea S. Larr
Commodore Charles M. Leighton
Stanley and Martha Livingston
Robert and Margaret McCullough
Michael C. McMenemy
Mr. and Mrs. Albert Pratt
Thor H. Ramsing
Mr. and Mrs. Rudolph J. Schaefer III
James M. Schoonmaker
E. Newbold Smith
Frank V. Snyder
Sparkman & Stephens, Inc.
Robert G. Stone, Jr.
Mr. and Mrs. Michael B. Stubbs
Alexandra T. Thorne

Dark Harbor 20 Owners:

Harriet Aldrich Bering
Douglas Dillon
John L. Gardner
Dudley, Ethan and Haven Ladd
Charles M. Leighton
John B. Rogers
Daniel K. Thorne

CONTENTS

1

I was lucky: I had a goal. As far back as I can remember I wanted to design fast boats. First they were powerboats, like the early runabouts I saw on Lake George and Gold Cup hydroplanes I watched racing there in 1914, when I was six. But after my first sail on Barnstable Bay on Cape Cod the boats I wanted to design all carried sail. That commitment drove me to learn and understand (to the extent I could), and this is something I still enjoy — more now, I think, as I am free of professional bonds. Finding the way on the water was best of all.

I was nineteen when I worked at my first job in 1927. Sherman Hoyt had found an opening for me in the office of Henry J. Gielow in New York. I knew Sherman, a great racing skipper about my father's age, from sailing in the Six-Metre Class. He was also a yacht designer and worked in Gielow's office on sailing boats, although the principal business there was the design of large power yachts. I did brokerage plans: small-scale accommodation drawings of boats that had been listed for sale. The work was menial, and little more than paid for my commutation to Scarsdale and lunches, but I had the satisfaction of a regular job in my chosen field. I thought, as I still do, that one thing leads to another. The nature of those things will unfold in what follows.

I came to work with little to support my hopes beyond intense interest satisfied by sailing and reading. After high school, at my parents' insistence, I had attended MIT but dropped out after less than a year. I was suffering from jaundice at the time. For years I had studied, photographed and drawn boats with great concentration. With a good eye for boat shape, I had the ability to express it through the conventions of a lines drawing, a skill that had come with constant sketching. Structure was a less pressing concern for me then, although frequent visits to the building yards of City Island had shown me how a wooden boat was put together.

Typically my experience on the water was far more complete and valuable than my schooling. I say typically because so many of my colleagues had also learned their lessons on the water. Today I could not recommend that course because analysis of all the design elements provides assurance that a new boat will behave as expected. There are still surprises, but they are far less frequent than they were. Computer modeling and performance prediction can and should eliminate much of the guesswork that was accepted in the 1920s and 1930s. Of course, a sound engineering background has always been valuable, as demonstrated so well in the work of Nathanael Herreshoff, whose ability with structures made him the greatest yacht designer of all time. I worked as I could to overcome my lack of technical training, and my experience on the water was a big help.

My sailing education began inland as my grandparents spent their summers at Lake George, where several families of the next generation had cottages of their own. There were cousins and friends of similar age, and there was a fine sandy beach where the water deepened gradually. We all swam by the age of four or five years. Although there was virtually no sailing on this Adirondack lake, motor boating was active and by 1914 our small family fleet included two launches — a 30-footer with a fair turn of speed and a power dory with a single-cylinder, make-and-break engine for power, turning a controllable-pitch propeller. These were supplemented by several smaller boats including two beautiful cedar canoes made in Peterborough, Canada. One was a racing canoe, light and narrow. The other was for general use and was more rugged in both structure and size. As a boy I enjoyed these boats routinely and became fully at home on the water. Today I appreciate those canoes, especially, as examples of true art and I am ashamed to admit that I have no idea where they have gone.

The First World War played its part in changing all this. After my father's return in 1919 from army service in the Tank Corps, we spent our summers on salt water, first on Sandy Neck, which forms Barnstable Bay on the Massachusetts Bay side of Cape Cod, and for several years during the middle 1920s at Edgartown on Martha's Vineyard.

On the Cape we lived near the lighthouse on the tip of Sandy Neck, which then we reached, normally from Yarmouthport on the mainland, by outboard-powered skiff across the bay. We left the family car at the Yarmouthport fish factory, or freezer. We rented a small cottage from a local fisherman, Shirley Lovell, and acquired two boats, a very small gaff-rigged centerboard sloop called *Corker*, and a rugged small skiff fitted with the outboard. With none of the interruptions of town or club life, my brother Rod and I spent all our time in one boat or the other exploring the Bay.

Corker was delivered by truck from Osterville on an exciting day. She was launched near the fish factory and her simple rig went together quickly so that the inexperienced family crew were soon sailing down the narrow channel between the flats and following it across the bay. I do not remember the details of our arrival at Sandy Neck, but the first moment under sail I shall never forget. The quality of silent yet positive propulsion, the slight heel angle in the light air and the small train of waves opened by the hull had the quality of a new magic that has stayed with me ever since that day.

Sometimes we could have used a little more magic. Experience was our only teacher then, since neither Father nor Mother had more than rudimentary sailing ability. A nice afternoon sail gave us both exercise and embarrassment when, as the tide ran out, we realized that the only way we would get home for supper was on foot. By climbing over the side onto the eel grass we saw how the water dropped from our knees to our ankles, and quickly, pushing as hard as we could, got *Corker* back into the channel and sailed to our mooring.

Our sailing was a family project. Father, although used to the water, knew no more than we about sailing. He was the captain. Rod, Jr. was quick in his handling of rigging and mechanical devices of all kinds. He became sail-handler and crew. I enjoyed the tiller so much that the others gave up trying to pry me off. The rotation of positions that might have been reasonable was minimal because we gravitated to our roles. Happily this relationship was lasting. It continued through our professional lives as we worked together, each attending to the share of the work he did best, in the office and on the water. Rod took care of rigs, structures, and getting the new boats built, while I was responsible for general design, particularly the lines. I have from those early days concentrated on hull shapes and their influence on performance. The subject still fascinates me, although increasing age has brought with it a loss of agility as well as less tolerance of discomfort, and my active enjoyment of sailing has become less. Reluctantly I admit today that the important place in my life once occupied by sailing has been replaced by a computer.

As Rod and I learned sailing, Father played a continuing role, less active but equally supportive. Later, in what became Sparkman & Stephens, he played a major part as guide and advisor in setting up the firm. This he followed immediately by

ordering the construction of *Dorade* — undoubtedly the biggest boost of our early years. In 1934 he turned *Dorade* over to Rod and me as business and family affairs took more of his time. Later I will describe how, in his eighties and fully retired, he came into our office to help us through our busiest years.

During those summers in the 'twenties we sailed constantly. We learned from our mistakes and later we learned from experienced sailors. Barnstable Bay with its tidal flats and currents was a good classroom. We gradually progressed to larger boats and extended our range. West of the Cape we found a 30´ Great South Bay sloop with a centerboard and auxiliary power. Shirley Lovell, our fisherman-landlord, helped us bring her around through the Cape Cod Canal. One day, on our own, we sailed this boat from Sandy Neck over to Provincetown. Returning, we were not alert to an approaching thunder squall and were caught off Wellfleet carrying too much sail. We luckily escaped real trouble, but there was more excitement than necessary. It was a good lesson.

Three summers at Sandy Neck were followed by three at Edgartown, Martha's Vineyard, where there was more going on both ashore and afloat. We took little part in the activity on shore but continued to live in boats, sailing constantly. We saw yachts of all kinds coming and going, but took no part in the locally organized sailing. For whatever reason, my attitude was to put down local efforts as regimented and wasteful of sailing time. Rod and I were equally committed to boats, but I usually sailed alone in a new C.D. Mower design called *Flapper*, something like a conservative Laser. Rod, more mechanically inclined, spent many days in his outboard-powered skiff. On family picnics we went together, taking the skiff or sometimes both boats to explore Katama Bay and the reaches of Edgartown Harbor. This was in the early to middle 'twenties when a small outboard delivered about two and a half horsepower. We had a cousin who started racing outboards in those days. We rather scorned racing around courses, whether under sail or power. To us the real racing happened offshore.

We literally devoured the boating magazines so that we had to draw lots for which one either Rod or I could see first. I think the ones we scrapped over were *Yachting, Rudder, Motor Boat, Motor Boating,* and the British *Yachting Monthly.* We read all the articles and studied all the photographs. In the 1920s ocean racing was gaining participants and the number of long races was growing. We watched for the boats described in the magazines, and I remember well the day when John Alden's fisherman-type schooner *Malabar IV* sailed into Edgartown after winning the 1923 race to Bermuda. I sailed around her and around again without getting up the courage to say something to the famous designer. Five years later he would invite me to sail with him to Bermuda in another *Malabar.*

Malabar's visit came during the time Rod and I were increasingly anxious to be off cruising. Father did not share our enthusiasm; he had a wife and a daughter to be home with instead of roughing it with his boys. But he was a most understanding and supportive parent, and before the season of 1924 he acquired a tiny auxiliary yawl called *Tradscantia. Trad,* as we called her, was about 26′ overall with a gaff-headed rig and moderate draft. The mizzen was tiny but we felt its importance. In those days a 26-footer did not have the accommodations worked into that length today, but she had a trunk cabin and two people could sleep below, two more under a cockpit tent. She had been built by a very competent amateur, E.K. Merrill of Riverton, New Jersey, who shared our passion for sailing.

Trad was a great little boat and an important part of our learning as we brought her north and east through the Delaware and Raritan Canal, the Raritan River, the Staten Island Kills and on to the American Yacht Club on Long Island Sound, near our home in Scarsdale. Later we took her out to Edgartown, and this was our first real cruise. Our mentor that season and next was often Charles Dayton, a good friend of Father's. He helped me with the rudiments of piloting. The Merrills' son Owen, nicknamed "Jim," shared our interests and later became a crew member on *Dorade* and a draftsman in the early days of Sparkman & Stephens.

I recall *Trad* as a very attractive toy; she helped us to reach further, and reinforced the urge to cruise. By the next season our understanding parents had bought a real seagoing auxiliary ketch. She was *Sou'wester,* a boat we knew from our reading as the sistership of a ketch William Atkin had designed for William Nutting with thoughts of a transAtlantic race. *Sou'wester* was almost new, although she had been moved from the builder's yard in Port Jefferson to Chute and Bixby of Huntington, Long Island. She lay in their yard and we worked to commission her there as the sailing season approached. This 40′4″ x 11′6″ x 6′8″ ketch brought us many new experiences, including full initiation into the cruising fraternity. That spring we — Father, Rod and I — spent all our spare time in Huntington and found new friends there who were as committed to boats as we were, and whose experience was far wider than ours. Rod and I were lucky in Father's easy way of finding new friends.

The friend who was most helpful in bringing us new experiences was Robert H. Moore, a sailor from boyhood with ties to the New England fishing industry through his insurance office. He had a young family much like our own, which included two sons, Buck and Bobby, whose ages paralleled Rod's and mine. Another new friend was *Sou'wester*'s designer, Billy Atkin, who lived there in Huntington. He was helpful with the new boat and sympathetic with my ambitions and with our contrasting enthusiasm and lack of experience. After the usual commissioning chores, *Sou'wester* was launched and we sailed out of Huntington on a cruise to the eastward.

Again, we sailed to Edgartown and back. My mind holds some blanks and some vivid recollections. Many of the latter involve *Sou'wester*'s behavior. Determined to design yachts, I was constantly thinking and sketching shapes. Hull form was my big concern with its influence on performance and appearance. *Sou'wester* was heavy and consequently bulky. As experience grew, so did disappointment in her sailing ability. In the end she taught us the enjoyment of cruising, living on board and sailing into new harbors, but for us the joy of sailing was compromised when we worked with all our limited skill to sail *Sou'wester* to windward back and forth across the Sound and failing, until we had a fair tide, to weather a mark we had fought to reach most of the day. I think *Sou'wester* permanently set in my mind the feeling that there was something very wrong with a boat that was slow, particularly one that lacked windward ability. In one short summer I came to appreciate the difference between the pure pleasure of steering a smart and able boat and the drag, to me, of trying to sail one that does not respond.

Another recollection is of a windy afternoon when we sailed for shelter into the harbor of Westport, Massachusetts, as it breezed up. Sailing from Edgartown to the west we were disturbed, and I think too much alarmed, by the increasing strength of the wind. We decided we were ready to find a harbor. Today, looking back, I think we were more at risk when sailing into that narrow entrance than we would have been pushing along with a deep reef in the main or even with jib and mizzen, and reaching a more open harbor. Maybe I forget how poorly she sailed when close-hauled. I believe the rig was worse than the hull.

Thinking back to *Sou'wester* serves as a reminder of the changes in fittings and equipment that I have seen. *Sou'wester* had a short jibheaded (Marconi) ketch rig. The main and mizzen were set on mast hoops on large-diameter spars. Her auxiliary power was a single-cylinder Mianus two-cycle engine with make-and-break ignition. To reverse you had to reverse the rotation of the engine. Whatever the reason, if the engine ran more than an hour or so, the igniter became fouled with burnt oil and fuel, and I recall becoming adept in exchanging the igniter that failed for one that was fresh, cool, and clean. Meanwhile, when the hot one had cooled I would clean it and prepare it for another exchange. Thus I learned some of the mechanical skills associated with the one-lung engine. It was in *Sou'wester*, too, that I learned to avoid seasickness and got some experience with on-board cooking.

Aboard *Sou'wester* we had no instrumentation or communication equipment except, of course, a compass. We learned something about compass error, which became apparent when the boat heeled. George Sistare, the compass adjuster in Padanaram, diagnosed the cause as a section of iron pipe in the exhaust system which we had replaced by brass right there as we waited to continue our cruise.

As I was writing an early draft of this chapter in 1991, when I was 83, I heard the sad news of Buck Moore's death. Of course he was not the first of many friends to go. Only the week before I had driven to Christmas Cove, Maine, to attend a service for Pete Peterson, a long-time friend and guide when I visited Japan. But now we are looking at the 'twenties when our family and the Moores became close and did a lot of sailing together. My father was close with Bob, Sr. while Rod and I sailed with Buck and Bobby. The older Bob often said that he taught Rod and me to sail. Actually we had lived in boats from the time we had learned to walk and swim, but our learning lacked all formality and Bob took us in hand. He was an interesting and experienced teacher.

One of our best times was a cruise to Casco Bay, Maine, in Bob's mini-schooner *Widow*, a 30′ Atkin design and a reasonably smart sailer. The rig of this little cruising boat must have been a reflection of the vogue for schooners during the 'twenties, possibly coupled with Bob's association with commercial fishing. The rig is fast neither to windward nor running, but schooners can reach well, making them reasonably adapted to long races. However, the usually overhanging main boom makes for difficult handling as does the customary bowsprit. In the North Atlantic fishing fleet the rig worked well for heaving to with dories out, and the large crews were well able to handle the overhanging sails. The fishing schooners could reach fast as they returned to port with a trip of fish to bring quickly to market. But, on balance, I should not recommend the rig today.

Our first racing experience was due to Bob. He encouraged us to sail *Sou'wester* in a race around Block Island organized by the Bayside Yacht Club in which a limited use of auxiliary power was allowed. The result was a new experience but no silver. Measurement for time allowance was, I think, simple overall length, leaving sail area free. As budding yacht designers Rod and I worked out an extension of the mainsail for this race, a sort of raffee which we called "the circus tent." It was in no sense a technological breakthrough, but it belongs in this account largely to suggest Father's readiness to give his sons a chance to try out a radical scheme as well as the hope of the sons to use a casual (or incomplete) measurement rule as an invitation to gain advantage. I have frequently occupied both offensive and defensive positions on rule-beating. The approach seems now to be more sophisticated and more intense. It seems part of the game at the current, more aggressive levels of competition. I cannot say it was well justified in the Bayside kind of racing, but at that time the race was highly intense for me and for Rod. This subjective attitude makes it hard to apply the principle that ought to control perhaps all sporting competition: the existence of a common attitude among all the contestants.

During that summer with *Sou'wester* our family accumulated a good deal of sailing knowledge. As we summed up our ideas about boats we came to an opportunity to sell *Sou'wester*. During the next year, possibly for financial reasons, we sailed a 30′ one-design boat from Nova Scotia. We used her on Long Island Sound for day and overnight sailing while for more ambitious cruising Rod and I joined the Moores, father and two sons, in the Casco Bay cruise already mentioned. This Nova Scotia one-design, *Scrapper*, attracted us for two reasons: first she had been, we were told, designed by Bill Roué, designer of the champion fishing schooner *Bluenose*; and we were also told that she had been owned by Casey Baldwin, who was known to us through William Washburn Nutting's book *The Track of the Typhoon*, and a charter member of the Cruising Club of America. Later I became well-acquainted with Casey Baldwin and found him to be every inch the hero I had expected. These favorable circumstances did not prevent our new boat from leaking gallons through both bottom and deck. We tried to accept the discomfort and when, during the next winter, she was destroyed in a shipyard fire, none of us cried over the loss.

Once the leaks turned to our advantage. In May of the *Scrapper* year, still in school, Rod and I sailed off one Friday evening with a friend to the Sand Hole on Lloyds Neck. We beat over from Larchmont against the grey easterly that was soon to bring rain. We had supper and did everything we could to protect our bunks from the water dripping through the deck. Then we turned in for a miserable night. We were wet and we were cold. We discovered there was a limit to fun and we ran before the continuing east wind, shivering, back to Larchmont, thoroughly chilled and generally uncomfortable.

We tied up to our mooring (there were no slips then) and were enjoying our first pleasure in 24 hours in the hot showers of the Larchmont Yacht Club when word came that two new Six Metres were looking for crew. This was too good to pass up, and we found ourselves out again, feeling neither wet nor cold, because sailing in new Sixes with Clinton Crane and Sherman Hoyt was being in heaven. They had been two of the most successful sailors for more than 30 years; we knew their reputations well; we were in the right place at the right time.

I sailed in *Red Head* with Clinton Crane and Rod sailed in *Lanai* with Sherman Hoyt. Mr. Crane had left his early career as a yacht designer, versatile, successful and responsible, to become an executive of the St. Joseph Lead Co., but had continued to design racing boats for himself and his friends. Both of these new boats were his designs and *Lanai* became one of the best of a successful string. She was one of the first American Sixes to earn an international reputation. Sherman Hoyt was generally considered the best small-boat sailor on Long Island Sound. I have mentioned his association with the Gielow office and his help toward my first job. He designed some good Six Metres including *Lea*, a very fast Six under light Long Island Sound conditions. He later designed *Mistress*, the ocean racer owned by George Roosevelt, and he had an early success with his own Q-Boat, *Capsicum*, when she won the gold cup presented for that class during the celebration of the 300th anniversary of the founding of the Virginia colony at Jamestown.

Rod and I had equal enthusiasm for cruising and racing, but the itch to do more racing was taking precedence. In the spring of 1926, following the *Scrapper* season, the family bought *Alicia*, a boat of the Sound Schooner Class, designed by B.B. Crowninshield. She had been built in 1912 at the time of the NYYC "thirties" by a group who were not club members, and was one of a fleet of little schooners that were light and had been sailed hard. No longer new, *Alicia* needed shipyard work to make her tight, but as neither Rod nor I were paying it seemed worth it as she was quick and always fun to sail.

Alicia, built by Rice Brothers in Maine, measured 40′11″ x 7′11″ x 6′3″. The things that made her fun were related to her combination of Spartan accommodations, narrow beam and light displacement. Today her displacement/length ratio of 200 does not seem as low as it seemed then but her general character made her a great boat for a crew of boys rather than a family. Rod and I sailed her often with our friends, racing on the Sound and cruising in her to Mt. Desert, Maine, while the rest of the family made the trip by land. *Alicia* took us into the mainstream of yachting and we found it good. We raced on weekends on the Sound and sailed her in an early-season race to Block Island. On the Maine cruise, although we were not participants, we paralleled an Eastern Yacht Club race across the Gulf of Maine and thought we had sailed well. We had learned the racing advantage of doing everything possible to keep going well at night.

A day in that summer was special enough to stay clear in my mind, yet it was characteristic of the fun we had in our sailing. In *Alicia* that day I think we were four, Rod and I with our friends Buck Moore and Johnny Fox. We were in Padanaram, fogged in all of one day and anxious to go on toward Bar Harbor to meet our parents. In the morning the fog was holding and opinions were divided on the subject of getting on through Vineyard Sound and around Cape Cod and then on to Maine. Hoping for progress, I optimistically predicted that the fog would lift under the warmth of the sun, and we got up the hook in mid-morning. I think Rod, the real seaman, thought this was premature with the wind in the east and we agreed to head for Cuttyhunk where we could go in if the fog held.

The fog did just that; so after careful piloting took us across lower Buzzards Bay we sailed in past the tied-up lobsterboats and swordfishermen and anchored in the island's inner harbor. After a quick lunch, and possibly setting a second anchor, as the holding ground was not good, we took the towed dinghy ashore to explore Cuttyhunk. We found, as it was then, a large open hillside climbing to the south and sloping toward the water to the west. With energy I can only envy now we ran up the hill and into the bright sun while the fog still covered the sea below. As we scattered across the field of short grass we found, to our surprise and great pleasure, thousands of wild strawberries. We gobbled them up, and no dessert could have been so good. To top it off we watched the wind come around into the west. Back aboard *Alicia*, and as the fog lifted, we sailed up through Quick's Hole and on to the east through Vineyard Sound.

Racing *Alicia* had not merely whetted but advanced our interest in racing so that we were anxious to sail against the best competition. On Long Island Sound that meant the Six-Metre Class of day-racing boats about 33′ long, with a crew of four or five. Since they were not one-designs but built to the International Rule, which provided some variation, the Sixes were a great school for a young yacht designer. We had watched the Sixes since that chilly day when we had been recruited to sail in *Red Head* and *Lanai* with Clinton Crane and Sherman Hoyt. So we determined to sell *Alicia* and buy a Six. I think this led to our first meeting with Drake Sparkman, who came to play such a big part in my life. The sale of *Alicia* made possible the purchase of *Natka*, a good second-tier Six whose owner, Henry Plant, was building a new Crane-designed Six called *Clytie*.

Rod and I, usually with Father, had a good summer with *Natka*. It was fun, and it was another intense learning experience. We felt that we were sailing against the best in boats, crews and sails, and when we occasionally won the satisfaction was immense. Better still in some ways was the experience of always being in the fight. When we were beaten without making any bad mistakes we knew that the speed of a better boat had done it and we were in no way disheartened. Later, sailing my own designs, it was harder to be so philosophical.

The *Natka* summer was full of adventure and challenge. I remember one day when we were sailing north across the Sound in the usual southwesterly, following Sherman Hoyt in his *Saleema* by maybe two boat lengths. Both boats had to bear away for a tow of tug and barges headed west. Sherman cut things a bit fine and the wake of the heavy barge caught *Saleema* and swung her right up onto the barge's low afterdeck, almost hitting the captain, who was there peeling potatoes. As the man got up to push the boat free we swung off to avoid a repetition and passed to leeward of our famous rival. We waved as he got back on course, now well in our wake.

2

GETTING STARTED

I cannot say that my determination to design yachts became more firm in those years of family sailing, because it had been absolutely solid in my mind for years. But as I grew older and approached graduation from high school there was a sharper focus. My parents were willing if not enthusiastic about my career choice, and they had been very generous in their support of my and Rod's sailing. But there was difficulty about college because I didn't want to attend. I don't know just why. I think it was a profound suspicion of anything that suggested organized authority as well as two sources of impatience: I wanted to start serious design work, and I wanted to get married.

On page 20 is the 30´ *Kalmia*, the first S&S design with offshore capability. By no measure a breakthrough design, she took a first place in the long Gibson Island Race of 1929. She provided some evidence of youthful design ability and was a valuable experience in the year before *Dorade*. (Photo: Rosenfeld Collection 33855F)

My resistance was not lessened when I visited a well-known technical school on the banks of the Charles River in Cambridge, Massachusetts. In talking with one of the MIT professors, prominent in yacht design, I asked about the stability of a certain model with a very cutaway profile and consequently high ballast. His answer was that in a light-hulled and heavily-ballasted yacht there was no need to even think about stability. That is the way I understood it then. Today it seems almost incredible, so it is likely that I misunderstood him as he must have been thinking of stability as safety, while I was thinking of driving force; but the perception that he was talking nonsense made me more than ever dubious about such schooling.

This may be the place to say that I now have some good friends on the faculty of this same school who have made important contributions to the understanding of sailing performance and who further are committed and competent sailors. I have great respect for them and appreciate what they have done to improve the sport. Although I attended MIT for less than a year I have had a great deal of help from members of the faculty who have been good to me in more ways than I can describe. But back then I went to Boston and Cambridge full of suspicion and dislike for everything having to do with school, and naturally did poorly. I lasted until about April of my freshman year, the spring of 1927, when illness, which was genuine enough, forced me to ask for a leave of absence which became permanent.

The decision to leave college allowed me to start work while times were still good. The depression that began two years later would not have provided the same opportunities. Yet I regret not completing my education. In particular, I have had problems as a yacht designer due to lack of advanced mathematical training. Today yacht design deals analytically with quantities in a relatively new way. It has become more highly technical in every sense due to the use of varied materials and much electronic gadgetry, and today's light complex rigs and other elements call for skillful engineering and the understanding of its principles. Continuing development in the field of CFD (computational fluid dynamics) make this advanced study an important adjunct to yacht design.

My only guide in fluid dynamics was intuition guided by experience with models and the boats themselves. I firmly recommend that the beginner today follow my advice rather than my action and acquire a good technical education. If I were starting today I should try to get into fluid dynamics further than naval architecture as my feeling is that naval architecture in terms of statics is within the reach of anyone seriously interested, supported by rudimentary mathematics. The analytical side is complex and the specialists use advanced math which has, in my view, become essential for understanding the finer points of sailing performance. I envy my friends who have the new skills, including a fluency with computers which seems so natural to students today. As this story goes on I expect to consider various technical subjects and I hope that my shortcomings in expression or understanding will be forgiven by those who know these subjects better than I.

During the 'twenties the Six-Metre Class grew on Long Island Sound. The Seawanhaka Corinthian Yacht Club on Long Island was the center of this racing because of the club's association with the British-American Cup for competition between teams of Sixes, each country represented by four boats and sailing in Britain and America in alternate years. Other international racing in Six Metres included the Seawanhaka Cup, a match-race series, and the Scandinavian Gold Cup, a series of fleet races that, by eliminating boats that did not win races, sometimes came down to a match-race final.

One of my vivid recollections of that period has to do with the Scandinavian Gold Cup in 1927. A good fleet was sailing off Oyster Bay. I think *Lea* was the American boat, sailed by Sherman Hoyt. As we watched from *Alicia*, the little schooner, a tightly bunched group of boats approached the lee mark carrying large overlapping headsails which we called balloon jibs. One after another changed to a small working jib, without overlap. All, that is, except one boat, the Swedish *Maybe*. Surprisingly, she kept the big sail while rounding the mark and trimmed it hard on the weather leg, passing the leaders and going on to win. This was the first use of the Genoa jib on this side of the Atlantic. Sven Salen, *Maybe*'s alert owner, had seen, off Genoa, Italy, that big overlapping headsails could be used when sailing to windward when cut properly. The idea worked, and the Genoa jib became a standard of everyone's sail inventory.

Most of the foreign Sixes that came to this country then were prepared for racing in the Nevins yard at City Island where I visited often to study, admire and photograph boats. I had watched many of the American Sixes being built there. I compared the contrasting designs and was impressed by the beauty of the boats designed and built in Scotland by William Fife, Jr. His signature was unmistakable in the clean, nicely balanced ends, the midsection with a little more beam and a firmer bilge than most, and his use of a touch of sheer more than the minimum required by the rule. The after overhang was always carried out to a small transom, lifted a little right aft. His art did not stand in the way of performance. It was an exciting day when, a few years later, off Oyster Bay, I spent an afternoon on a tender with Mr. Fife watching an Eight-Metre boat that he had designed beat the American *Gypsy* for the Seawanhaka Cup.

The designs of Johan Anker of Norway were also frequent winners. His boats were rather full forward with more rounded forebody sections than those of Fife. Such a blunt entrance did not seem well-adapted to windward work in rough water, but the performance of Anker's boats suggested to me that the best results do not always hinge on one characteristic but rather on a consistent combination. Among designs I saw later I noted that Frank Paine incorporated a good deal of fullness forward. I sailed against a number of his Eight Metres and it seemed that the best was his own *Gypsy* which Ray Hunt sailed in the Seawanhaka Cup match noted above. Although *Gypsy* was the loser in that match, she was a fast Eight. She was a very narrow boat and the full bow seemed to work better with her than it did later on Paine's beamier designs. Thirty years later, a full bow was on the British Twelve-Metre *Sceptre*, badly beaten by *Columbia* in the 1958 America's Cup match. She was extremely full and suffered in the rough seas off Newport.

The relationship between beam and the full bow may explain what seems to me a consistent combination. A narrow boat is inherently well-suited to windward work in rough water, and if sufficiently stable should do well despite the rounded shape forward. Further, the narrow boat is lifted and shortened less by heeling than a beamy one. As the forebody lines normally become sharper toward the bow, the entry, blunted less due to heeling is, in effect, relatively sharp. In the beamier boat, the full bow when upright is still fuller when heeled. The advantage of the full bow must be that it lengthens more or shortens less with heel, and again the narrow boat, rising less, scores. It is still a matter of concern if the narrow boat lacks stability. This brings up questions of weather conditions at a race site and matters having to do with construction, as the narrow boat must have plenty of ballast. If that is impossible because of structural requirements the narrow boat will fail, whereas she should score if the combination of displacement and scantlings permit generous ballast. If the ballast can be low down, so much the better.

Rule requirements play a big part in finding the right combination. The effect of the course, specifically whether it is largely downwind, as in most very long races, or windward and leeward legs typical of many inshore courses, will determine major design objectives and dimensions and how they are combined. There are many possibilities, many elements. The right combination is not always as rational as I have tried to make it seem here. Surely, in my case, there was a lot of luck involved. Later we will think about the velocity prediction, the VPP, a product of the 'sixties and 'seventies. It partly, but only partly, replaces luck.

It was apparent during this time that racing yachts in all classes were growing in length and displacement and shrinking in measured sail area. All readers may not appreciate that the resistance of a yacht or ship has two major elements: friction which results from the area of the surface in contact with the water, and wave-making caused by bulk or displacement. Wave-making increases rapidly with speed; friction less rapidly, so at low speeds wetted area is the greater factor in hull drag, while at high speeds it is a high ratio of displacement to length that puts on the brakes.

The bigger hulls were generally seen to have been cut away in profile, which tended to become a triangle so that the increased length and the drag of the greater displacement, which was required under either the Universal or the International Rule, was offset by less wetted surface. Thus the big hulls, with their stability derived through great displacement, balanced by length, had the advantage in strong winds, while the character of both profile and narrow, deep mid-section minimized wetted area and contributed to low-speed, light-weather performance. The Genoa jib that was widely adopted after the Swedish *Maybe* showed the way contributed unmeasured sail area, and this helped the bigger boats in light going while allowing them to make the most of their power when it blew.

It seemed evident that a big boat with a small rig could outsail a small one with a big rig in a hard wind and that the reverse had to be true in light going. Estimates of hull drag could be made, although data was scarce, and sail forces could only be guessed at. The academic, analytical method that is now routine could have yielded estimates, but the foundation would not have been considered reliable. The working yacht designer then used his feel for performance — that is, his judgement or intuition — to select the combination of length, sail area and geometry that he considered most promising. So it is no great wonder that the line separating the light-weather from the heavy-weather boats was often missed. Surprises were frequent. The Six-Metre *Lea* provides an example: for years she was a winner in light Long Island Sound conditions, yet I understand she was intended to be at her best in the Solent, England, where teams raced on alternate years and much more wind was expected. For her time she had a long waterline but her ends were rather short and sharp, characteristics that would not be found today on a heavy-weather boat. Perhaps I should be cautious in stating an opinion that could well be time-dependent.

Rod and I were no longer shy in approaching the giants of sailing, and we managed to meet many sailors whom we admired and from whom we could learn. About two years after Sven Salen introduced the Genoa jib, Rod brought him home to our house in Scarsdale. About then I remember well going on board Harry Pidgeon's little cruiser *Islander* as she lay in New Rochelle harbor after his early singlehanded circumnavigation, and then taking him for a tour of Westchester County by car. Before my year at MIT my father and I had visited John Alden, whose fisherman-type schooners were so justly popular. During the same visit to Boston we called on B.B. Crowninshield, who had designed our schooner and for whom Alden had worked before setting up his own office. Both recommended college just as I do today, but to me the time seems different and the need more positive.

John Alden was the most active of the American designers of cruising boats, and the most successful in offshore racing. He owned and raced a series of schooners called *Malabar*, of which number four had won the 1923 Bermuda race. He was regularly near the top in the longer races of that time. Most of his designs were rigged as schooners, some as ketches, and the smaller ones as sloops. I think they all had auxiliary power although it was not quite as universally used then as it is now. They were known as "fisherman-types" for their appearance and type of construction. This was wood, of course, with sawn frames and rather plain finish. Ballast was usually iron, part of it on the keel and a good deal inside. The sheerline of these yachts was lively and attractive and the ends were short when compared with the racing boats of the day. In the 1920s and 1930s offshore racing in small boats was new and growing fast, as was extended cruising in small yachts, and Alden's fisherman-types had great appeal.

Bob Moore belonged to the Cruising Club of America and I think it was as his guests that Father, Rod and I went to CCA dinners at the Yale Club. Later we became members. John Alden would come down from Boston to talk and sketch boats. He had great facility with freehand sketches, which often were complete and very pretty, and it was said that the club napkins which served as sketching pads were often taken home to save the drawings.

Alden was a successful entrepreneur as well as a yacht designer. He was also an able and experienced seaman. His habit then was to build and sail a boat of his own, new every year. His name and his racing record made the boats easy to sell, and then he could repeat the process after studying the boat and improving the design. These were days of growing prosperity, and with a popular model he would arrange with the better Maine builders for a number of similar hulls. Except for one-design classes, generally developed by a group of owners, such as the members of a club, John's activity represented early recognition of the advantages of standard or stock boats.

As the fisherman-type grew popular with offshore sailors, boats for racing 'round the buoys were being built to the Universal Rule and later to the International Rule's metre-boat classes. The Universal R class of 20′ rating was active but fading on Long Island Sound where interest swung to the International Sixes. Universal-Rule racing continued in Marblehead with the larger Q Class (25′ rating). While the best Sixes were growing from 20′ to 23′-plus on the waterline, the R-Boats reached 26′. The Q-Boats were larger again, having grown to 32′ on the water. Starling Burgess was the most consistently successful designer of these yachts, although his one-time associates Frank Paine and Francis Herreshoff, Nathanael's son, did a number of Rs and Qs that were highly competitive.

In the early 'twenties these three worked together in the firm of Burgess, Swazey, and Paine of Boston. Another associate there was Norman L. Skene, whose book,

The Elements of Yacht Design, was helpful to me. Later revised by Francis S. Kinney, who worked for many years with me at Sparkman & Stephens, it is a classic and a guide to many young and not-so-young designers. About 1925 Starling Burgess moved to New York as design partner in the firm of Burgess, Rigg and Morgan.

It was in 1925 also that Clifford D. Mallory took the lead in reviving the North American Yacht Racing Union (NAYRU) to encourage sailing and to unify the rating and sailing rules. (NAYRU evolved into the United States Yacht Racing Union and then into its present form, the United States Sailing Association.) In 1927 NAYRU and the European authority, the International Yacht Racing Union (IYRU), agreed that the International Rule that governed the metre classes would be applied in the U.S. as well as the rest of the sailing world for classes up to the Twelve Metres (about 65′) in size, while the Universal Rule would be accepted abroad for larger yachts. This was supported fully in New York. I think the New York Yacht Club must have been a little sorry to see a substitute for its own Universal Rule, but its retention for larger boats kept it in place for the America's Cup, the main interest of the NYYC. Conservative Boston and Marblehead were not so quick to comply and the Universal Rs and Qs held on in Marblehead for several years.

Supporting NAYRU and the New York Yacht Club, a class of Ten Metres was formed in 1927 and built by Abeking and Rasmussen in Germany to Starling Burgess designs. Good racing in that class of boats of about 60′ in length encouraged the construction the next year of Twelve Metres and Eight Metres. All of these were built by A & R and shipped to Halifax, from where they were sailed into the U.S. to avoid customs duties under the provisions of the time. In the first year my father and I crewed in a Ten Metre called *Branta*, and the next year I made the same trip in one of the Eights. Neither class was built to out-and-out racing standards as both hull and rig were a little heavier than required by the rule. The accommodations, too, had been arranged for some comfort so that these boats were appropriate for the cruise from Nova Scotia to the Sound, our destination both years. This was my first offshore experience. It included the run to Halifax in a small passenger steamer. I practiced the use of a sextant and picked up the rudiments of celestial navigation with the help of the Roosevelt brothers, Phil and Jack, who were traveling to bring in one of the boats. It was a great chance to learn and to meet many active sailors.

One event of the sail in *Branta* has remained in my memory. As the boats had no auxiliary power and we faced a headwind at the time for departure it was decided that we would leave Halifax under tow. One of the Ten Metre owners had a large fisherman-type schooner, *Michabo,* powered by a big slow-turning diesel also of fisherman type, I think a Fairbanks-Morse. In the headwind this would give us a good start. In the light afternoon breeze all was fine, but after dark the wind freshened and the sea made up. I was trying to hang on and get some sleep in a fo'c'sle pipe berth as the bow of this long-ended racing boat banged into one sea after another. First the berth lifted as we drove into it rather too fast, then the bunk dropped and I felt as though the only way I kept with it was the force of the deck pressing me down. Then the repeat. It was a relief to be called on deck toward midnight and to be told that we were dropping the tow. I was given a sharp knife and crawled forward to cut the tow line. As we set short sail on the starboard tack it was a revelation to feel the difference. Comfortable once more, we eased into the same seas. Later we went over to the inshore tack. As the sun rose on a new coast, green and white and blue, we experienced the joy of cruising.

A tow is apt to be troublesome and can be dangerous. That night off the Nova Scotia coast the conditions were in no way severe and the discomfort we felt on the lively racing yacht could hardly have been sensed on the big towboat. Once under sail the seas no longer broke over the bow and washed down the deck; the noise was mostly gone; and the motion was so much easier we felt we were in a different world. We sailed *Branta* easily because we were not racing and the boat and gear were new and untried. The rest of the trip was pleasantly routine. The next year some of the same crew brought in an Eight Metre. I am reminded of the fact that in those days small boats had no communication with the rest of the world when I report that, in this case, our excitement came when we sailed into Marblehead to learn that Lindbergh had landed in Paris.

As far back as I can remember I had drawn boats, mainly small sketches to show the outboard appearance and studies of lines on a very small scale. Soon after leaving MIT I set up a drafting table at home and started working seriously on plans from which a boat could be built. My interest centered on the Six-Metre Class, many of which I had watched building on Sunday morning trips to the City Island builders. And I had sailed Six Metres, with experiences I have described, so it was natural to go to work on a Six-Metre design.

The work was primarily a systematic exercise in design and drafting, working for the first time with the tools of the trade, including splines or battens held in place by lead weights, or "ducks" as they are known. Skene's *Elements* guided me in working out the basic hydrostatics and the rating. After completing the lines and the sailplan I carefully made ink tracings on linen of both. The pencil work had been easy as I had made many studies only a little less formal, but with ink I was unpracticed and slow. The drawings were presentable when finished, although anyone who knew drawing could see that I had very little practice in ink tracing.

I was pleased with the result and I took the drawings in to New York City where I called on *Yachting* magazine in the persons of Herbert Stone, the editor, and Sam

A Six-Metre Boat Design with Interesting Features

AT the conclusion of the recent international six-metre races off Oyster Bay, most of the critics agreed on at least two things, i.e.: American designers had been left far in the rear by their foreign contemporaries, and "something should be done about it."

Just what should be done about it is a question. But at least, the ideas of young designers should see the light of day, in the hopes that they might succeed where more experienced naval architects have progressed but little in the past year or so. It is with this idea in view that we publish the accompanying plans from the board of Olin J. Stephens, II, of New York, which show a six-metre boat with possibilities.

The dimensions of this craft are as follows: l.o.a. 34′; l.w.l. 22′ 10″; beam, 6′ 4½″; draft, 5′; sail area (measured), 525 sq. ft.; sail area, actual, 589 sq. ft.; displacement, 8620 lbs. In explanation of the design, Mr. Stephens has the following to say:

"The design is intended primarily for light weather. In any design the most important factors of speed seem to be long sailing lines and large sail area, with moderate displacement and small wetted surface. Then comes beauty, by which is meant clean, fair, pleasing lines. Though *per se* beauty is not a factor of speed, the easiest boats to look at seem the easiest to drive.

"To produce long sailing lines there are two methods available. First, by using a long water line coupled with fine ends; second, a shorter water line and full ends. The former method has been used in this design. The water line is about the longest of any existing American 'Six.' Though this long water line would ordinarily result in small sail area, this has been avoided by reducing the girth and girth difference measurements to the very minimum, which also lessens the wetted surface. The measured sail area is good, while with overlapping jibs of various sizes it may be said to be ample for the lightest of weather."

To predict what a boat will or will not do, from a study of her design, is a dangerous undertaking, as experienced designers and critics well know. Nevertheless, this design shows a great deal of promise, and it would be decidedly interesting to see her built and tried out.

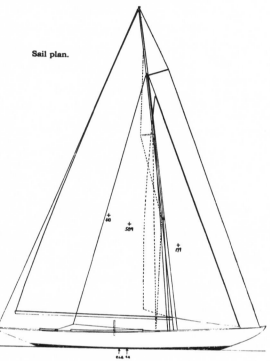

Sail plan.

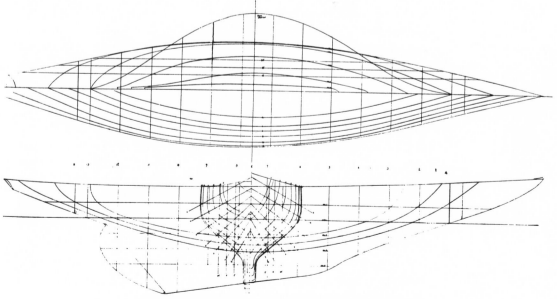

Lines and sections of the six-metre boat designed by Olin J. Stephens, II.

Wetherill, his assistant in charge of plan publication. Sam took the plans for that purpose. Evidently Sam was sympathetic with the aims of a young and ambitious designer. Neither then nor since have I lacked confidence in my ability to design a good boat, but this was a very nice boost to my morale as well as a chance to get my name and work out into the open. I carried prints to several boat-owner friends whom I hoped might build this Six but did not find the kind of acceptance I had received at *Yachting*.

In the course of showing the plans I received many kind words, not all of which I accepted at face value. I particularly recall a talk with the father of one of my sailing contemporaries who congratulated me on the fact I had gotten out to see him even though he was not about to build. He told me that it really didn't matter whether one knew much about his work, the important thing was to hustle and to cultivate the ability to sell. This was his recipe for success, but I have always preferred the better-mouse-trap theory and have tried to follow it in my work.

I was more prepared to accept the advice I received from Starling Burgess. He treated me and my small roll of plans very patiently and commented seriously on the design and the drawing work. He encouraged me and recommended several books more advanced than Skene. These included Atwood's *Naval Architecture* (the name Pengelly is now coupled with that of Atwood) and W.H. White's *Manual of Naval Architecture*, both English works that I was able to find and buy in New York.

The summer of 1927 was spent sailing and working on more drawings at home. In the fall I started work at the Gielow office. This was not exciting but it was regular and it put me in the atmosphere of professional yacht design as a member of an organized group. It offered another way to learn. However, in something like three or four months I found an opening with Philip Rhodes who was working on boats much more to my liking. Phil must soon have realized how much I had to learn as I labored and stumbled along on the construction drawings for a straightforward wooden boat. It was clear how little familiarity I had with the conventions of drafting, but he was helpful and I think I learned pretty fast. Nevertheless, I never became an expert draftsman, except maybe in the drawing of lines.

The job with Rhodes lasted only a short time until I resigned to join Drake Sparkman as a partner to handle design. The arrangements were informal and experimental, to be extended or not depending on how things worked out. Drake was an active yacht broker and a good sailor with many friends in the Larchmont and New York Yacht Clubs. He raced for several years in the Victory Class. He had a great interest in boats and the ability to sell them. He was then associated with Roger Haddock, a much older naval architect who, in retrospect, had ability as a designer of powerboats but seemingly not much feeling for sail. He was retiring but agreed to help out on any powerboat designs. The first-ever S&S powerboat plans were done by Roger Haddock. I think he also took a good look at my other first plans to see that they were not too far off the mark. Assuming that I could produce, the arrangements were ideal. Luckily I could.

My thoughts about business and Drake's meshed well. We were both conservative in the sense that we wished to do our part to make a proper living but we had no great desire to become rich. The last thing either of us wished to do was to run risks in the hope of gain. During the history of the firm that became S&S we never borrowed a penny. We did not require much capital. Both Drake and I were able to put in small amounts to buy stock when we signed papers of incorporation, and that was all we needed. Other partners came in as stockholders later.

Our individual incomes depended entirely on what we could earn as commissions, although later when accounting required an overhead charge we gave ourselves small salaries augmented by a share of the profits, of which there were always some because our overhead costs were minimal. These, of course, grew as we added salaried draftsmen and designers and clerical help, but we were careful to keep them under control. As time passed we seemed to acquire the reputation of being expensive, and this was because we tried to do pretty complete plans and had to do time and material work instead of, or in addition to, a commission on a boat's cost. Our margins were small but positive and that is what both Drake and I preferred.

Our first project was a small one-design class for the Junior Yacht Racing Association of Long Island Sound. The building of a class of 20 boats to the plans of a novice designer seems a bolder step now than it did to me then. Drake never said anything, but probably Mr. Haddock took a good look at the plans. Drake would not have considered himself qualified in a technical sense even though he knew boats. Work with Drake began quickly enough to get the Junior boats built before the end of the '28 summer. The boats, originally named the Sound Junior Class, are about 21′ overall, 15′-plus on the water with about 6-1/2′ of beam. There was nothing radical about the design, but neither was it a copy of any existing boat. The ends are shorter than was the racing fashion at the time. It was gratifying, after launching, to find that flotation, balance and stability were all as expected. Today I should say that, fortunately, the design did not pretend to look like anything except a practical 20′ boat. The shape and proportions seem appropriate to the size. I have never liked long ends on small boats as they simply add weight, particularly when coupled with a small boat's necessarily high freeboard. Small boats need reasonable beam for stability. Today when short ends and wide beam are fashionable this hardly needs to be said, but in the 1920s these points were not so clear.

Some of the boats of that first design are still sailing as the Manhasset Bay One Design Class. In July of 1978 and again in 1988 I was an appreciative guest at dinners arranged to celebrate the fiftieth and sixtieth anniversaries of the class.

The Sound Junior Class sloop of early 1929 was S&S design #1, still sailing as the Manhasset Bay One Design. This is just a simple small boat, fortunately showing no serious faults, easy to build and to sail. A useful start. (Courtesy of Sparkman & Stephens)

While still working in the Gielow office it was tempting to visit the office of *Yachting* magazine in the same building. I stopped in from time to time to talk boats with Sam Wetherill, who had placed my earlier Six in his design section. He often sailed as mate with John Alden, and he helped me again by arranging an invitation to sail in the 1928 Bermuda Race with Alden in his new *Malabar IX*.

John Alden ran a good ship in every way. Gear, equipment and sails were of the best and the crew sailed the boat hard. The food was good, too. It was a wonderful introduction to deepwater racing. We had a close race with the new *Dragoon*, owned and designed by Robert N. Bavier (father of Bob, Jr., my younger contemporary, who has been at the center of the sailing scene for many years). A nice sailing breeze gave us a close reach on the starboard tack, but on the third

day *Malabar* and *Dragoon* slowed to a drift. Searching the horizon for competitors we spotted the Herreshoff-designed yawl *Rugosa II* broad on our lee bow. Built new in 1928, she carried a yawl rig on the hull lines of a New York 40. (I should say "carries," as today she is owned by Halsey Herreshoff, grandson of Captain Nat.) We watched her move ahead as the wind filled in from the southeast. We could only slat and drift until it reached us. The new Hand-designed schooner *Yankee Girl II* and *Dragoon* got the new breeze before we did, and that was our Bermuda Race.

When our anchor was down, I dove over the side to visit the other boats and hear about their races. As one boat after another came in, the day went on — a short swim and on deck another story. It must have been only youth and enthusiasm that kept me out of the hospital as the sun raised on my shoulders blisters the size of silver dollars.

Two other facts of this race may be worth noting: first, my brother Rod sailed in the crew of *Teal*, R. Graham Bigelow's Alden schooner, while another Alden design in the race was *Elizabeth*, owned and sailed by Lynn A. Williams of Chicago. On board was Lynn, Jr. whose activity in the field of rating rules paralleled my own over many years. Further along we will come to know him better.

I stayed with *Malabar* in Bermuda and made the return cruise as navigator. The large target formed by North America was hit easily enough. We took the boat to Marblehead where John had asked me to sail with him in his new Q-Boat *Hope*. John Alden was an expert and successful designer of offshore boats, and also an extremely able offshore skipper and experienced seaman. On short courses he was less experienced and less able so that we did poorly. As a boat I thought *Hope* could have done better. Despite our showing, the experience of racing in a new area and against a new fleet was both enjoyable and instructive. I also took satisfaction in a job offer that John made to me. But by that time I felt that I was on my independent way and I did not want to alter course.

That first experience of Bermuda added up to a lot more, and I was fortunate in its repetition over many years until ties to and responsibilities with the America's Cup interfered. The green hills and white roofs were part of the race's appeal. In those early days, after the finish, with a local pilot at the wheel, we relaxed and watched the brilliant water change color where it shoaled as we approached the narrow passage called Two Rocks and joined the gathering fleet in protected Hamilton Harbor. Ashore, before automobiles were permitted after World War Two, there were horse-drawn carriages and many bicycles. The excitement of a new country — all that, and sailing too.

To design boats one needed a place to work and a little special equipment. The gear I had accumulated at home consisted of a few splines and ducks and a planimeter to measure areas. I think it was Drake who thought of asking Henry Nevins whether he had room in his drawing office that I could use. Nevins was agreeable, and so it was that I was given a board in the Nevins yard's drafting room where detailed drawings were made for special fittings and other layouts needed in the shop. When busy I did my own work; at other times I worked under the direction of either Charles D. Mower or George Crouch. Mower had a large Universal-Rule M-Boat building in the yard and Crouch had one of the racing motor boats with which he had great success. It was a good opportunity to see what a top-flight builder needed in the way of plans and to observe the building of several very different boats.

After sailing with John Alden, the rest of the summer of 1928 was spent in the Nevins drafting room. On weekends we raced our Six-Metre *Natka*. The drawings

for the Sound Junior Class must have been done there. I remember no feeling of disappointment in a quiet summer.

That summer the Eight-Metre Class was active, following the acceptance by the Seawanhaka Corinthian Yacht Club of a challenge for the Seawanhaka Cup from the Royal Northern Yacht Club on the Clyde in Scotland. During the previous winter three Eights had been built at the Nevins yard to designs by Sherman Hoyt, Clinton Crane and Charles Mower. After a series of eliminations, the Marblehead Eight-Metre *Gypsy*, designed by Frank Paine and sailed by Ray Hunt, was chosen to defend. In the Seawanhaka series she lost to the challenger from Scotland.

The able manager of the Nevins shop was Rufus Murray. I understood that the traditions of the Herreshoff yard at Bristol, Rhode Island, had been carried to New York by Rufus Murray who became yard manager for Henry B. Nevins, whose yard at City Island was the top building shop in the U.S. during the 'twenties and 'thirties. Although I doubt whether Murray had any formal engineering training, he was a real engineer in a practical sense, and he had certainly benefited from association with Captain Nat, who was the greatest engineer in yacht design. Murray was unparalleled in his knowledge of the nature of wood and how it should be put together and fastened to form a yacht hull. I did not work in the shop; but I like to think that a little of Rufus Murray and his background rubbed off on me, and surely more on Rod, who later spent several years helping to build yachts at Nevins. Maybe we have in a small way continued a fine tradition.

Sailors, of course, all know the legend of Captain Nat and the Herreshoff Manufacturing Company. In the summer of '34 Nathanael G. Herreshoff was living in Bristol, Rhode Island, in semi-retirement. Not so much earlier he had done two designs that I knew. One was the R-Boat *Gamecock*, owned by Commodore George Nichols of the New York Yacht Club, while the other, designed a little later, was the centerboard yawl *Belisarius*, owned by Charles B. Rockwell of Bristol. She has been sailing until recently and is much admired. Her home now is the Herreshoff Museum in Bristol. In 1934 I went to Bristol with Mr. Crane when the J-Boat *Weetamoe* was given an altered keel at the Herreshoff yard, and I was introduced to Captain Nat by Mr. Crane. Though it amounted to no more than shaking hands, it was an exciting day.

Nat had two sons, both involved with designing boats, though of very different character. Francis designed many successful yachts for both cruising and racing. These included *Istalena*, probably the fastest of all the M-Class yachts racing in the late 'twenties and early 'thirties. He also did the well-known and beautiful *Ticonderoga*. One of his most interesting and fast designs was the R-Class *Live Yankee*. The structure as well as the form of *Live Yankee* was radical, as she had no regular wood keel, her widely spaced frames being fitted to her lead keel, supporting longitudinals. Over these she had double-diagonal planking which was rabetted into her keel and rounded into her deck with no normal deck edge or planksheer.

Captain Nat's other yacht-designing son Sidney followed the engineering interests of his father, including steam engines and all things mechanical, and remained associated with the yard at Bristol. He had a lovely, fine-lined little motor launch, *Bubble*, which he sometimes used to follow the racing off Newport. She moved so quietly and with so little fuss that no one ever objected however close he might come in to study a boat's behavior. Halsey Herreshoff, who is active today, is Sidney's son. He has followed the family's interest in sailing boats, studying naval architecture at the Webb Institute and MIT. He has been a crew member on three S&S Twelves, *Columbia, Courageous* and *Freedom*. That he has not sailed as skipper is only because he is so valuable in the crew. On any Twelve I would immediately nominate him as most valuable player. On *Columbia*'s foredeck he was the youngest man in the crew, while in both *Courageous* and *Freedom* he navigated. On both his judgement of the lay line was decisive in more than one important race. He is just as valuable on shore; he knows exactly who can do what in the Newport-Bristol area.

Getting back to that quiet summer of 1928, a client of Drake's, Arthur Hatch of Stamford, decided to build a small boat for afternoon sailing with some below-decks accommodations. She was to be just over 30′ long, a length which reflected a hope, probably more on the part of the designer than of the owner, that she might get into some racing, where a minimum length of 30′ was often required. *Kalmia* was built at the Minneford yard at City Island. By the time she was launched in the spring of '29 Mr. Hatch had offered her to the Stephens family to sail in the Gibson Island Race, down the coast and into the Chesapeake. We were quick to accept and were successful in winning the smallest class. Our closest and best competition was from the slightly larger *Hotspur*, also a new boat that year, designed for the writer Alfred Loomis by Linton Rigg. After a short stay at Gibson Island we sailed back to Long Island Sound in company with the Loomis family, which gave us a good chance to compare the boats and discuss their characteristics.

The design philosophy applied to *Kalmia* was a very simple one. The pleasure of sailing any boat, as well as its race-winning potential, seemed to me dependent on its windward performance, supplemented if possible by good light-weather speed. None of the competitors of that day had the high offwind speeds that we see today in the ultralight-displacement boats (ULDBs) and the big dinghies, so that if you could save time in light going and in windward work you were likely to enjoy your sail. This early experience has colored my view of displacement to this day, and that is to favor heavy over light as it offered power for upwind performance. *Kalmia* exemplified the type, and the combination of moderate to generous displacement, low wetted area and low-speed design due to a low prismatic coefficient — meaning a relatively large midship section and fine ends — seemed to work out. Looking back now the design seems pretty crude. The study of boats and books had satisfied me that the ends should be sharp and balanced, and that the midsection should have the area to give a prismatic coefficient of about 0.50 including keel area. This means that the displacement was exactly half the volume of a prism having the midsection area over the full length of the waterline.

Kalmia was built with conventional single planking over bent oak frames. She carried lead ballast, all but a very little outside on her keel, differing in this from many small auxiliaries of the time. Her ends were rather long to accommodate a fairly large rig, all inboard, without a bowsprit. Her jib-headed mainsail, though not radical, was a little advanced for the time.

Winning a small class in an off year (no Bermuda Race) was no great accomplishment, nor was the design of this rather ordinary small boat, but *Kalmia*'s performance seemed to give confidence to both prospective clients and my associates, offsetting likely doubts due to my youth and limited background. So the summer of 1929 brought an end to a rather quiet period and it is hardly an exaggeration to say that I have been trying to catch up ever since.

The next project was another piece of continuing good luck. While racing in the Six-Metre Class we had become acquainted with another owner, Lewis G. Young. He raced a Norwegian-built Six, a good boat designed by Johan Anker, but he had very little success and he had some ideas of his own about a new boat which he asked me to work up into a design at the very beginning of 1929. His ideas were not too difficult, so here I had the opportunity to work into the class I knew best.

Thalia, as the new boat was called, was built by Nevins in the summer of 1929. To be raced on Long Island Sound she was designed for light weather. Her forward overhang had U-shaped sections while aft the sections were sharp. Her below-water profile was almost a triangle. This saved wetted area and minimized a girth measurement that was then taken around the keel costing length or sail area with increasing keel depth amidships. The triangular profile had a slight bulge under the mast. Her midships section was rather large, following the character of *Kalmia*.

Thalia was launched after the end of the racing season. We were lucky in finding a tune-up partner when Sherman Hoyt offered to keep his Six, *Seleema*, in the water. Both boats were taken to the Columbus Day rendezvous of the Cruising Club at Lloyd Harbor. The weekend was occupied with informal racing in which *Thalia* performed well. Fortunately, despite a degree of euphoria, I realized that the boat had faults that could be corrected another time. In particular, when reaching in a breeze, and sailing fast, she pulled a very disturbing wake on her weather quarter. She seemed to move well in light weather, and the impression she gave those who watched the trials was good despite the realization thar *Seleema*'s bottom was rather

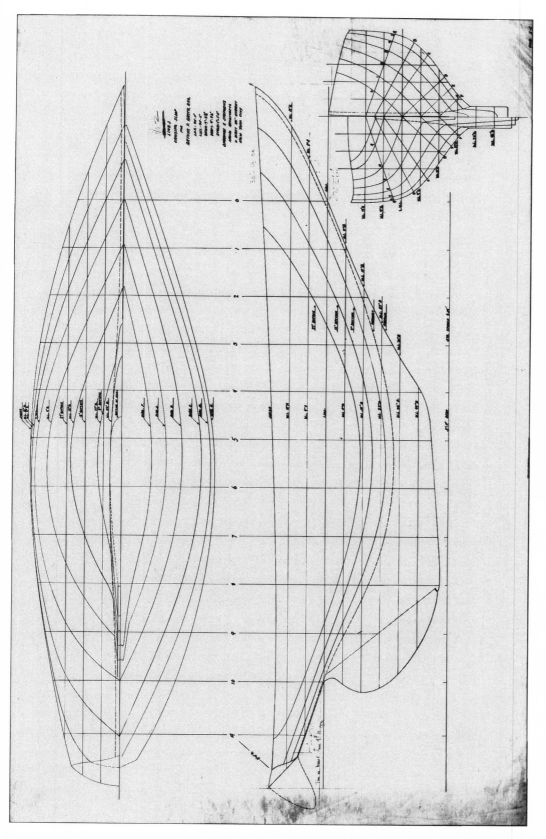

Kalmia's lines are shown here. Her shape conforms to principles outlined in the text: balance between the ends and between hull volumes above and below the waterline. Generous displacement coupled with a large mid-section (low prismatic coefficient) suggests ability at the lower speeds of windward and light-weather sailing rather than high-speed reaching. (Courtesy of Sparkman & Stephens)

foul because of the time she had been kept in the water. *Thalia*, of course, was new and clean. Again this was great good luck, as was Sherman Hoyt's willingness to keep *Seleema* in commission. I still appreciate the great help of Sherman Hoyt in those early days.

The best thing about *Thalia* was the lesson her performance drove home, namely that the midship section could be too large. On a fast reach this simply put on the brakes. Still, the mere fact that someone new and young could design a passable Six Metre created interest and a generous degree of acceptance. It still surprises me to think of the willingness of a number of new clients, who soon followed, to take a chance. As autumn became winter S&S had orders for four new Sixes, one Eight Metre and two new cruising boats or offshore racers. In early 1929 people were taking chances.

With this my time in the Nevins drafting room ended. As the building of these new yachts was to be done by three City Island yards, Nevins, Minneford and Robert Jacob, it made sense to find space to work somewhere nearby. We found a ground-floor office, really a store, right across the street from Nevins, and we took on two assistants. One was an elderly marine draftsman, a Mr. Clark; the other was a young friend, Jim Merrill, the son of the builder of the little yawl *Trad* which we had owned several years earlier. Jim shared my interests and somehow had learned to be a good neat draftsman, something I never accomplished, although I could make a good lines drawing and in fact could do it fast, which helped a lot that winter.

I did all the lines and most of the calculations. The others shared the other plans. Our first project was a larger version of *Kalmia*, for H.S. Sayers, owner of the Minneford yard and a City Island resident. The next was a Six Metre called *Mist*. She was for John K. Roosevelt, a truly expert navigator, who had helped me several years before to learn celestial navigation on one of the Halifax trips. *Mist* was to be a real Long Island Sound boat. She was long and narrow and deep. By avoiding penalties at her ends and girth point, she was able to carry a large rig with a very high foretriangle. *Mist* became a prototype of the Eight-Metre *Conewago*, not overly successful in her first year but later a Canada's Cup winner.

Without continuing in detail I can say that 1929 was a good year. There was one development that seems worth mentioning, namely a meeting I had with Mr. Johnston deForest, who was then chairman of the Seawanhaka Corinthian Yacht Club committee for the British-American Cup. The team races were scheduled in the U.S. for the late summer of 1930. In October of 1929 the stock market crashed and the ever-growing optimism about economic conditions was abruptly reversed. Just when I was ready for a big year with orders for four new Six Metres I heard that the team races might be canceled or postponed. Conflict with the America's Cup, also planned for 1930, was cited as a further reason favoring a change. I went to see

Mr. deForest in his New York office with the best arguments I could think of, such as the likelihood of British Six-Metre sailors coming over to see the Cup races, and a little later the 1930 date was confirmed. I have never known whether my visit influenced this decision, but it seemed to me that the effort and the activity had in some degree been worthwhile, and I felt better for having done something, however small, other than being resigned to disappointment.

Because the International Rule classes, the metre boats, were so prominent during this period, I will briefly explain the rule as the sum of hull and rig measurements which, after division by a constant, indicated a measurement in metres. The parameters consisted of Length taken between girth points at the bow and stern plus the square root of the Sail Area as defined by measurements of the spars, plus the Freeboard. Displacement and Draft were defined as functions of waterline length. Using computer format the rule could be defined as $(L+SA^{0.5}-F)/C$. C, the constant, currently 2.37, was changed to balance other changes in the rule which was modified from time to time by the Keelboat Committee of the IYRU at its yearly November meetings in London.

The character of the winning boats had changed, growing longer and narrower and carrying less sail in even the few years I had watched the class. Experience had shown that the value of length up to about 23′ on the water was greater than the drawback of the greater required displacement, especially if the section shape was such as to minimize wetted area. This encouraged a deep vee-shaped midsection which logically terminated in sharp ends. The sharp ends minimized the increase to the L measurement as related to the waterline, so that the measured sail area had been held almost constant or could be taken as slightly less in view of the added power of the Genoa jib.

That description could be applied to the four boats designed for the 1930 season, and directly to *Mist*, with a larger rig than the others, that permitted a higher foretriangle. The others had slightly more U-shaped ends and shorter rigs. Two of the boats, *Comet* and *Meteor*, went to Charlevoix, Michigan, where their owners from Chicago and St. Louis spent summers. The fourth Six, *Cherokee*, owned by Herman Whiton, sailed in the Sound and won the class championship.

Of all the events of that winter, 1929-30, the most exciting was the sale of the family business, the retailing of anthracite coal, which made it possible to build the boat the family, or part of it, had been considering with hope for a long time. Reasons for the sale are not entirely clear to me except that my grandfather, whom I believe was the second-generation owner, had reached retirement age. Probably contributing factors were the fact that neither Rod nor I was interested in continuing the business as we were clearly committed to sail, and the competition of heating oil as an alternate fuel. The new boat was to be called *Dorade*.

For years, I had prepared for this time when I could do a design intended for what I wanted to do most, serious offshore racing. But now when that moment came I was a busy young man with several commissions on the drafting board. There were three of the Six Metres just mentioned along with an Eight Metre and a 30´-waterline fast cruiser/racer. The planning of *Dorade* was more rushed than relaxed, but it went along smoothly.

Familiarity with racing boats, especially in the metre classes, as well as my experience in the Nevins yard, had convinced me that the fisherman-type could be improved upon and beaten in offshore racing. In short-course racing I hoped that good details and well-balanced lines could bring about winners, but for offshore I believed in a more radical type, although based on sound theory.

Dorade's design was very different from the Alden and Hand schooners which were her principal competitors, but not a complete break with the past even though it has been so described. Her construction was based on Herreshoff methods. Hull shape was a little more radical as her beam was narrow and her depth greater than normal; but there are models in the New York Yacht Club, especially a G.L. Watson design called *Dora* from 1890, which *Dorade* surprisingly resembles. If her jib-headed yawl rig seemed new it was only in the change from gaff to Marconi in common with the trend of the time. The yawl rig had been around as long as the schooner.

But *Dorade* did look very different from Alden's boats. The popular fisherman-type had a combination of outside and inside ballast, and the ballast that was inside and higher contributed less to stability. Frames in the Maine-built schooners were generally sawn and doubled to reinforce the necessary joints. Both ballasting and framing contributed to rather heavy displacement. John Alden had developed the type skillfully so that reasonable speed was combined with roominess and moderate cost. John had a very good eye and his schooners carried his unmistakable signature. But it seemed that anyone who was serious about racing-yacht design could visualize a faster combination, and the key was in City Island construction.

Weights and lines routinely received my first consideration — weights having an importance above all. Structural members were generally in accordance with the scantling rules that had been applied under the Universal Rule. Today I am uncertain of the source, though I believe Lloyd's New York had made tables that were based on Herreshoff's practices for wooden boats organized as a set of requirements rather than the informal guide which was the starting point. We had closely spaced steam-bent frames with the so-called floors, transverse connecting members, on each pair of frames. Wherever there was doubt we went to the heavier, stronger choice. The planking was one important member that was over the specification of the rule. In spite of this conservative approach we retained the weight advantage

Dorade's lines and sail plan are shown here. Compared with *Kalmia*, her long lean character can be recognized to promise better downwind performance. Narrow beam makes her tender but she can move well under all conditions. Outside ballast provides a wide range of positive stability. The jib-headed yawl rig is exceptional only as it departed from the schooner rig so common in ocean racing in the 1920s. It offered windward performance comparable to that of the conventional sloops and a rating bonus that meant that the mizzen and mizzen stays'l were almost free. As *Dorade* had no engine power, steering control for narrow waters was given by the small mizzen. (Courtesy of Sparkman & Stephens, here and on page 46)

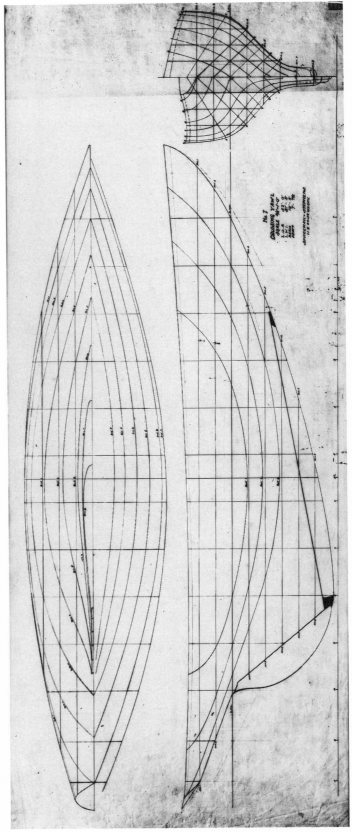

over fisherman-type construction that was to give *Dorade* some winning margins.

The bent framing in particular was much lighter than the double-sawn fisherman-type framing made up of short sections overlapped to support the joints. By using wider frame spacing, part of this doubled weight could be saved, but only at the cost of heavier planking needed by the greater span between frames. Similar weight-saving was made in the decking where beams were placed at each frame, permitting relatively light deck planking. Most of *Dorade*'s deck beams were spruce, lighter than the oak of the fisherman-type, and offsetting the closer spacing. Where we could we allowed the deck beams to run right through the deck openings, but where a clear opening was necessary we used oak beams at either end. Such savings permitted a higher ratio of ballast to displacement. All of this, except a little trimming ballast, was outside on the keel where its longer lever arm contributed more to stability than was possible with the combination of outside iron and whatever went inside on the more conventional boats.

I drew *Dorade*'s lines in the same short period as those of two new Six Metres. *Dorade* had essentially the same beam-to-length ratio as they did. Actually the figure was slightly lower, and this looked reasonable to me because her waterline endings were carried out rather than snubbed as were those of the Sixes. I figured that, although her proportion of ballast to displacement would be lower, the inherently greater stability of the larger boat would balance the loss of ballast. In contrast to the winning boats of today her lead keel was long and well-spread forward and aft rather than concentrated. I wished to minimize her pitching in a chop and it worked that way, presumably because of her narrow beam which made it easy for her to slice through a sea. I am sure that this characteristic helped the action of her rig as there was so little sea-induced quick motion to shake the wind out of her sails or shift its apparent direction.

The lines carried out principles that had guided the design of the smaller racing boats, but for seagoing use the ends were shorter as the long-ended racing types pound in a rough sea, so the load waterline shape was finer at both ends. This led to my feeling that, as I believed in small beam, to minimize wetted area and resistance due to wave encounter, a ratio of beam to stretched waterline length corresponding to the racing boats would give sufficient stability. In these choices there were two errors relating to the fact that the weight estimates were too light so that the boat floated deeper than expected and the initial stability was marginal. Because *Dorade*'s lines were fair, showing no discontinuity between underbody and ends, and because she was not required to meet any class limitations, and because she had good freeboard, the deeper flotation did not hurt her performance. Today I would assume that the greater draft helped her to windward, and though her wetted area was increased it was relatively so much less than that of her chief competition that her light-weather performance remained superior.

Dorade's length overall was (and is) 52′-0″; her datum waterline length was 37′-6″; but being heavy the flotation line was close to 39′. Her beam was 10′-3″ and her draft 8′. Sail area was 1100 sq. ft.; displacement 34,000 lbs.

As *Dorade*'s weights were already over our estimate we never added ballast, but before the 1931 season we reduced the sail area. As to her lines and proportions, there was no discussion with others. That may have been a mistake as her lack of beam would have been noted and more beam would have almost certainly improved her. More beam soon came on other boats like *Stormy Weather* with the advantage of increased driving power from a more upright rig and a more relaxed crew.

The jib-headed (masthead) yawl rig was taken for granted, partly for presumed rating advantage, plus yawl for maneuverability as we had no auxiliary power, and jib-headed for windward efficiency. The spar sizes were based on Skene as I had not yet reached the more theoretically correct method I followed later. These sizes again were conservative as was the entire rig. Rod joined in laying out the rig and the deck but he was still working at Nevins. His big part came as *Dorade* was built.

The accommodations were practical and conservative. As there was no engine, there was extra length under the cockpit, but width was restricted. Despite that limitation we decided to use narrow built-in berths in the main cabin with narrow transoms and a built-in table. The berths were fine at sea, no way to roll around, and we tolerated them in port. The galley was aft, adjacent to the cockpit. We had a Shipmate stove, burning coal or charcoal, with a kerosene Primus for warm-weather

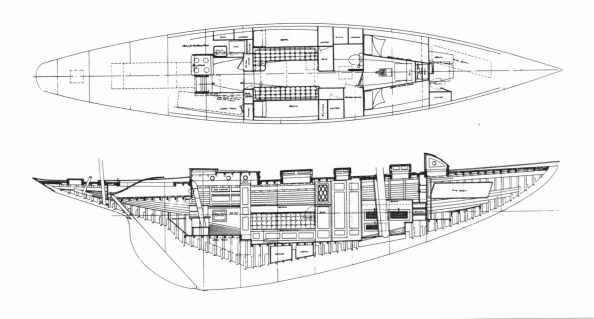

cooking. Forward of the main cabin there was a toilet room to port and lockers to starboard, and farther forward a stateroom with berths either side and an entrance to the fore peak.

The deck plan was unusual on two counts. First was the provision of a generous supply of winches. Each halyard or sheet had its own. They were the single-acting type with the crank on top, I think made by Nevins, copied from Merriman which at some point had acquired the patterns from either Lawley or Herreshoff. Second was the first use of the *Dorade* vents utilizing an idea of Rod's, by which a cowl vent was fitted in the top of a box large enough to hold a good deal of water and scuppered aft to drain what water entered. Through the deck inside the box was a stand pipe, equal in diameter to the cowl and high enough to be open above any likely water level. It is still the most practical way to get air below with a minimum of water. Despite some questions about their appearance, these vents have been found useful and very widely copied.

I was disappointed, though not too surprised, when Henry Nevins said the yard was just too full to promise the early delivery we needed to prepare for the Bermuda Race of 1930, and we were happy that Henry and Dick Sayers of the Minneford yard were ready to take on the new boat with the understanding that they would provide the necessary manpower and that their shop manager would be ready to cooperate with Rod in managing the building work. This was successfully carried through. Mr. Nevins kindly allowed Rod time off to supervise the work.

Rod started at the usual beginning, joining their loftsman in laying down the lines full size on the mould loft floor, and went on, spending something like an hour a day at the yard, which was next door to Nevins. There were no serious hitches. I regret that I cannot recall the name of the Minneford boatbuilder who deserves considerable credit in his readiness to accept a person as young as Rod, then 20, to watch over his shoulder and often give directions. Rod, for his part, double-checked the lofting, and went on to watch with great care the selection of all the wood, utilizing his experience with Rufus Murray of Nevins. Throughout the building he watched the material, wood and metal, and the quality of the fastenings and the way it all fitted and maintained the lofted shape. We knew well what we were getting and Rod built on that experience for the rest of his life, doing similar work for our clients over and over. We had complete confidence that *Dorade* would stay together.

The spring and early summer of 1930 was a busy and exciting time and I can't remember details of our first sail. We prepared for Bermuda with much hope and confidence in our boat's strength and speed. In contrast to today I do not recall much thought about rating. I doubt whether it was ever estimated during the design stage. We knew she would be fast and she was. That was enough. As the Bermuda Race start approached we sailed to New London.

3

The scenario must be as old as sport. Competition builds along certain lines which suit the participants and thus a norm is established. From year to year marginal advances are the rule. Then along comes someone, something of an outsider and more single-minded in his efforts to win, who seizes an opportunity that is obvious to him though unrecognized by the routine participants. The new player exploits a new way that offers a winning margin. I have wondered whether this is good for the sport, yet I recognize it as part of the game. It keeps competitors on their toes. In 1929 I sensed the opening.

I saw the contrast between John Alden's Maine construction details and the City Island construction that I knew. Steam-bent frames would be lighter than the Down East sawn frames, and incidentally would take less space from the interior. For both reasons displacement could be reduced, making the boat easier to drive. Then lead ballast, all outside, would offer the needed stability with less beam. The efficiency of the jib-headed yawl rig, especially when sailing to wind-ward, would permit the boat to be driven without too much sail, helping to keep the rating down. I was confident in the City Island way, and Dorade was the result.

On page 48 is *Dorade*

On page 48 is *Dorade* under sail. The three headsails represent a step between a good single Genoa in light going and the two lower jibs and stays'l in stronger winds. Reef points for two deep reefs are shown in the main; there is one set of reef points in the mizzen. Despite low initial stability, reefs were seldom used. (Photo: Rosenfeld Collection 61205F)

The fundamentals worked well enough so that *Dorade* made a fine record and became the prototype of the coming offshore yacht. She was strong and safe, a carefully thought-out boat for ocean racing. She was very fast on the wind and in rough water but she was far from perfect; the original rig was too big and the beam was too small. In the long run the easy identification of ways she could be made better was a piece of very good luck.

Although I have spoken of confidence and fundamentals, as I think back now I realize I had very little to guide me beyond reading and thinking. I think it is fair to say that as years have passed I have "done my homework" in that I have done more reading and thinking on the various aspects of sailing-boat performance and have learned a good deal. The big change has been the use of quantities. We have numbers for all of it now. I will come to more detail on that, but with *Dorade* the design work was strictly comparative and intuitive.

The data base that is a taken-for-granted essential today was not available. The fundamentals then included a good ratio of sail area to wetted surface and a corresponding ratio of sail area to displacement, that is to the two-thirds power. On the other side of the equation was stability to carry sail. These two essential features are directly opposed and yet had to be combined and optimized. With today's computers and the data they swallow this is a mathematical problem, not too hard. In the 1920s and 1930s it was a guess. In a way it was easier then, but chancy. The ability to measure and predict speed came later when I met Kenneth Davidson, almost directly as a result of building *Dorade*. Once you know the quantities there is no limit to the number of combinations that can be tested. When to stop the computer? Guessing and hoping was easier and quicker, but a greater gamble.

Rating rules were then, as now, a guide and a challenge. The balance of conflicting elements should be such as to promise the best ratio of performance against rating. Time allowances for handicapping are inversely proportional to the rating (its square root) which increases with length and other speed-producing measurements. The measurements and the rules by which they are combined have become more and more complex, a sophistication resulting from quantitative understanding. The rule of the Cruising Club of America to which *Dorade* was to be measured was an adaptation of the rule used by the British Royal Ocean Racing Club after 1926, and it was the first rule in ocean racing to take account of the three basic parameters of yacht performance — length, sail area and displacement. Written as L*SQR(SA)/SQR(B*D), (computer format) where B and D are beam and depth, it paralleled the current Universal Rule applied to racing types, while omitting the length component of displacement in the denominator. That rule devised by Nathanael Herreshoff was used in the racing classes in the form

0.18*SQR(SA)/(Displacement)$^{1}/_{3}$. The logic is that the speed-producing parameters, length and sail area, increase rating, while the drag factor, displacement, reduces it. There is, however, a disadvantage in the rigid relationship between the several factors which does not mirror their influence on speed as proportions change.

I do not remember attempting then anything approaching the kind of analysis that I would apply today, and if I am thinking straight the rule strongly favored smaller boats. This is something neither I nor the designers of two larger boats built for the 1931 transAtlantic race seemed to notice. Although during *Dorade*'s design I was pretty relaxed about the rule, my interest grew fast as I became accustomed to thinking in numbers such as seconds per mile related to potential speed. The effect of a rule on a design, hoping to gain some advantage, became a subject that remains an active interest of mine to this day.

Dorade looked fast, and her record confirmed her looks, but her form is not one that would be followed today. Being narrow and deep she lacks the stability to best propel her displacement, moderate though it is. For her time she had a high ratio of ballast to displacement, and the ballast is fairly low. It is interesting to consider how long the actual chunk of lead is: approximately half the length of her waterline. This would be frowned on today. By modern standards the aspect ratio of her rig is low. She even carried a bowsprit during her first season. This was removed in the spring of '31 before the transAtlantic race of that year.

So what made her win? *Dorade* was a remarkable success despite faults I have noted. These were more than offset by her good features. She was also sailed well and raced hard — but so were many of the boats she beat. The answer must be that, especially after her rig was cut down by removing the bowsprit and shortening the main mast, the combination was right. Particularly, the narrow beam and deep section combined to minimize her wetted area so that it took only a small rig to drive her. Thus, although she was relatively lighter than most of the competition, her rating was not high. This lightness helped her reaching and running. The long races in which she did so well were mostly sailed off the wind. She had several really great characteristics, being always easy to steer and control no matter how hard she may have been driven. She was and is (I am confused about tenses as she is still sailing) seakindly, and she went beautifully to weather in both light and heavy wind, and even better if the water was rough. It must be admitted, though, that her rolling has become legendary, and she was sometimes very wet on deck.

Dorade's first real race (to Bermuda) was an easy one. We had an able crew, including Father, Rod and me. There were three more who sailed with us the next summer to England, Buck Moore, Johnny Fox and Jim Merrill, plus Arthur Knapp and Marshall Rawle. The breeze was all under 18 knots, mostly less, and she liked

Dorade's transAtlantic crew is seen here right after finishing in Plymouth, England. L to R, standing — Eddie Koster, RS Sr., Jack Fox, Jim Merrill; front — Rod, Jr., OJS II, Buck Moore. Note one cigarette and a pipe. There was no smoking below. (Photo: Author's Collection)

that, especially in that first year before her rig was reduced. Her gear held up except for one incident. It was during a period when the wind had worked well into the west and we were carrying a spinnaker when the halyard let go and the sail dropped into the water. Fortunately we recovered it intact. The block had hung from a wire strop around the masthead and fatigue had weakened the wire. Rod got another halyard up there fast and we were able to quickly reset the same sail, but we learned to attach all such blocks with a metal-to-metal fitting.

In the afternoon before our expected landfall I worked up a sight that put us on a course about ten miles above the Kitchen Shoals mark near the finish. We corrected our course to reach down a little and the next morning we were clearly too low, just about doubling the length of the expected beat up to the finish. There was some compensation in the fact that we saw twelve larger boats ahead of us toward the finish and on the way passed them all, crossing the finish line ten seconds ahead of the leader. After finishing we hailed a committee boat near the finish line to hear that, although official time was taken only at the lighthouse, *Malabar X* had finished enough ahead of us to have saved her time. Later the smaller *Malay* finished soon enough after *Dorade* to save her time on both larger boats to become winner overall.

Looking back, that beat, as we ticked off one boat after another, is still a high point in my sailing experience because it confirmed all I had hoped for in *Dorade* — a real sea boat that could go to windward with the out-and-out racers. The sheer fun of steering a boat that could go like that should have been enough, and there was more. Each boat we passed added to our satisfaction until, in the final seconds we luffed to nick the biggest of the group.

In the lee of the islands there was very little sea but there was just enough slop to hurt the schooners with their greater beam and less-efficient rigs. *Dorade*'s narrow hull sliced through that chop, just loving it. Our tacks were long as we approached and became shorter as the lay lines grew closer. The breeze was moderate, maybe ten to twelve knots and just shifting enough to let us take advantage of the headers. We were racing every second; some of the others were cruising, but it took nothing away when we heard later how observers at St. David's had seen a tiny spot of white come in over the horizon, and how rapidly it grew. We heard that bets were made on who it was and when it would finish. I already had friends in Bermuda. Their appreciation of our last few miles eased the disappointment of failure to win.

After the finish we were ready for relief and invited aboard a genial black pilot who took the tiller and, though surprised that we had no engine, soon allowed that he was happy to take hold of such a lively and responsive charge. I guess some of the crew celebrated with a beer or two; I don't remember, but I know how our pilot entered into the spirit of a good sail, up through the reefs and Great Sound and Two Rock Passage into Hamilton Harbor where we dropped the hook.

Soon we learned officially about *Malabar X* and a few hours later we learned about *Malay*. Though we had lost enough time doing the extra windward distance to have beaten both boats we felt that *Dorade* had done well. I was happy with the boat if not with my navigation. It was great to be in Hamilton in our own vessel. I had been there in April for Six Metre sailing and remembered wondering how I was going to feel the next time I sighted Bermuda. I again visited around, swimming, while guarding better against the sun than I had two years before. It was fun to hear the nice things competitors said about our boat. One evening we had a great party. The crowd that came aboard almost sank us. Their weight put water deep in the normally self-bailing cockpit. Rod and I were teetotalers but Father was a proper host and was just as excited as any of us. I appreciate now, far more than I did then, that he had bet heavily on the ability of his two sons. Perhaps then, in Hamilton Harbor, he was thinking of that. He had a good time.

Although it was still early summer when we returned from Bermuda I had other new boats calling for attention. The first two Sixes, *Comet* and *Meteor*, had left for Lake Michigan after a few good early-season races. *Mist*, Jack Roosevelt's Six and Herman Whiton's Six *Cherokee* were just getting started. The Eight-Metre *Conewago* had, I think, made the passage through the canals to Rochester, New York. She missed out in the trials for the Canada's Cup but was later bought by Rooney Castle, winning subsequent trials and successfully defending the cup he had won in the Crane-designed Eight *Thisbe*. It was *Thisbe* that had beaten *Conewago* in that first season.

Plans for *Dorade* centered on the transAtlantic race scheduled for 1931. Mother was somewhat negative and the grandparents on Father's side seemed even more so. The intensity of Rod's hopes and my own eventually brought them around, and the grandparents provided us with a new hand-sewn Ratsey mainsail. Because the hand stitches were pulled tighter than stitches by machine the seams were less likely to suffer from chafe. The new sail was designed for a cut-down rig which we decided was advisable. A Kenyon speedometer was installed, one of the first, courtesy of Ted Kenyon. As the spring of 1931 came there were many lists to be compiled and checked off — food, charts, instruments and a hundred others. I remember painting contents on cans of food after removing paper labels to prevent them from blocking the limbers if there was water in the bilge. We had very little of that. One of the last of many jobs and activities was to pick up good water at Block Island before sailing to Newport for the start of the race to Plymouth, England. There we took on ice and eggs and milk, and rechecked as much as we could. We were ready.

As many readers will know, we had a good race. We had made a lucky decision about the course to follow. During the winter and spring the magazines ran articles about the choice of courses, basically south to get a boost from the Gulf Stream or farther north to shave distance by following a great circle. We had speculated with the other entries and noted an apparent preference for the Gulf Stream, although I was inclined toward the shorter course where I also saw the prospect of more wind. Fog was likely but my only concern was that, in my experience, fog was generally not accompanied by wind. I think the pilot charts suggested this, and I recalled that Bill Nutting had made a fast crossing from Baddeck, Nova Scotia, some years before in *Typhoon*. Casey Baldwin was one of his crew and I had met Casey in the Rhodes office. I wrote Casey for his opinion as a resident of Nova Scotia and a sailor who would be acquainted with fishermen. He said that fog was unlikely to kill the wind and that we should have plenty to keep us going. There was another consideration, too. If most of the fleet, as I believed, were to take a southern route, and we went with them, we would be racing most of the fleet. Other things being equal this would be one chance in ten. If we went north the odds were one chance in two, at least as I saw them. So, on July fourth, our good friend Bob Moore, father of crew member Buck, towed us out to the start. In a southerly breeze of about twelve knots we bore away from the rest of the fleet and sailed along the south shores of the Vineyard and Nantucket and then off a little more for Sable Island, the Grand Banks of Newfoundland and Cape Race.

During the first four days we had fog and we carried a good sailing breeze, not a lot but enough to keep us moving about seven knots. Our sole communication equipment was a small receiver tuned to a government weather station. "Some fog" were the words repeated and repeated. Once we broke out of it and hailed a Portuguese fishing bark. North of the Virgin Rocks we were startled to see what we took to be bottom and eventually reported it to the Hydrographic Office. A line of position showed us well clear of shoal water. We did not sight Cape Race but we were not far off, I think about 80 miles. As we got farther north and east we had more wind and it worked around behind us. We set the spinnaker and we rolled, sailing dead downwind, and after some hours we jibed and kept rolling. We did a 200-mile day and then another, jibing and rolling, and in our best five days we did more than a thousand miles. The wind was fresh but not too strong. We never shortened sail. Toward the end of this period we sighted the American liner *George Washington* and asked her to report us. I think that was on our fourteenth day.

We were approaching the far side of the ocean and the wind gradually lightened but held. On the evening of the fifteenth day our sights put us about 30 miles west of the Scillies. Rod had been wanting to go up the mast and finally I said OK.

Nearing the masthead he looked forward and called "Land ho." The wind that was left went gradually lighter and it was on the morning of day 17 that the *Lizard* came abeam. We set a flag signal, reading "what are we," and it was an excited crew that read the response "you are first."

We swept the area with binoculars and found nothing resembling the competition. That excitement had hardly passed before a big square-rigger sailed by us heading down the English Channel. Quite a day. But we were still racing and we kept her going while we made ready for port. We cleaned up as best we could. We sailed into Plymouth without too much evidence of a 17-day voyage.

Though it is properly known as "old," it was for us a new world on the other side of the Atlantic. As we finished we were warmly greeted by Bobby Somerset, a legendary figure in offshore racing and then Vice Commodore of the Royal Ocean Racing Club. The little news of the other boats suggested that they were a long way off. At the yacht club we received word that mother, wife and sister were hurrying south from the Lake District where they had been touring when we were reported from the Lizard. Then there were hot showers and clean clothes and dinner with Bobby S. at his nearby home, with the form, if not the dimensions, of an old-world castle. How does one describe the excitement?

It was two days before *Landfall* and *Highland Light* came in over the horizon in a close race for what they assumed was first to finish. I hope our brashness was excused when we went out to meet them with our family on board. We could almost see their jaws drop as they recognized their smaller competitor; but they were extremely gracious and *Landfall*'s owner, Paul Hammond, had presented a beautiful Plath sextant which I won as navigator of the winning boat. I treasured this until, years later, it was removed from our home by a burglar.

After a few days ashore we returned to the Channel and, with the augmented family aboard, sailed on to Cowes. Luckily the wind was fair and moderate and for brief excitement we had only the rough sea of Portland Race to sail through. That we hit suddenly with hatches open. Immediately the deck was flooded and more than a little water found its way below. *Dorade* passed the Needles in the evening and, well after dark, dropped anchor in Cowes roads.

We all enjoyed the pleasure of morning in a new harbor. Where before there had been only a few spots of light, now we found green trees and tile-roofed houses and another castle; and off the castle a yacht, the most beautiful yacht ever. It was the King's (or should I say G.L. Watson's?) *Britannia*. I have often told how Susie, my wife since the previous October, came on deck and, seeing *Britannia*, demanded, "Buy me one of those."

The excitement continued with dinner at the Royal Yacht Squadron's castle and a visit to the Royal steam yacht where our crew were introduced to the King. At dinner I sat next to a very elderly Squadron member carrying on a lively conversation. Later I was told it had been years since this individual had been able to hear conversation. I must have shouted but it seemed to go well. On the Royal yacht the King was most gracious and seemed interested in our young crew. Father, much the eldest, would have been 46 although he seemed old to the rest of us. We really believed that no one who started sailing at more than 10 years old could truly learn sailing, and we let him know it. I fear today that, in the event, we took all he had done for his two sons as the normal action of a parent rather than the amazing expression of love and confidence that I appreciate now.

Dorade's only race in Cowes was a Squadron regatta. I'm not sure how they gave us a rating but we sailed hard, setting a ballooner and small mizzen staysail on a reach, still with a reef in the main. Although we did not win, we placed, and received a beautiful silver plate with the Squadron symbol inlaid in gold.

We prepared *Dorade* for the Fastnet Race, in British tradition the counterpart of the American Bermuda Race. While much of the course is alongshore, the Channel and the Irish Sea have strong currents and highly variable winds, and the Fastnet has the reputation of being tough. We added two men to our crew. One was Briggs Cunningham, active in the Six-Metre Class and later skipper of *Columbia* in the 1958 America's Cup. He was a good sport to join our sea-adapted crew for his first offshore race. The other, a good sport too, was Commander Hawkridge of the British Naval Reserve and, in civilian life, in fishing-boat insurance. He knew the waters. I think our urgency to drive the boat and to win frightened him a little, especially as we pushed hard across the Irish Sea toward Fastnet Rock.

This hard push was the highlight of the race for me. We had rounded Land's End well up with the best in the fleet and were determined to hold our position. As the wind built from astern, all carried spinnakers. It was getting dark with the wind beginning to whistle as the larger boats either dropped their spinnakers or had them blown away, which was the case with *Highland Light*, near us. I went off watch about then and lay down on my chart-table berth at the foot of the companion ladder. We were sailing fast and I thought it was wonderful as I felt her roll, first with the main boom hitting the water and then the spinnaker pole almost doing the same. I could hear the water coming in over the bow and rushing down the side deck, moving fast, much of it over the cabin trunk and companionway. It sounded a little like Niagara Falls, yet I was protected from the activity above and happy to sense the speed as the wind continued to build. Toward the middle of the watch Father called down from the deck to say that they thought up there that we should douse the spinnaker. I watched the Kenyon speedometer over my bunk for a short time, admiring the way the hand on the dial went into its second round, better than ten knots, and I turned over, saying only "let's hang on." Not much later I sensed a deeper flood over the deck and Father came below. Exercising parental authority he ordered me on deck to observe the true conditions. Putting on foul-weather gear I squeezed through the almost-closed companionway and perched on the after end of the cabin when another sea almost swept me into the cockpit and I yielded. "Yes, get it off." One crew member has recalled that the sail blew away just then, but I think the crew saved it.

As we went on with the speedometer in almost the same range Commander Hawkridge was really worrying. I think he had confidence in the boat but, with wartime experience in a destroyer, thought we were going fast enough to sail right onto the Irish coast before dawn. I guess we might have done that by sailing at 13 knots but not at the 10 or so which I knew was our maximum even with the hardest driving. So it was well into daylight with a moderating breeze when we sighted land and adjusted our course to round Fastnet Rock, still with the big boys. Going back to the east it breezed on again, but even with driving we could not hold the bigger and faster yachts. We finished well up in the fleet to win on

corrected time by a healthy margin.

That was *Dorade*'s summer. The crew spent a week or so in London and returned in the liner *Homeric*. *Dorade*, too, had been lifted into a cradle, well-protected between two deckhouses and easily boarded from the ship's deck. Many passengers with whom we made friends let us show off the boat. Reaching home we were given a New York welcome complete with ticker tape and a welcome talk by the deputy mayor. It was an experience, fun, but best was getting back to normal family life and work.

In the next chapter I will tell something about my next summer with the Six

At left, touring cars form a line for New York's welcome-home parade up Broadway to City Hall for *Dorade*'s crew. The crew had been picked up from the liner *Homeric* by a tug and and taken to cars lined up at the Battery. Evidently the city favored Packards. It would be fun to have one of them today. Here, unusual formality on the part of three Stephens's, ready to disembark from the *Homeric*. (Photos: Courtesy of Sparkman & Stephens)

WELCOME HOME DORADE CREW

Metres again in England, living in Cowes and racing in the Solent. After Cowes I went to the Clyde as a member of *Jill*'s crew. With Seward Johnson sailing we took the Seawanhaka Cup back to Oyster Bay. Rod took *Dorade* in the Bermuda Race in 1932 and won the smaller class while Alden's *Malabar X*, in the bigger class, won overall.

In 1933 I stayed home while Rod took *Dorade* on a summer cruise to Norway, Holland, England for the Fastnet, and back home. He had a very different crew which included the old master Sherman Hoyt, "Ducky" Endt, Porter Buck, and a cook new to sailing, David Leson. As in 1931 they took a northerly route going east. But returning from England they sailed north again. That was plausible for late summer-early fall, clear of the hurricane paths, but cold and against the prevailing winds, meaning a lot of sailing close-hauled. Most yachts sailing from east to west have gone for the easterly trades much farther south and later in the year. Rod did a great job, again winning the Fastnet after enjoying the Scandinavian and Dutch coasts and making exceptionally fast crossings, especially coming back. He was later given the Blue Water Medal of the Cruising Club of America.

I had a very different summer. One of Drake's brokerage clients, Horace Havemeyer, had brought over a top British Twelve Metre named *Mouette*. Due to the depression it looked as though he would have no racing in the class. So he backed us in the charter of one of the Twelves designed by Starling Burgess, and on weekends we did all we could with the older and heavier boat. Drake and I took turns as skipper and both were able to make our benefactor work to win. We had occasional wins of our own including the Astor Cup on the NYYC Cruise.

I am often asked whether my wife Susie enjoyed sailing and I reply with a qualified "Yes," although when there was 'round-the-buoys racing on a large boat with good friends and several professionals, as it was that summer, no qualification was needed. Racing a smaller boat of our own, as in the early Six-Metre days, she liked the excitement; but as I became busy professionally and sailed always with clients there was seldom a good place for her, or later for our two boys. *Iris,* "our" Twelve, unlike the America's Cup boats, had very decent accommodations below and she, with all of us, enjoyed that sailing. We spent frequent nights on board.

Dorade's reputation and Drake's effective promotion brought new work. I was particularly pleased that we were able to arrange for the construction of two new offshore boats at the Nevins yard as this spelled confidence in the quality of the result. *Stormy Weather* was strictly for offshore racing; *Edlu* was for more comfortable cruising. Both were proportionately wider than *Dorade*. Times were not good and *Stormy*'s owner drove a tough bargain. I mention this because it is notable that this boat, inches less than 40′ on the water and 54′ overall, was built in 1933-34 for $20,000, the owner's stated limit. A boat of similar dimensions today would come into the $800,000-dollar-range. *Edlu*, slightly heavier and more complete below, cost a little but not a lot more.

Interestingly enough *Edlu* became the winner of the 1934 Bermuda Race. *Stormy* was well up, though not a winner. Rod and I sailed *Dorade*. She was well up, too; I think we had a second in class. At this time I began to think seriously about rating rules, and I was pleased to see the heavier *Edlu* hold off the more extreme *Stormy Weather*. I was also glad to see the newer beamier boats do better than narrow *Dorade*.

Perhaps *Dorade* deserved an assist toward *Edlu*'s win. We were sailing in a typical fresh sou'westerly breeze at dawn of the third day. We had slowly sailed through to leeward of a bobbing light in the small hours, and as dawn came we could see the reefed-down *Edlu* on our weather quarter. We were carrying full sail. Though heeled well over we were making good weather of it and moving faster than our competitor. *Edlu* could see this, and it was not long before we could see her main going up to the masthead and a larger headsail being set. Then *Edlu* began gaining on *Dorade*. As I have noted, she became the winner.

Sadly, Father and Mother had separated after the transAtlantic summer, and Father had made a gift of *Dorade* to Rod and me. Her success, as much as anything, had made us busier and busier and we decided that we would have little time for sailing in our own boat. We finally concluded that we must sell her. Drake found a buyer in James Flood of San Francisco and we reluctantly said goodbye to a great friend. Word that she had continued to sail fast by winning the Honolulu Race in 1935 alleviated some regrets. She was in good hands. I am pleased that as I write this in 1998 she is still in good hands.

4

The early success with Dorade was paralleled in the Six-Metre Class when four new boats performed well and one of them, Cherokee, won the Long Island Sound championship. I was fortunate in knowing the class from following it closely and from sailing Natka, our family Six. It was lucky that I had recognized the faults in my first Six-Metre design attempt, Thalia, and corrected the worst of them. I am ever grateful for the help of Clinton Crane who, I know, directed several clients to me. He was the most successful designer of Six Metres in this country. Doing the designs as an amateur he apparently did not wish to take on work which might have gone to one whose livelihood depended on it. All of the early design work went well, and by the fall of 1933 in the small storefront office on City Island I and two assistants had to move fast to keep up with it all. Not helpful, I had to travel frequently between City Island and 44th Street near Madison Avenue, where Drake Sparkman had the main office and the brokerage department.

In late '34 we moved the design work to the same building. I normally drove downtown, following, through the Bronx, Fordham Road and the Grand Concourse, and I remember one day approaching the then-new Bronx Courthouse when the car radio shifted programs to describe the Hindenburg fire as it was happening. I have always liked travel by car. I feel in control and I like to have with me the things I may need.

During these summers in the 'thirties I spent a lot of time on the water sailing in all of the new boats, the Sixes and fast cruisers. Before becoming too busy I sailed in dinghies on winter weekends. Frostbiting in small boats began on New Year's Day in 1931. One of the original participants was a dinghy we had built for *Dorade*. Designed to carry the whole crew, she was high-sided and slow. During the two winters following I sailed often on weekends and designed several of the boats. Length was restricted to 12′ and sail to 72 square feet. Dinghies were fun, but as the recovery from the depression brought new work in larger boats I did less and less frostbiting.

One of my most happy recollections of the years following 1930 was the annual early spring trek of the Six Metres and Sound Interclubs to Bermuda. The Trimingham brothers and some friends in Hamilton had brought in four new Sixes designed and built by the Norwegian Bjarne Aas. They were excellent all-around boats and, in 1930, were successful in winning against an American team, one of whose boats was *Thalia*. Although she wasn't impossibly bad in light going, the Bermuda weather was much too heavy for her, as she dragged that big wake whenever the wind picked up. Despite the fun of the racing and the opportunity to learn, I spent some wakeful nights while the wind whistled outside the window, fearing that the next race would not go well if the wind held. But nothing would turn off that wind. Yet what is more fun than sailing to windward in a strong wind in a good stable boat well-suited to the conditions? During later Bermuda visits I had that pleasure, but not in 1930 with *Thalia*.

Fortunately other Sixes were being built. It was too late for owners to cancel if they had doubts. I knew that all of them were bigger and more powerful boats and I was confident that the displacement was better distributed. Still I was impatient when the first of the new Sixes of 1930 went overboard. She was one of two sister-ships for owners who summered in Charlevoix, on Lake Michigan, and both were built by Henry Nevins. Mr. N did his best to hold me in check to give these new wooden boats a chance to swell and tighten their planking. It was blowing hard from the northwest when finally Rod and I could wait no longer to get out under sail, optimistically saying that the breeze was fading. We sailed the new Sixes over to moorings that had been prepared at Larchmont. It was good to feel their power, and to see that the new boats sailed without a breaking quarter wave.

Below is the Six-Metre *Nancy*. The author sailed her as a member of the winning American team in the British-American Cup in the Solent, England, in 1932. Each of four boats took one race. A headstay has replaced the jumpers of 1930. Though the head of the working jib is still low, the Genoa could be carried right up to the mast. (Photo: Beken of Cowes)

Our newest design in 1932, a boat named *Nancy*, was owned by three good sailors from the Seawanhaka Corinthian Yacht Club of Oyster Bay, all involved with Wall Street. She had been designed and built expressly to compete in the British-American team races, to be sailed that year in England. The bad financial situation led them to ask me to sail *Nancy* in England and I jumped at the chance. My teammates were two more S&S boats that had come out in 1931 — *Bobcat*, owned by Bob Meyer, and *Jill*, owned by J. Seward Johnson of the medical-supply firm. I should note that Seward Johnson was not only an S&S client but later was very helpful financially with our early tank-testing efforts. Briggs Cunningham's Crane-designed *Lucie* made the fourth team member. This was the first American team to win in the Solent, with each one of our boats winning one of the races. There was little excitement to the racing. Our boats were marginally faster and we had become familiar with the local conditions. There were some limited team tactics, like luffing to hold back a competitor for the good of a teammate. This may explain the distribution among winners. Later in the summer *Jill* went to Scotland to race on the Clyde where she recovered the Seawanhaka Cup.

Preparing to race in the Solent our team worked hard. Did we work too hard? If winning is important, so is thorough preparation; but it may be that too much preparation overwhelms the sport. I wonder whether in 1932, as possibly even in 1931, we may have let the effort to win take precedence over the "sporting" reasons to be there. None of us felt so at the time, but to the extent that our intensity foreshadowed attitudes that have become universally accepted today, I look back with concern at the 'thirties. They might now be recognized as the entering wedge of something unfortunate.

Our hard work consisted of getting to England three weeks before the match. There we lived in a team house and went sailing every morning. We studied the unusual tidal conditions resulting from entrances to the Solent at opposite ends of the Isle of Wight, and we placed small buoys at points of interest regarding depth of water or strength of current. When the races started we felt we knew the Solent better than the native sailors.

Despite our serious effort we gave Bob Meyer, our team captain, a fright when, returning from a weekend in London, he saw the four boats of the team high and dry on the Shingles Bank. That day, in a practice race, one after the other had hit the sand hard on a falling tide and as it dried out the boats were stranded. Fortunately the water was smooth as the water rose and the boats returned to their moorings without damage.

Our new offshore boats did well, too, during the first years of the firm. Different was *Brilliant*, a schooner, and in no sense a racing boat. Launched in 1932, she is still beautifully kept and sailed for training at Mystic Seaport. She was built by

The schooner *Brilliant*, at left, was launched by Nevins at City Island, New York, in 1932 and is still actively sailing out of Mystic Seaport in 1999. This 1930s photo shows her traditionally-rigged, with fitted topmast and square yard. The square-sail was seldom used, and after the war the gaff main was replaced by a jib-headed sail on a pole mast. Walter Barnum, *Brilliant*'s owner, wanted the ultimate in seagoing ability and all-round quality and came as close as humanly possible. *Brilliant* is very different from *Malabar IX*.
(Photo: Rosenfeld Collection 68101F)

Nevins for Walter Barnum, who asked for the ultimate in seagoing ability and safety. I have always believed that the first assurance of safety must be the ability to stay afloat, to keep out the water. This implies strong construction, and this client was all for the best that could be found in materials and workmanship. *Brilliant*'s long and active life shows what Nevins could do.

For my part, in design, I tried to stick to the basics of clean, balanced lines, the avoidance of extremes in displacement or beam, and providing low wetted area to the degree permitted by adequate lateral plane. In overall geometry and keel profile I looked for guidance to the study I had made of *Terns III* and *IV*, both designed by the British writer on deepwater cruising, Claud Worth. I parted from Worth, however, to favor stability by putting as much ballast as possible outside on the keel. *Brilliant* sails well and her motion has never been criticized as unduly quick. I think of her as an early success and still a standard in seagoing ability.

The autumn of '33 brought two important new orders noted briefly in the previous chapter. In contrast to *Brilliant* both owners wished to race, although one boat,

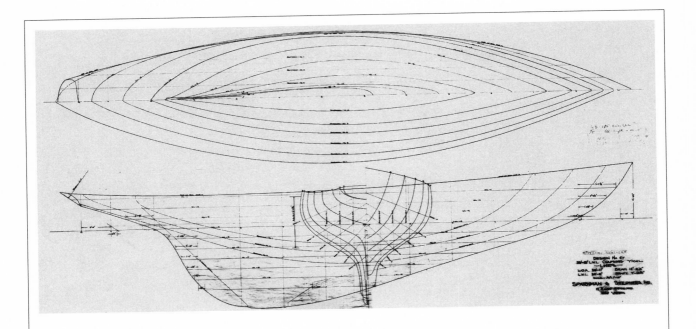

Here are lines of *Stormy Weather,* interesting to compare with *Dorade* on page 44. The greater beam is obvious in the body plan, illustrating the sections. A more cutaway profile saves wetted area. Interestingly, except to Bermuda in 1934, it was not until 1999 that the two met in organized competition. Reports from Italy say that the racing was close, with *Dorade* beautifully restored and with new sails, and *Stormy* awaiting restoration. When *Stormy* is restored, and with a little wind, no doubt the later, beamier design will be justified.

to be named *Edlu,* was to include cruising space and comfort. The second was *Stormy Weather,* designed for Philip LeBoutillier as an out-and-out racer like *Dorade.* Both of these boats benefited from construction by Nevins and from more beam and thus stability. *Edlu* was heavier, while *Stormy* had about the same relative displacement as *Dorade.* Both had their racing successes, *Edlu* when she won the '34 Bermuda Race. That was the last race Rod and I sailed in *Dorade,* and our part in *Edlu*'s win has been described.

The story of *Stormy Weather,* beginning in '34, includes a long list of victories, her most notable summer coming in 1935 when, with Rod in charge and Phil LeBoutiller, Jr. in the crew, she won the transAtlantic race to Bergen and went on to take the Fastnet in British waters. As he had done in *Dorade* the year before, Rod sailed her home. She is still one of my favorite designs, probably the best I could do without the later help of model testing. She combines fairly long easy lines with small wetted area and good stability. Like *Dorade* and *Brilliant* she is still sailing.

Although pleased with the performance of the new boats, the feeling that I had done my best was, in its implications, troubling. Somehow I felt I was beginning to grope a little for the next step. On two designs of late '34 I tried a slightly lower prismatic coefficient, and when they raced the next summer I was a little disappointed in their performance. Analyzing performance is difficult. It is easy to explain doing poorly, which may involve handling, sails, luck. When you do well it's the whole combination. Poorly, one small slip and you're out of the money. To do better I needed something new and positive, and that came along through Professor

Kenneth Davidson of the Stevens Institute of Technology in 1933. I will soon tell more about Ken Davidson and his work, but only after going further into the simple design principles that I had been following.

Those principles were performance-directed and were governed by observation and comparison with the best I could imagine, leading to analysis of the differences between designs. *Dorade*, for example, was certainly too narrow. As a result she heeled too easily and too far, losing drive from her rig and forcing her crew to live in a limited space and remain balanced at a high angle of heel. Out of that fault came *Stormy Weather*, a boat with two feet more beam, faster, roomier and more stable.

I think I was fortunate in the ability to see these faults, for my armament of academic knowledge was small. I always had a target, frequently in the form of existing types which I thought I could improve upon, such as the fisherman-type schooner. And, as the story of *Dorade* shows, I was just as critical of my own efforts. There always were tradeoffs, such as the battle between wetted area and stability. Evaluating the effects of the differences was guesswork. To get the better often meant having to live with the worse. In a beamier boat, did added sail area and stability compensate for increased wetted area and drag due to encountered waves? Performance was dependent on the outcome of this tradeoff. As a minimum, I took care to produce fair lines with good balance at the ends, both of which I was convinced are important to performance and also to appearance. I am still sure of this. I guess a good eye for a boat helped.

While considering principles of design, I think it would be a mistake to suggest any real difference between my way of thinking and the methods of some other designers such as Starling Burgess with whom I later collaborated. I believe we had a great deal in common in our understanding of yacht performance. If I was lucky to become busy in years that were leaner for others, it may have been the result of two things: my youth and an intense commitment to ocean racing. I may have been on my own in applying racing-boat principles to cruising and offshore racing designs.

It may not be evidence of a kind disposition, but I was always critical, always looking for faults. Features in other boats that I admired, I copied. I think it helped me to have very little respect for practices of any kind just because they existed. I was young, skeptical, critical. Despite such views I studied the books and magazines and admired English types more than those I saw at home. I have mentioned the influence of Claud Worth, the English doctor, writer, and designer, whose *Tern IV* I greatly admired. Those who know Worth's boat and my *Brilliant* design may see his inspiration; both are shaped and built not as racing yachts but as sea boats intended to survive the worst weather and to make good passages. To me passagemaking and winning races called for very different designs. Race-winning meant small wetted area, in turn a shorter keel and deep sections, with as much outside ballast as possible. Worth would not have approved those characteristics because they make for speed rather than comfort. But to me the ballast outside made for safety for a greater range of positive stability.

The purpose of a design must always be considered, for purpose leads to type. Owners' wishes are apt to be pretty well-developed, and they form the principal guide. Racing? Cruising? Homeport and sailing area? Class? With a racing boat designed to class rules, like a Six Metre or Twelve Metre, it is easier to be specific. A class is chosen and the designer's judgement applied to the expected weather and sea conditions will provide many of the answers, which are largely left to the designer. The cruising boat is more complex and compromise is the key.

In racing boats rating rules, of course, go a long way toward defining a design. The shape of the Six Metres and the one Eight Metre that I designed in those early years was intended to get the most out of the International Rule. Then, as now, the difference between girth and height at the ends was added to length, taken slightly above the flotation line, plus the square root of the sail area. Sail area was taken as the sum of the main triangle — boom length times hoist — divided by two plus 85% of the foretriangle. The sum was divided by a constant to give the class rating, expressed in metres.

The balance of sail area and length, as well as the ways of measuring sail area, inspired several experiments. In about 1927 Sherman Hoyt had designed a Six, appropriately named *Atrocia* because of her strange rig, in which the mast was in the center of the boat and the jib must have made up 75% of the total sail. He took advantage of the seemingly undervalued foretriangle by putting well more than half of the boat's sail area into the jib. The boat was not fast, maybe due to the fact that the jib was on a boom, evidently for quick and easy tacking (it was before the era of the Genoa jib). On our boats, the forward triangle was high but rather short on the base as I felt that the Genoa and main would work together better that way. Later the base would become longer, but nobody ever did anything like another *Atrocia* rig on a metre boat. Had a limit not later been placed on the allowed foretriangle height of the International-Rule classes, the big jib would be used today.

The Sixes to beat in the early 1930s were Clinton Crane's. The rigs were conventional, with rather small foretriangles. The hull design was more interesting. The International Rule provides that the girth difference aft is divided by three while forward it is taken one and one-half times actual value to discourage scow types and in recognition that a normal hull form is sharper up forward. Clinton Crane took full advantage of this cheap stern girth by using a wide and low after overhang with a narrow U-shaped bow. By contrast, the ends on the S&S boats were closer to a balance, possibly losing some upright advantage in sailing length that I hoped to recover through better heeled performance due to a more nearly horizontal heeling axis.

I knew from the beginning the importance of the right builder. Fortunately I knew and was known by the builders of City Island where nearly all of our early designs were carried out. Some yards are more careful than others in their adherence to the design. And no matter how careful they may be it is the builder, right down to the man fitting a small piece of wood, that makes decisions affecting the strength and the outcome of the weight calculation. Some yards also, especially those accustomed to building commercial vessels, which must take rough treatment, tend toward making everything a little heavier than planned. Yards that specialize in racing boats need to be careful to avoid such choices and to deliver hulls that are both light and strong. From Henry Nevins through his whole office staff to the lowest position in the yard each man knew his job and did it well. I was happy whenever I

could arrange for Nevins to build a new boat. This became routine for Six Metres, but it was especially satisfying when a fast cruiser — a racing/cruising yacht — was worked into the shop. The right balance between lightness and strength can mean everything in a racer.

It would not be fair to forget the Minneford yard in City Island. At first they were second to Nevins, but later they took the top place. They built many good boats to our plans. The first was *Kalmia* and the last was *Freedom*. Their aluminum Twelves were excellent. *Dorade*, of course was built there, and a number of wooden boats, including the Twelves *Constellation* and *Intrepid*. Then *Courageous* was built there in aluminum. The Minneford yard was owned by H.S. Sayers, who was not a boatbuilder but had real-estate interests on City Island, where he lived, and in the east Bronx. His two sons in succession managed the yard and accepted the responsibility for organizing a highly competent group of boatbuilders.

We were neighbors to both yards in our storefront office until 1934, and most of those years were the bottom years of the depression. The depression surely made a difference to the City Island yards. There must have been much unemployment, during the 'thirties. That may have helped our new office because both Nevins and Minneford were available to build our smaller boats, not having more or bigger boats such as Nevins especially had previously built. With a small but growing business, I was less aware of the depression than most.

Theoretical advice or discussion of yacht design was difficult to come by in those early days of Sparkman & Stephens, although the study of statics, hull form, and stability is rather simple. As I have said, I found that observation and intuition were my best tools. Today we have far more quantitative guidance in yacht design, thanks to the computer's ability to handle complex and repetitive arithmetic. Remarkable work on theoretical hydrodynamics was done back in the eighteenth century, soon after Newton (1695), but it was too complex to follow through by hand. The computer's memory and quick, accurate arithmetic now make possible even such operations as the solution of massive sets of simultaneous equations, recognized early in the 1700s by Leonhard Euler and others. We can now be more nearly certain of the effects, separately and combined, of the most important characteristics of design and engineering work. But in the 1930s such knowledge was mainly theory. Ken Davidson quantified the empirical part of it in the small towing tank. Undoubtedly some designers depended more than others on their calculations. Naval architecture as statics was well-developed by my time, and fully covered by some textbooks, such as the Atwood and White books that Starling Burgess recommended to me. Weights were fundamental, as they remain. By the careful and complete measurement of the volumes and densities of the entire structure and equipment, and the summing of each part's weight and position, the weight and center of gravity of the entire boat was able to be determined. The key words are "careful" and "complete." Both are difficult, introducing more or less uncertainty. Those words still apply as the computer has made calculating weights easier and quicker.

While there has been a technical revolution in construction and calculations, our understanding of the statics of yacht design has changed only by defining and fairing the hull surface points by computer. In our time the lines were faired on paper with splines, while areas were taken with a planimeter, a small rolling instrument with which an outline of any closed shape was traced with a pointer while a vernier dial registered the area. Heeled stability, to the extent that section shape caused it to depart from the straight line given by the metacentric height, could be taken with an integrator, which was a more complicated planimeter that provided centers or centroids as well as areas. Ratings and some other calculations were done with logarithms. I did most calculations then with a slide rule. Today computers and electronic calculators have completely displaced these instruments, which were then the normal working equipment of the naval architect.

My understanding of hull resistance was limited by the interpretation of ship data. Its application to yacht forms was nowhere documented. An Englishman, William Froude, had provided the fundamentals of model-testing in the 1870s, and an American Navy Admiral, David W. Taylor, later used Froude's method to publish the results of tests made on a systematically designed set of models, using a range of proportions appropriate for most naval and commercial vessels. But yacht geometry and scale are so different from those of ships that the way to use such data was uncertain. Their use was in the nature of study rather than design. Subject only to such reservations, I found Admiral Taylor's book *The Speed and Power of Ships* a useful guide. I became familiar with it and found it helpful as a supplement to observation in selecting hull proportions, especially the prismatic coefficient.

This coefficient, usually designated Cp, is a number that indicates a hull's fineness. It is the ratio between the volume of the hull on the one hand and the volume of a prism or block having all sections equal in area to the area of the largest hull section and a length equal to the waterline length of the hull. Cp is the percentage of that block occupied by the hull volume. In other words, the block is a prism as long as the boat's waterline, all sections the same size from end to end. That would be like a scow and would have a coefficient of 1.00. In a typical yacht hull the smaller sections toward the sharpened ends result in a value slightly above 0.5, the volume being just over half that of the scow. To represent three dimensions by two, solid by flat, naval architects normally plot a displacement curve or curve of areas in which the area of each design station along the length of the boat is marked as a linear measurement and a curve passed through the points. Over the years there have been many theories advanced as to the best shape for this curve in its effect on hull drag. None have defined a shape better than a fair continuous curve with the center of buoyancy near the mid-length or slightly farther aft, and a mid-section neither too large nor too small as measured by the prismatic coefficient.

I was glad to find any guidance on the prismatic. It was a challenge to select the right number, and any such number must be a compromise because we know that the best coefficient depends on the boat's speed, varying considerably over a range that depends on the wind strength and the point of sailing. Textbooks give the values as they differ with speed. Intended for ships, how should these values be applied to the different shapes and variable speeds of yachts? Probably rightly, I had diagnosed the trouble with *Thalia*, my early Six, as the result of too large a midship section, meaning too low a prismatic, concentrating the displacement amidships. Using a higher value on subsequent boats worked well, and I have ever since worked within a narrow range, numerically between 0.50 and 0.535, applying the higher values to heavy-weather boats and the lower for boats to be sailed in light winds — i.e. slower sailing. This number applies to the hull forms typical between the 1930s and about 1970, when the keel was faired into the body of the boat and was itself fair in outline. Because there was no way the keel and hull could be distinguished consistently the volume of the keel was taken as part of the hull. Today, as most keels are distinct from the hull, it is usual to omit the keel from the calculation, and to use a higher numerical range. Whichever method is used, this and all similar coefficients seem best applied in a comparative way, observing the effect from one design to another.

I know that it was felt around our office that I was something of a fanatic about the prismatic, and that I may have required unnecessary changes in lines drawings that did not quite fit the number I had selected for a particular boat. This I sensed as a little in-house joke. Aside from Admiral Taylor's work there were a few other textbooks and technical papers on ship design that I was aware of. One was the book *Ship Design* by G. S. Baker, an English naval architect and sometime colleague of Froude. My copy is dated 1933 and I have had it since about that time. Today the literature on the design of yachts is far more extensive.

In the 1930s, when I was still in my early twenties, my education was advanced by three visitors to that first design office on City Island. Located on the street level on City Island Avenue, it was easily and frequently (if often at the cost of interruption) a tempting place for visitors to come in and talk boats. One of the pleasant occasional visitors was Fred Dellenbaugh, who passed along a tool of basic naval architecture that carries his name. There was nothing new in Fred's theory, but the convenient form was his. The Dellenbaugh coefficient formula provides a simple way to estimate the stability of a sailing yacht. It finds the heeling moment with an assumed wind pressure of one pound per square foot of sail area applied at the center of effort of the rig. With knowledge of the righting moment, the heel angle is easily found. The formula then gives the expected heel angle at the assumed wind pressure.[1]

Another interesting visitor to the City Island office was a member of the Herreshoff family, Francis, a cousin of the better known L. Francis Herreshoff and nephew of Captain Nat. If he had an occupation it was unknown to me. He turned up every month or so at City Island to look at the new boats and talk design. His greatest interest was in model boats and he persuaded me to do a couple of model-yacht designs which were moderately successful although I had little time to follow them in detail. His contribution also related to fore-and-aft balance, particularly important in models for the sake of their steering. He used a word of his own, "corrajingle," to describe a set of lines in which the shape of each section, from bow to stern, was notably similar to its neighbor, and so to all the others. It was a guide to the eye. This seemed both a good and an effective principle. Often when the force of compliance with some rating rule suggested abandoning this principle, I have been tempted to ignore it, and I have been sorry if I did.

Dellenbaugh's visits to our storefront office on City Island Avenue were extremely helpful to me, and the Herreshoff calls were interesting, but more valuable yet was the arrival of Ken Davidson. He was teaching at the Stevens Institute of Technology in Hoboken, New Jersey, and thinking about model-testing sailing yachts. He had seen a movie Father had made of our transAtlantic race in *Dorade* and heard about what I was doing. In the winter of 1932-33 he came to City Island to talk boats and to look for small models. His twin objectives were to find some small models to test and to stir up interest in his work.

Ken described the work he was doing at Stevens in the college swimming pool, where he had arranged an endless line running over demountable pulleys at either end of the pool. In order to change the speed with which the models were towed, the constant-speed electric drive could be varied by adjusting the pulley diameter. He had rigged a rather crude yacht model so that it carried on deck a light spring scale that indicated the force needed to tow the model down the pool. The readings

---

[1] Fred put this in simple (computer format) terms as Dc=57.3*SaHt/GM*Displ). Dc (Dellenbaugh coefficient) refers to the angle. Sa, Ht, and Displ are sail area, height of the center of pressure and displacement. GM is the metacentric height, the vertical separation between the center of gravity and the point on the hull centerline directly above the center of buoyancy as the boat heels. The constant, 57.3, is the number of degrees in a radian of angular measure and has the effect that the denominator in the fraction represents the product of righting arm for one degree and the displacement, which is the righting moment for one degree. Dividing this into the total heeling moment, measured by the product of area and height, gives the expected heel angle at the assumed wind pressure. Conveniently, one pound per square foot occurs at around 13 knots of apparent wind. This is rather low for an average, but at angles in the low range the righting moment falls close to a straight line so that projections to more wind are easily made. The parameters entering this simple formula should be readily available from estimates at the start of a design, and later, with more precision.

were noted by an observer who walked alongside the model as it was drawn through the water. The observer-assistant was Allen Murray, then a student at the school. For years to follow he was Ken's right-hand man at the tank. His care and good judgement contributed greatly to the usefulness of the tank.

Ken's visit was successful on both counts: Rod could supply a model of the Six-Metre *Natka*, and I was immediately anxious to learn what I could. The first phase of learning required several years. Thinking back I am not sure how far into the future Ken could see. He solved problems as they came up, although I don't think they were always expected; but the steps he took were consistent and progress seemed steady.

The *Natka* model was one of a pair that Rod had made from the lines of Fred Hoyt to test rigs. *Natka* was almost new but had not been a winner in her first season, and her owner was replacing her with a new Crane design. We found that she took care of us well enough when we gave her the right chance. She was a good boat for learners. One of the models had the boat's typical Six-Metre rig, with a small foretriangle. The other was more like *Atrocia*'s, all foretriangle. The models were hard to control and the test results were inconclusive. It was not long before one of these was in the Stevens swimming pool. Force readings were repeatable considering the portable, and rather crude, nature of the test rig. The differences between the earlier and later models seemed reasonable, as did the full-scale expansions, although there was no accurate guide to measure the drag of the full-scale yacht, as *Natka* had gone ashore in a fall storm some years before.

The next step was crucial. It paved the way to all of Ken's later work. To our considerable disappointment at that time the firm of Sparkman & Stephens was saddled with a small boat called *Gimcrack*, 34′ overall and fairly light. We had built her in partnership with the Nevins yard as a demonstrator for one-design racing on Long Island Sound, but the order had gone to Norway in the form of the International One-Design Class, so *Gimcrack* was available for experiment and test. Ken produced and calibrated a very nice spring dynamometer with an oil dashpot, while Rod and I arranged to use a carefully cleaned-up *Gimcrack*.

Our test consisted of two phases, towing and sailing. In both we measured speed in two ways: a combination pitot and impact tube extended ahead of the boat on a bowsprit, and a chip log was launched over the stern. While sailing we simultaneously measured speed, heel angle, and apparent wind speed. I sailed the best windward course according to the wind strength. Later the apparent wind angle was found by working back from these data and the tacking angle. Previously when the wind was calm, a Nevins launch towed *Gimcrack* on a long line while we steered out of the towboat's wake. We measured speed and, with the dynamometer, drag. A detailed description of these tests and the results is given in a paper, now considered a classic, that Ken presented to the Society of Naval Architects and Marine Engineers.[2] The derivation of sail force coefficients which this work made possible gave the tools to predict the windward performance of yachts whose model had been tested.

While these full-scale tests were being done, a small-scale model of *Gimcrack* was made and tested so that the results at the two scales could be compared and correlated. It was here that I think Ken made a clear advance over previous small-model tests. To explain we have to review the fundamentals of ship-model testing.

I have mentioned the work of William Froude who, in the 1870s, had made ship-model testing a practical procedure following a series of tests similar to ours, but using the British naval vessel *Greyhound*. Froude theorized that the hull resistance comprised two main parts — that resulting from friction between the skin of the ship and the water, and that caused by the bulk of the hull as it pushed the water out of the way and made waves. Friction could reasonably be considered as proportional to wetted area, and the balance, called residuary or wave-making resistance, could be proportional to the bulk or displacement of the vessel. Although the total resistance, the sum of both friction and residuary, could be measured, this did not determine their relative contributions to that total as drag changed with speed.

Froude realized that because these two kinds of hull resistance required different scaling methods, one of them would have to be calculated. He found reasons for selecting friction. By measuring the drag of long slender planks he found a general rule for relating drag to the speed, the wetted area and the length, and with this he could compute the friction drag for either a model or a ship. He found that the remaining drag followed a rule he called the law of similitude, according to which the drag was proportional to the displacement when the model and ship speeds were related as the square roots of the lengths. While there have been later refinements, mainly having to do with newly recognized small elements of friction drag, Froude's method has been the foundation of all further model testing.

Davidson was not the first person to try testing small models, but the expanded results had been inconsistent. Earlier yacht tests had not led to improved designs. However, hydrodynamic friction was becoming better understood. Froude knew that an index using length and velocity was better related to skin friction than speed alone. A little later this became known as the Reynolds number after it was formulated in terms of length, velocity, and viscosity by Osborne Reynolds, who particularly studied fluid friction in pipes. Reynolds also noted a range in the number in which the friction was particularly difficult to predict. Investigators found that fluid flow took place in two regimes: one, described as laminar, took place at low

---

[2] Kenneth S.M. Davidson, "Some Experimental Studies of the Sailing Yachts," *Transactions of the Society of Naval Architects and Marine Engineers*, November 1936.

Reynolds numbers while at higher numbers the flow became turbulent and drag became greater. Drag in the transition range could not be accurately predicted.

Although Reynolds published his results in the middle of the 1880s, Admiral Taylor's highly respected book, published first in 1910, and in revised form in 1933, describes frictional resistance in Froude's terms, although there is an appendix describing Reynolds' pipe experiments. So it may be said that when Ken Davidson started his work there was more known about friction drag in hydrodynamics than was being applied in naval architecture. His recognition of this condition led him to the practical use of small models somewhat over 3′ long and weighing about 30 pounds. Practice in Twelve-Metre tests has varied from the small models that were tested through the 1960s, and then (following some upsetting results in America's Cup trials of 1970, to be discussed in a later chapter) models that were one-third full size, or approximately 15′ on the waterline and weighed about one ton.

Ken took two major steps in departing from the standard testing technique. He used the Reynolds number in computing friction drag, and recognizing that this number, when applied to the small scale he used, put the models in the transitional area between laminar and turbulent flow, he induced turbulence by roughening the stem with sand. Then, using friction coefficients appropriate to the Reynolds number of the model and the full-size yacht, he calculated the drag caused by turbulent friction and expanded the residuary resistence according to Froude's law of similitude at corresponding speeds.

With the completion of the *Gimcrack* model and towing tests it was provisionally clear that one small model gave accurate results. This lent encouragement to the analysis of the sailing trials. Their objective was to determine the propulsive force of the sails, and to put this data into a form that could be applied to forecast the wind-ward performance of other yachts. Knowing the stability and resistance of our test yacht, and using the relation between wind velocity and force, it was not hard to find driving and heeling forces and the associated coefficients to apply to other rigs. It was also easy to compute the related aerodynamic lift and drag coefficients which Ken could compare with aircraft data. This all went smoothly and the results seemed reasonable. Writing after the event it does not now seem that it could have been easy. Even with present instrumentation, it is hard to be sure of the wind direction and strength. Ken demonstrated exceptional judgement and ability.

Ken was entirely responsible for all the technical background. I was an enthusiastic follower and sometime practical advisor. Rod handled rigging and climbing and kept *Gimcrack*'s gear in order. Ken, Rod, and I normally sailed *Gimcrack*, and we all worked together to record the data. Later J. Seward Johnson, of Johnson & Johnson, contributed toward the construction of the small tank that took the place of the swimming pool; I think he helped on some of the out-of-pocket costs of

these tests, too, but the expenses were very small. As the depression minimized design work, so it gave time for something much better. I think this is a good example of what can be done with brains rather than dollars. Seward Johnson had successfully raced the Six-Metre *Jill*, and on the results of the tests he ordered the design of a new Six called *Jack*. She was built to a model that had been tested against the *Jill* model with very good results.

When *Jack* came out it did not take long to find out that she was no match for the older boat. Fortunately this failure, both a surprise and a severe disappointment, served to pinpoint an omission which we all had failed to catch. It now strikes me as a blind lack of foresight when I say that all the tests had been made for drag only in the upright condition. *Jack* was fast downwind when she was upright, but slow when sailing to windward. None of us had thought about the role of the keel and hull in offering lateral support against the side force that heeled the boat. Forced to think a little about windward sailing, I realized how little I knew about it and Ken realized that his tests would have to be made with the equivalent of the sail force applied across the model. The dynamometer would have to measure these transverse forces as well as the straight drag. In turn these conditions called for a supporting rail for the dynamometer to run the length of the test area. In practical terms this meant the end of swimming-pool tests.

The middle of the 1930s was hardly an ideal time to raise money for a yacht towing tank. Business was still depressed. Much racing then was a province of Wall Street. The first tested yacht had failed. Somehow Ken, with help from Johnson, managed to raise the money he needed for a tank a hundred feet long. The Stevens Institute provided space in the Navy Building, and Tank One came into being. The rest, in a word, is history. It could be a long story, of which I have tried to tell the beginning. Many good years followed and they led to an end of sorts which I hope is not an end, although part of this story has to be the end of the smallest models used in Twelve-Metre tests. With developing studies the value of models of a size well below the sometime-standard 15′ to 18′ waterline models has been reconfirmed.

Using the new tank with the lateral dynamometer showed clearly that the trouble with *Jack* was a lack of keel area, and possibly a hull form that was not good when heeled. Seward Johnson had faith enough to build another Six Metre which he called *Mood*. She was not the world-beater I should have liked. A new boat designed by the amateur designer Herman Whiton was as good if not better, but I was satisfied that there was now a way to find assurance, if not certainty, that if the tests compared favorably a new design should be better than a preceding one of the same type.

I feel sure that Ken believed that the measurement of side force was original with him. Until early in the year 1998 I had heard of no previous instance; but then I learned through Mr. Martin Black, an English student of the life of G.L. Watson, the leading Scottish yacht designer of the turn of the century, that in the Denny tank in Dunbarton, Scotland, in 1900 Denny and Watson tested models during the design of *Shamrock II*, using lateral dynamometers to measure side forces generated by leeway. It was common knowledge that models had been tested then, and that after Herreshoff's *Columbia* had beaten *Shamrock* a disappointed Watson had said that he wished that Herreshoff had a towing tank, but the measurement of side force was generally overlooked. Possibly that was due to Watson's apparent disappointment with the outcome for which there could have been any number of other reasons such as the uncertain flow regime. The models were relatively small then, although larger than ours. No effort was made to induce turbulence.

It is interesting to recall that Laurent (Jack) Giles of England came to New York around 1937 to use the Davidson facilities in the design of the Twelve-Metre *Flica*, and soon after arranged to build a duplicate tank-testing facility in England. This was interrupted by the war, but he must have been unaware of the Denny tank and its earlier work.

Davidson put together model predictions of hull drag with sail-force coefficients to find the expected speed made good to windward. His usual practice was to test at four angles of heel (0, 10, 20, and 30 degrees) using the side-force values to permit the application of the force associated with the heel and the height of the rig of the boat under test. With knowledge of the sail area and the side force, the wind speed could be predicted for each point.

These tests in the Stevens tank gave a boat a partial velocity prediction program (known today as a VPP) consisting of the best windward sailing speeds at the wind strengths consistent with the heel angles. Although upright resistances were routinely measured, I can recall no effort to predict downwind speeds until later. That came after the war when Paul Spens, who divided his time between the Stevens Institute and Southampton University, prepared a technical memorandum extending the range of the *Gimcrack* coefficients for application to reaching and running conditions. Improvements in the tested designs followed steadily for about 30 years. Further along I shall try to suggest what happened then, but I don't claim to know why, after years of success, the use of small models suddenly seemed to lead us astray. Plausible reasons have been given by better theoreticians than I.

I enjoyed working closely with Ken Davidson during those early years, but I was not alone in appreciating his work and using his facilities. Another early design supporter was Clinton Crane, whose interest had turned to the Twelve-Metre Class. In the winter of 1935-36 he designed *Seven Seas* for Van S. Merle Smith after testing models in Hoboken. I believe that Philip Rhodes and Bill Luders among others followed and soon became clients of the tank.

The usefulness of these models grew out of their moderate cost, quick construction, and general convenience of use. At that time we could often build and test a model of a $10,000 Six for less than $500. Usually one or two of the small models were sufficient to confirm a design for a small fraction of the design and building costs, while a 20′ model of a boat like a Six Metre, with testing, could be more than the cost of the full-size boat. Equally important, we thought there was no other facility that used a lateral dynameter and this had become absolutely vital. Such equipment is in use today, making 15′-to 20′-waterline models available and useful when cost is secondary. Even today, with the larger models, it is customary to induce turbulence as Ken Davidson did.

Once the work in Hoboken had become somewhat routine our office made steady use of the tank. Most of our designs were tested, and all of them were influenced by towing work. I think it is fair to say that the work went successfully. At the same time it must be said that the tank does not design a boat; it simply allows ideas about hull form to be evaluated. The designer must determine the form to be checked. If the check is not an improvement one has to go back to an earlier form or keep trying to find the way to make some improvement. Often our steps were small, if not backward, and we were limited to testing windward work. Yet the tank provided a new analytical tool of great importance to yacht designers. The crucial advance was that we now had numbers to replace guesswork. We had a yardstick, which I found very valuable. It seemed to open the way to new possibilities in speed and performance.

5

I have been lucky in so many associations. Clinton Crane was a very helpful friend. Evidently what he saw in the Six-Metre Class gave him confidence, because in the spring of '34 Frederick Prince, then the owner of Weetamoe, *the J-Class yacht of Mr. Crane's design, invited me to sail as a member of her afterguard in the coming trial races off Newport to select a defender of the America's Cup. The invitation came through Mr. Crane. I'm sure he engineered it. The opportunity opened a new door for me to experience all the details of sailing a big boat in an America's Cup summer and to meet the people doing that kind of racing.*

ASSOCIATIONS

Weetamoe is shown on page 86 on a close reach. She was Clinton Crane's Cup-contender design for 1930. *Enterprise*, with an experimental aluminum alloy mast, just beat her out in the 1930 America's Cup summer. Mr. Crane arranged a place in her afterguard for me in 1934, and I found the experience in so big a boat invaluable. For reasons hard to explain, *Weetamoe* was unable to do well and we were excused by the Cup Committee. (Photo: Rosenfeld Collection 69358F)

Clinton Crane might have sensed my interest in the class because, during the year before, I had done a J-Boat study, the source of a half model, which Drake publicized to a degree. More likely, as a designer himself, Mr. Crane must have realized that I had America's Cup ambitions. The resulting model was illustrated, with me holding it, on the cover of *Scribner's Magazine*. Of course there was hope, way in the back of my mind, that a J-Boat client might appear, but that was never serious. Those 1933 lines were never used, but they gave a starting point for real work that came three years later. Who knows whether a model and a little publicity might not have planted a seed?

Weetamoe was one of four Js, yachts about 125′ long, built as defenders in 1930, and although not selected she made a good record and was widely considered to be the best of the four. Frederick Prince, her owner, had made a great deal of money in the turbulent market following the crash of '29 and had bought *Weetamoe* from the building syndicate. Because her stability had seemed marginal she had received a new keel of Mr. Crane's design which lowered her ballast. We started the trial races with great hopes sailing against Harold Vanderbilt's new Burgess-designed *Rainbow* and *Yankee*, Frank Paine's Boston-based J-Boat owned by Chandler Hovey. It was disappointing when we found that we could not quite stay with either of these competitors.

The value of the summer to me was not lessened by our inability to win. I saw big-boat racing close up. I realized that aboard *Weetamoe* our afterguard did not quite have the intensity or the skill required to compete for the America's Cup. Clinton Crane must have felt this very keenly because the design was his, and this was the second season of America's Cup defense trials in which the boat had been handicapped in the same way. We discussed design questions which had led to the keel changes, and between the first and second trial series more keel work was done. It helped me to see how this was carried out at the Herreshoff yard in Bristol. It was during one of the visits to Bristol that Mr. Crane introduced me to Mr. Herreshoff. Although I recall discussing the keel with Mr. Crane, we never went into other problems such as tactics, navigation and sails. I think Mr. Crane's instincts as a gentlemen made him reluctant to criticize his friends who made up the afterguard; but they did not do justice to the boat. Uncertain handling makes it difficult to assess a boat's potential; but with *Weetamoe* neither new keel seemed better than the original form.

Disappointment with *Weetamoe* took our attention away from the other trials during which *Yankee* was regularly beating *Rainbow*. It was again in the final trial series, and reportedly after adding ballast, that *Rainbow* beat *Yankee* by one second in the final race of an even match to gain selection. Length, offsetting the weight it made necessary, was now recognized as a decisive factor among the contenders of 1934.

During the periods of racing I lived on Mr. Prince's diesel yacht *Lone Star*, and when I could I went back to work in New York, generally on the overnight Fall River Line steamer which picked up passengers in Newport. That line, to be in service only a few years longer, was one of the last of many that carried passengers and freight between New York and the New England ports in old sidewheel steamers. Announced by the whistle and plume of steam as the ship approached, passengers crowded onto the Newport landing, and I can still feel the superiority of an unholy snob as I rode across the harbor in *Lone Star*'s varnished starboard launch to board the night boat — differentiated, one rather than many, above them all as the big paddles stopped the ship alongside the pier. That éclat is lost now. We have billionaires today, and they have plastic speedboats, faster, more practical to maintain, and better boats in many ways. But the small, round-bottom, bright-finished wooden launch with the helmsman's cockpit forward of a sedan top, and a hand with a boathook stationed aft in a well, is something that has passed from the sport and was wonderful while it lasted. Maybe we were snobs but we knew how to live. I am grateful for the chance to have felt it. Today even the megayachts lie in slips with the world of onlookers passing by. Convenient and democratic but hardly distinctive. Do the new owners realize what they've missed? Should we admit such feelings?

As a member of a J-Boat afterguard I'm sure I, with others, felt such distinction. We lived a pretty special kind of life. Some, as I did, lived on one of the large diesel yachts moored in the harbor, Brenton's Cove, with all the comfort of a luxury hotel. Others lived ashore in one or another of the grand cottages. On *Lone Star* we had breakfast and dinner on board, served by a uniformed steward. It was rather formal, although we didn't go to the black-tie stage. Wine was there, although I didn't take it then, and tea or coffee. Lunch was generally on the sailing boat at some interval in the tuning or racing day, sandwiches and soda pop. I consumed a lot of orange soda. In the evening there was usually bridge, but I did not join in the expert games where the stakes were in no way related to my lifestyle. I usually read, and during that summer I remember the long romantic poem *Tristram* by Edwin Arlington Robinson which had been recently published.

Harold Vanderbilt's *Rainbow* defended the Cup successfully in 1934, but only due to luck and skill, and by a small margin. She did not seem to be as fast as *Endeavour*, the Nicholson design that Tom Sopwith brought over as challenger. *Endeavour* was unusual only in her beautifully balanced lines and in her steel construction which was lighter than the bronze used for the hulls of most J-Boats. Bronze had been preferred because it was naturally anti-fouling. However, the steel hull could carry a higher proportion of lead ballast. In 1937 *Ranger* had a steel hull for the same reason. With *Ranger* the steel caused concern when, through the whole season, the paint never adhered properly. *Endeavour* had been in the water another season and her painted surface looked fine.

In the success of *Rainbow* following *Enterprise* Mike Vanderbilt demonstrated his ability as a sailor and manager. To me, his qualifications were those of intelligence and determination, aided by a clear view of his purpose, and guided by his sailing experience. I should not list him with the world's greatest helmsmen, but his other qualities made him a consistent winner. To win against Tom Sopwith and *Endeavour* called for everything he had.

Endeavour's lines deserve study by anyone interested in hull shape. They are hard to describe in the sense that they have no single feature that calls for first attention. I see the lesson that says "distortion doesn't pay." The water doesn't like bumps or hollows. I have been sometimes guilty of failing to heed this lesson, and unfortunately many boats built to the now-past IOR Rule seemed to gain rating advantage through the use of unfair points. Of course, on balance any benefit is a matter of degree; but what attracts the eye seems to please the water.

After a quiet 1935 the next summer became the year of the "thirty-twos," the New York Yacht Club one-design class. Thirty-two applies to the waterline length of these boats. Their beam was 10′-7″, and overall length was 45′-1/2″. Designing such a class brings with it the need to satisfy a number of different demands, and this became a difficult challenge. The boats were well-built and attractive in appearance and the accommodations were good. The worry was that they carried more

weather helm than they should have — certainly in the opinion of some owners. They steered by tiller and seemed to pull pretty hard. The original mainsails seemed to be tight on the leach. Most owners arranged to free these, easing the helm considerably. The next winter a small amount of ballast was added in existing deadwood at both ends of the keel, and the tack of the jib was moved forward to the stemhead. This further relieved the helm.

There were questions, too, about whether the thirty-twos were as fast as they should have been. They were intended to race under the CCA Rule. Speed questions were acute after an early Long Island Sound race in a fresh northwester when on a windward leg a class of the smaller Six Metres that had started five minutes after the thirty-twos sailed past the bigger boats. Racing performance seemed generally better as the summer advanced, and such worries largely evaporated after the Labor Day Vineyard Lightship Race in which thirty-twos took first and second places and actually passed a bigger Ten Metre during a beat to the westward after rounding the lightship. To me the explanation was the relation between the length of the boats and the length of the different seas they were meeting. In both cases the smaller boats made a better fit to the seas. Today it is an article of faith that weight must be kept out of the ends of a boat to minimize the radius of gyration, a measure of the ability to react quickly to an applied force, as in pitching, thus permitting the boats to follow more easily the surface of the water. This is often,

*L*one Star, the diesel yacht of Frederick Prince, was my "home away from home" in the summer of 1934. The living was good, if a little formal. I took full part in the sailing but few other activities. The starboard launch, mentioned in the text, is carried in davits abreast of the funnel.
(Photo: Rosenfeld Collection 42614F)

perhaps usually, true; but the most important fact is that the natural pitching period of the hull should not be close to the period of encounter with the waves. The helmsman can often adjust the encounter period by a small change in course while losing little in the theoretical speed made good. *Dorade* was an example of an excellent rough-water boat despite a very long ballast keel. With her narrow beam and sharp entrance she sliced easily through a short chop and rose nicely to the longer ocean seas.

There is a story leading up to the design of the thirty-twos. After *Dorade*'s success, in 1932 I received a letter from Guy Rex, of Hobart, Tasmania, inquiring about the feasibility of a smaller version of the same boat. Recognizing the problem of beam, which would only be worse in a smaller boat, I replied that a proportionally wider boat about 32´ on the water, and otherwise much like *Dorade*, should do well. In a short time we received instructions to go ahead. The new boat, built in Tasmania, was named *Landfall*, and Guy Rex reported that she performed well.

A little later I met Albert Fay, who was then a student at Yale. He wished to build a small cruiser/racer, about as much boat as he could build for $10,000 (remember the date). *Landfall*'s design seemed a good starting point. More experience suggested even a little more beam, and *Starlight* was built. She seemed attractive and fast. The next year there was a similar, but again modified, 32-footer. So we had a good base of experience to build on when the New York Yacht Club let it be known that the club was ready to sponsor a new one-design class in the spirit of the old NYYC thirties. Several designers submitted proposals, and ours was picked. Twenty of the class were built at the Nevins yard. I know that Drake was the principal reason we were given this project, and not only for his sales talents; he had organized the offering with Nevins, the builder, and the sailmaker, Ratsey, to provide a simple, complete package. In a short time the 20 boats, all that Nevins could build for the next summer, had been ordered.

From the Junior Class and *Kalmia*, through *Stormy Weather*, *Edlu*, numerous others, and now a New York Yacht Club class of twenty boats, and still to come, *Ranger*, Drake had supported me and the whole office by lining up the new designs. He had the confidence and respect of many contacts and friends in Wall Street and the NYYC, major centers of sailing activity, as well as in the wider sailing community and he stressed design to his clients. He did this because he was so interested and wanted to see the design department succeed, and the time and effort he put into that support was a personal sacrifice. Although second-hand yachts are less costly than new ones, and the selling commission is proportionally less, the time and effort necessary to lining up a new design is so much more than the time required to make the sale of an existing boat that Drake was giving up potential income by concentrating on design. Drake and I were well aware that he could have

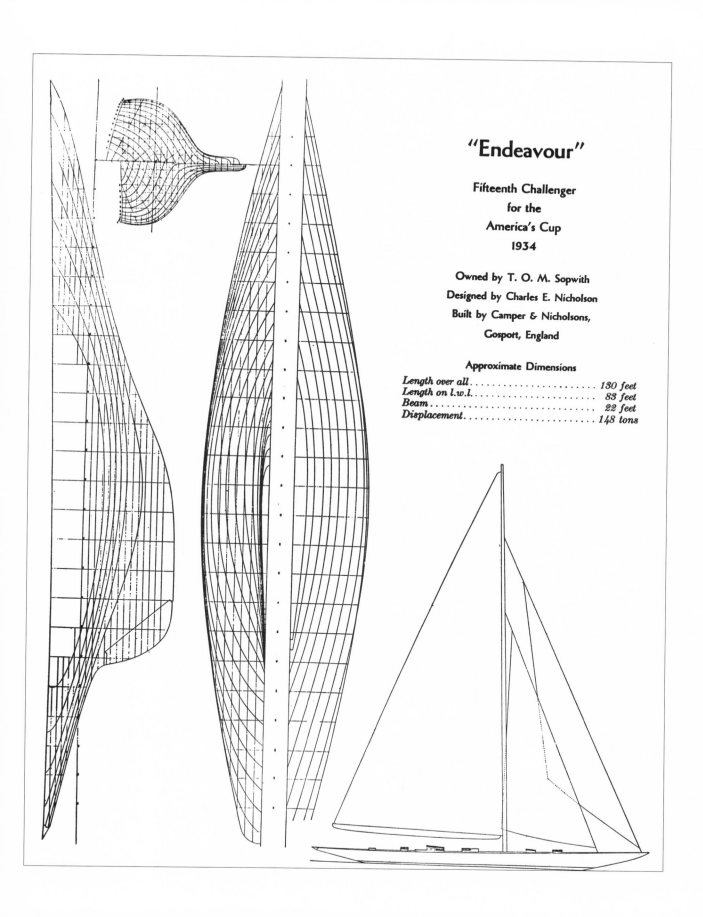

"Endeavour"

Fifteenth Challenger
for the
America's Cup
1934

Owned by T. O. M. Sopwith

Designed by Charles E. Nicholson

Built by Camper & Nicholsons,

Gosport, England

Approximate Dimensions

Length over all . . . . 130 feet
Length on l.w.l. . . . . 83 feet
Beam . . . . 22 feet
Displacement . . . . 148 tons

bettered his earnings by selling existing boats, yet he continued to bring in the projects that were my support. I appreciate to this day all he did.

Drake was about 10 years older than I and had been in the navy during World War One. He lived in Larchmont, where he was married to Katherine Tierney of New Rochelle. He had a yacht brokerage office on 44th Street in New York City. He was a member of the NYYC and chairman for some time of the model committee, which has made the clubhouse and its model room at 37 West 44th Street the place in New York all sailors want to visit. He also belonged to the Larchmont Yacht Club and sailed a Victory Class one-design owned by its commodore, James B. Ford. Drake was a good helmsman and generally stood first or second in the class. During all the time I knew him he was a teetotaler as I was, though since traveling in Europe I have often enjoyed wine with dinner.

Drake came into my life as the result of selling a small boat to Father. Later, when I was actually working at home on designs, Father went to him for advice, and when Drake realized my determination he was sympathetic. He made it possible for me to get a start and then much more. It was in the spring of '28 that we arranged an informal partnership, agreeing to make it formal when I came of age if the first year had worked out. We were both taking a chance. Drake was a conservative, in politics more than I; but in business policy we agreed to be cautious despite the chance we took to start up. We did not need much capital and proved that by never borrowing a penny. At the end of the first year Father encouraged us to incorporate. Sparkman & Stephens, Inc. came into being in 1929, soon after my 21st birthday

To repeat, Drake supported the design side of the business in every way. This was not only welcome but made possible the good start we made. From beginning to end we had complete trust in each other and both worked hard to perform well. I think our clients appreciated that. We had one business, although we kept the department accounts apart for the purpose of individual compensation. In the beginning I counted on Drake for most business decisions, but as I gained experience he left more to me so that later, when it came to dealing with Washington during the war, it was mostly in my hands, though not without his interest and advice. I think I was a little more patient and tolerant of red tape than he could be.

When World War Two ended and we remained busy with navy minesweepers for Korea we decided to move the design department to a lower-rent area than the 44th Street headquarters. The design department took a floor at Madison Avenue and 28th Street. The daily walk from Grand Central Station at 42nd Street was probably good for Rod and me. It became harder to keep in close touch with Drake, but as yacht activity resumed he was right there again, playing his part in the *Columbia* arrangements with the NYYC brass in 1958. I remember his riding with me between New York and Newport before the Cup races. We must have made a very early start because I remember crossing the Mount Hope Bridge just as the sun came up. Something impelled us to stop in the middle and relieve our kidneys from the 135´ height. Still kids, I guess.

Very early in the 1960s I learned that Drake had lung cancer, from which he died during the winter of 1963-64. Late in August of 1963 (I had just returned from Cowes) he had brought in two good projects: a new Twelve for America's Cup competition — *Constellation* and the *America* replica for Rudy Schaefer. I remember taking charge of the Twelve while Gil Wyland tackled the new *America*. That one was a big job to do fast. The Twelve meant models at Hoboken, and the first ones were not too good. By that time Drake was in the Memorial Sloan-Kettering Hospital where I visited him. Finally, after a visit to Hoboken, I came back with word of a really promising model and I remember how his face lit up with the news.

It was tough to realize that Drake had gone. I had depended for more than 30 years on his support, both personally and as a source of design work. He had founded and supported the firm, and perhaps the way things continued was a measure of his success. The organization he left was small but sound. We had no debt and the overhead costs were well under control. Drake's brother Jim was active and experienced in the sale of powerboats and Bob Garland, who had been with us since our founding, had a worldwide clientele for boats of all kinds. Our design work was largely predicated on racing success which, with luck, continued. The scarcity of real hardy cruising designs troubled me, but we had some good ones that the owners liked. So work went on.

In 1936 Susie and I sailed with Jack Shethar and his wife and family aboard their new NYYC thirty-two *Valencia*. We enjoyed good sailing, but the pleasure was especially keen because of a meeting at the NYYC Cruise rendezvous at New London. There I was invited aboard *Vara*, Harold Vanderbilt's motor yacht. Rod had been sailing that summer on board Vanderbilt's *Rainbow*. Rod was there, and Drake, and of course Mr. Vanderbilt. The subject was a new J-Boat for the defense of a second challenge from Tom Sopwith, and the suggestion was that our office should collaborate with Starling Burgess on the design. Starling was said to be willing. There were details to be worked out, but it sounded like a great opportunity and I was ready to go.

Somehow I had no concern about the large size of a J-Boat. I had studied the class and had drawn lines before the '34 challenge. I knew then that there was no realistic chance of doing a J-Boat design, and now, two years later, despite any possible personal ambition, I was happy about the joint commission. I might have been nervous about Starling's reputation for eccentricity, but I have always discounted much rumor that I have heard. I did not know him well at the start, nor did I realize how active he had been in fields other than yacht design, especially in early aircraft and flying boats. What I knew I respected, and in our work together we concentrated on the new boat. We did not make dinner-table conversation by asking each other questions.

My collaboration with Starling Burgess was a good deal like that with Mr. V., whose friends called him Mike. His reputation for serious application to his interests was well-known. His keen analytic intelligence was applied in varied fields in addition to sailing and business, including bridge and the yacht-racing rules. He and Rod had sailed together in *Rainbow* and their mutual respect was obvious. They had become real friends, which made the contact very easy for me. I did, of course, come to know Harold Vanderbilt better as time passed. It may be notable to record that he did ask questions, and many, showing a keen and highly intelligent interest in all phases of design, from model-testing to final details of structure, accommodation and rig.

Mr. V. said that he would be glad to get us started right after the cruise, although he could not guarantee construction. That would depend on his ability to form a syndicate. Starling was not at that first meeting. He met with Drake and me when the cruise was over to discuss his ideas and the basis of our business agreement, which Drake settled with him. One of the many ways Drake helped me was by handling most such details, letting me concentrate on design.

Starling was living in Wiscasset, Maine, and working under an arrangement with the Aluminum Company of America and the Bath Iron Works on the plans of an experimental aluminum-alloy destroyer. I knew Starling as a very successful designer of fast sailing boats, and I was familiar with his recent work. I know now, so I don't remember whether I realized then, that he was the son of Edward Burgess who had been responsible for designing three Boston-based America's Cup defenders in the last century. I know that I did not appreciate the extent of his early association with flying as an associate of the Wright brothers. I believe that Starling was the first to build a plane that took off from the water. At the time of the First World War he took a contract from the government to build a hundred Wright-licensed planes but his plant was destroyed by fire before the planes had been built. He was the same age as my father.

As we immediately agreed that we liked steel as a hull material, Bath seemed an ideal place to build as this was the material used in the navy destroyers they were building. The only serious alternative would be the Herreshoff yard in Bristol which had experience with both steel and bronze; but neither Starling nor I considered that the yard had quite maintained its earlier standard after its sale by the Herreshoffs. The yard's most recent big boat had been *Rainbow*, Starling's design of 1933-34, and he preferred Bath. In the end we had bids and I recall that Bath's figure was substantially lower than Herreshoff's.

We also agreed that a small independent drafting room should be set up in Bath and that we would hire a good chief draftsman to take direct charge of its operation. We offered the job to Henry Gruber, a very able German draftsman who had worked for Starling in the late 'twenties before returning to Germany. Knowing his great interest in the kind of work we were about to do, we suspected that his failure to accept our offer may have been due to a good deal of pressure to remain in the Germany of Hitler.

The result of our next offer made us happy that Gruber had not been ready to join us. Drake's friend Jed McCullough arranged for a meeting with Gilbert Wyland, whom he recommended highly. McCullough had known Gil during the building of a diesel yacht at the Luders yard in Stamford, Connecticut. Gil, in fact, was working on studies of a similar but larger boat for McCullough and we had met him already in connection with that work. He was then employed by the New York Shipbuilding Company and lived in New Jersey. He had graduated from the Webb Institute of Naval Architecture about 10 years before this time. Gil was an enthusiastic sailor. Due to the depression his employment since leaving school had been mainly on powerboats and ships, but evidence of his sailing interest was shown by the fact that he had made a voyage to the Caribbean and back as a member of the crew in one of the last four-masted schooners.

Starling and I were favorably impressed and arranged with Gil to take charge of our work in Bath as soon as he could properly leave his job at New York Ship. We had rented a single large room in a business block near the Iron Works. After Gil's arrival, we arranged to take on two good marine draftsmen, Geerd Hendel and Henry Menke, borrowed from Bath's drafting room, thus forming a team of five to get out the plans. As models had done so well for me I was naturally anxious to make full use of them now. Starling felt, as almost everyone else did at that time, that small, 4′ to 5′ models could be misleading and thus dangerous. We talked with Ken Davidson and agreed to test two models of J-Boat proportions, one small (about 4′ on the water) and the other much larger (I think with a waterline length of about 16′). The larger model would be tested in the navy tank in Washington. Because of differences between tank procedures in expanding the model data, Ken did not wish to compare full-scale predictions but said that he would expand his results first to the size of the larger model, saying that he could predict her drag with confidence. From this point we could go on to estimate the drag of the full-scale boat in any way we thought best. Test results satisfied Starling that he could trust the small models. The best of those we tested became *Ranger*.

Meanwhile we agreed with Mr. Vanderbilt to make some tests of another type. These were to help us decide the question of size. Both Starling and I felt that it would pay to go up to the maximum waterline length of about 87′ which, according to the Universal Rule governing the class, required the considerable displacement of 165 tons if the full rig was to be carried. As the displacement required to justify full sail was a function of length, and *Rainbow* was about 83′ on the water, her displacement was 142 tons. Less displacement would have meant less sail. So to test our judgement we loaded some 23 tons of lead into *Rainbow* and took her out for informal trials against *Yankee*, whose owner, Chandler Hovey, was exceptionally generous in making her available as a trial horse for a project directed toward his yacht's defeat. These trials showed that *Rainbow* could carry the extra weight without loss of speed. We felt that this confirmed our hopes for the big boat.

Studies of the Universal Rule showed that it was related to the International Rule by both similarities and differences. It used a very simple formula by which 18% of the product of the waterline length and the square root of the sail area was divided by the cube root of the displacement. The International Rule requires the same relation between length and displacement, causing similar hull geometry, but here the sum of length and sail area is taken, meaning that to increase one the other must be reduced, thus discouraging extreme length. Long before it had been found that heavy displacement was favored by the Universal Rule by allowing more than balancing sail area. A ceiling, based on waterline length, had been placed on the displacement that could be taken for credit. In the smaller R and Q classes the longer waterlines combined with the maximum allowed displacement had done best. But this was no certain indication that the best waterline in the larger J-Boats would be the maximum.

The history of the J Class in the preparations and matches of 1930 and 1934 offered no clear guidance. In the last of the business boom leading up to the 1930 series, four new boats were built, and their length range was from 79′ (*Enterprise*) to 87′ (*Whirlwind*). *Weetamoe* and *Yankee* were in between, at about 83′ and 84′. During the early trials *Weetamoe* was the leader with *Enterprise* next. *Yankee* was not too far back and *Whirlwind* was trailing badly. We found no support here for the idea of the big boat.

Yankee was interesting for her generous beam and the typical full bow favored by her designer, Frank Paine. Crane's design, *Weetamoe*, was narrowest of the four and followed the current trend toward a cutaway, almost triangular, underwater profile. Her wetted area was small, giving her an advantage in light weather. Burgess' *Enterprise*, the shortest, and thus the lightest, had a little more beam and keel area than *Weetamoe*, and only came fully to life for the final trial series when she stepped a light and slender aluminum mast designed with the help of Starling's brother, Charles, who had worked with the light structures of dirigibles as a civilian engineer with the navy. Increased stability and probably reduced windage drag, due to a lighter, smaller mast gave *Enterprise* the edge over *Weetamoe* by a small margin. The older boats *Resolute* and *Vanitie* entered some early-season races but were outclassed by the newer ones except in the lightest of weather.

Between 1930 and 1934 *Weetamoe*, now owned by Frederick Prince, and Gerard Lambert's *Vanitie* sailed in many of the important NYYC regattas, of which *Vanitie* won a surprising number. This may have influenced Mr. Crane and Mr. Prince to make a radical change in *Weetamoe*'s keel before the trials for the 1934 Cup match. I have referred to the disappointing results and to a second change in midseason that failed to help. *Yankee* also underwent changes to her forebody and rig with much better result. Until the final trial series, she won consistently against the new *Rainbow* as well as *Weetamoe*.

As Starling had been largely satisfied with the small models we promptly made a sort of double-purpose test in the form of models of *Rainbow* and *Endeavour*, then the fastest of the J-Boats, and we tested these models in the Stevens Institute tank in preparation for our series of new models. *Endeavour*'s lines and *Rainbow*'s had been published after the 1934 America's Cup series. The designers had agreed to exchange and publish their lines, not then recognizing the potential of model testing in Davidson's sense. The fact that these showed the superiority of *Endeavour* over *Rainbow* confirmed the general opinion of the two boats. Although my recollection is not certain, I believe we also tested *Rainbow* with and without the extra ballast.

None of this told us why in 1930 the smaller boats had all done better than *Whirlwind*, the biggest. Why she had not done better might or might not have had anything to do with her length and weight.

6

RANGER

Starling very kindly invited me to make my home with him during periods of work in Bath, which began in 1936. He was living with his wife Nanny in one of the old houses in Wiscasset which had been preserved with others from colonial times. Wiscasset is still one of the finest examples of early New England for which it was an important port, active in shipbuilding and the lumber trade. It was a pleasure just to be there and I appreciated the kindness of my hosts. They were building a new house on a small island, about eight acres in extent, on the harbor just west of the town. During the next spring they moved in and I visited them there. Typical of much I have seen, this island, their home, where I stayed in the spring of 1937, is now transformed. The entire lovely small Maine island is now the site of an nuclear power plant.

The time I spent with Starling was not revealing in a personal sense. Had either one of us been different we might have come closer. We were both all business, and although I felt he was a generous mentor I did not realize then how much he had done in the early days of aviation. Too late, I have realized how interesting that subject would have been. At mealtime we talked boats, or the houses and history of Wiscasset. In the evening he left me to myself, recommending his classical music disks or the poetry of George Moore, a slight glimpse there of personality. I knew, of course that Starling was considered eccentric, in his several marriages if nothing else. I avoided any reference to that. Our lifestyles and our backgrounds were different and we lived each within his own enclosure, connected only by a path labeled "sailboats." I was happy when Starling invited me to work with him in Washington in the early days of the war, evidently feeling that I might be helpful. I went there for a few days but only to explain that S&S was deeply involved in navy work and I was responsible.

Starling and I drove the twelve or so miles from Wiscasset to Bath in the morning and returned late in the day. Work in the office was begun by drawing the lines of six models, three of which were the responsibility of each of us. As I remember it we each had a board and drew a set of lines while each of the draftsmen took our instructions to do a second and later a third model with slightly different characteristics. All were at the maximum waterline length of about 87′. The variations were primarily in beam, in the lateral plane, and in the shape of the ends.

Starling was way ahead of me in his technical background. He applied this directly to matters having to do with the rig when we reached that stage of the design, but we seemed to be guided by parallel thinking about our hulls. Our approach to minimum resistance dealt with the fundamentals of wetted surface, the right prismatic coefficient, a center of buoyancy slightly abaft the center of the waterline length and an intuitive feeling for fair lines. We both placed a high value on good stability, but made no attempt toward numerically evaluating its effect on speed, which later came out of the model test results.

Because I was in New York when not in Bath, I think I spent more time at the tank in Hoboken than did Starling. Mr. V. came to the tank several times and discussions of the models and their performance was much on both our minds. During that period in the early fall I flew to Bath several times with Mike for discussions with Starling. There were also negotiations with the yard. That part was easy as the yard, particularly in the person of Stark Newell, Bath's president, wanted the job and would do it essentially at cost. I don't know the details, but the cost estimates were needed by Mike in his search for supporters. In the end Mike's brother, William, shared the cost, and arrangements with the yard were made and the design work continued. When the boat had been set up on the keel Mike visited from time to time but there was little formal communication on the design of *Ranger* except for progress reports to approve payments. In May the boat's launching was an important day for us all but Mike did not make it the occasion for a big party. The whole experience was extremely friendly, businesslike, rather informal, no frills.

The office in Bath brought my first experience with calculating machines: we had two, an old hand-powered Monroe and an electric machine called a Friden. Both would multiply and divide as well as add. But it was one step at a time: no programming. I think Starling could persuade them to find roots. I was accustomed to use a largish 20″ slide rule for most calculations or logarithms for greater accuracy. It would be almost 30 years before I had my first electronic digital hand calculator, now routine and ubiquitous.

I was 29 in 1937, and Starling was 59. This collaboration with a much older man had both drawbacks and advantages. The difficulties were few and the advantages many. It was not too hard to accept certain rigidities of procedure when Starling followed habits of a lifetime such as the way that weights were tabulated. I said to myself that I, as the junior, should avoid friction by accepting his ways when I saw nothing that would detract from the final result. Meanwhile the work was progressing and I was learning.

Cost was still a problem. Recovery from the depression was slow and Mike had found only his brother as a partner in the syndicate to build *Ranger*. We were glad to be going on with our work. Several models looked faster than the best earlier boat, and our group was beginning to produce more than lines drawings. Work on the hull design seemed quite straightforward, except that the size and scale were new to me as was the metal construction. Construction planning was in the hands of Gil Wyland, well-acquainted with steel, who consulted with Lloyd's and Bath about details. We went a little beyond the routine in two respects. One was the extensive use of welding, which would save weight in the hull and allow just that much more lead in the keel. The other was the keel itself which, at about one hundred tons, was probably to be the heaviest lead casting ever made.

The design of the sailplan and rig involved more that was new to me, particularly in a structural sense. The area came right out of the rule, as did the limit height of both mast and foretriangle. We considered it a matter of course to take the maximum allowed. Distribution of area between the main and foretriangle was optional and we used the mainsail dimensions of *Rainbow*, not only because they seemed right, but also to allow us to use her sails. New sails were to be few. She had one really beautiful main among other good ones. Mike had great confidence in that mainsail, and he had carefully protected it from the weather as one had to do with the cotton sails of that time. This reliance on older sails troubled the then-reigning sailmaker, George Ratsey of Ratsey and Lapthorne, and I remember well how earnestly he worked on me one day on the porch of the Larchmont Yacht Club, pressing his opinion that only a new sail had the "life" needed to make the boat win. Fortunately Mr. V's beautiful but old main retained all its drive. "Life" remained undefined. I can't help contrasting this canny approach with the extremely lavish use of sails in more recent America's Cup seasons.

Although minimum weight and center of gravity were rule requirements, the design of the spars was more complex and newer to me than the hull work. I found that Starling determined the required overall mast stiffness by a method I had previously worked out for myself. This took the boat's righting moment at a maximum sailing angle as a measure of the force applied by the mast working through the lever arm provided by the spread between the centerline and the chainplates. The righting moment divided by that distance gave the total chainplate loading to be carried by the shrouds and supported by the mast step. The mast can then be treated as a long column, with allowable stress dependent on the spar material, and the actual stress a function of the length of the panels and the degree of fixity at the ends as well as the column loading. In the ideal case the ends may be either fixed, as though buried in concrete, or pin-ended as though resting on a point. Because a mast is not a true example of either one of these conditions, a mix of end assumptions and factors of safety must be used.

There was no well-accepted method of finding the distribution of loading along the mast to give the loading at the different spreaders. Starling's experience had given him a chance to test possible assumptions so that he had a great deal of data. I had taken similar measurements on a smaller boat. We based transverse distribution on measurements of rigging loads that both of us had made under sail with dynamometers on the shrouds, and we took the loads on stays to be largely dependent on backstay tension as they were set up.

Starling's America's Cup experience had given him two very valuable boundaries on mast stiffness. *Enterprise* had been rescued from apparent failure in 1930 by the arrival of a light and slender aluminum-alloy mainmast, the first to use that material. Starling said it had been designed in conjunction with his brother Charles Burgess whose vocation was the design of dirigibles. This mast just missed being entirely too slender. It barely was kept in place in a critical heavy weather race against *Weetamoe* when Starling used a spare halliard to form an eye looped around all the shrouds at the deck and hoisted to the lower spreaders to hold them in place. Soon the rules were changed to require more substantial masts.

At the other limit was a pair of masts Starling had designed for use by *Rainbow* and *Weetamoe* in 1934. These were relatively heavy, and were long on the fore-and-aft axis. They stood with virtually no deflection and were considered more than safe.

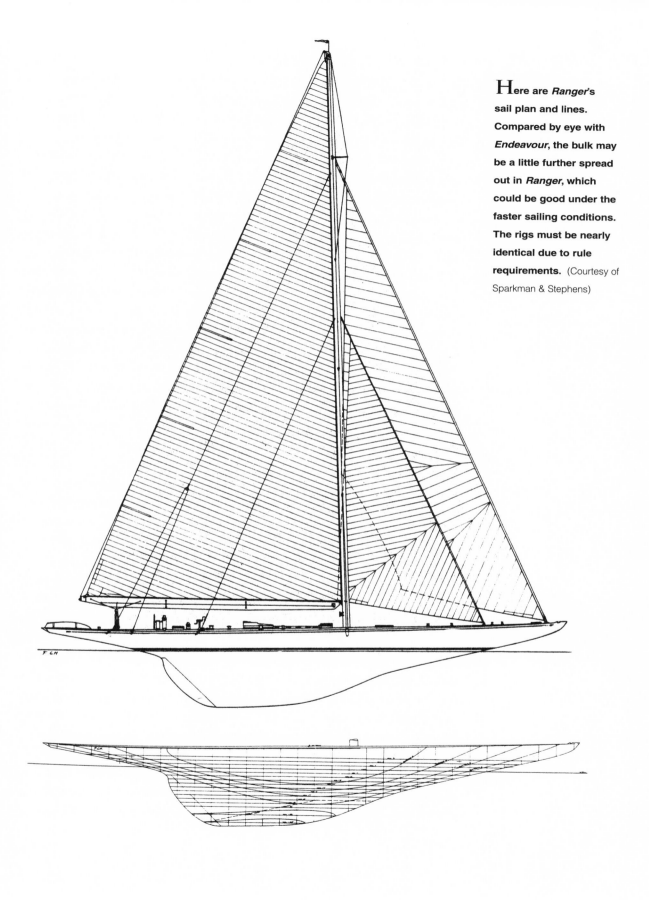

Here are *Ranger*'s
sail plan and lines.
Compared by eye with
Endeavour, the bulk may
be a little further spread
out in *Ranger*, which
could be good under the
faster sailing conditions.
The rigs must be nearly
identical due to rule
requirements. (Courtesy of
Sparkman & Stephens)

For *Ranger* we knew that we should work between factors derived from these masts, finding a place between the two extremes while observing the new requirements.

Load distribution was a subject that Starling had studied in detail. I have in my notebook formulas on spar loading that he shared with me. These helped primarily to determine the needed rigging strengths. As we studied these rigging elements we decided that we could use the same heat-treated steel rod shrouds that were used on *Rainbow* even though the new boat would load them more heavily. The solid material greatly reduces the elastic stretch that occurs in wire cable. For the same reason, and also to minimize parasitic drag, S&S had started to use elliptical-section aircraft rods as shrouds for smaller boats. Those on *Ranger* were round.

Before this had been done the two geometrically similar models, but different in scale, known as geosyms, had been tested at the tanks in Washington and Hoboken. Starling was, I think, a little surprised, although also pleased, to see how well the results matched. At this point we were ready to use Ken's Stevens Institute tank with confidence. As our lines were faired, six models were made for testing there. The results were pleasing. Several looked better than our yardstick, *Endeavour*. One of Starling's looked especially good. We studied the data and watched the models run down the tank and made some alterations, not only in the one that looked best but also in one or two others; but we found we could not improve the one that showed up so well. We had hoped to do better because this model for all its promise had slightly more displacement than it needed for maximum sail area, and it even looked a little lumpy down in the lower forebody. This was hardly visible, not really unfair, but a slight swelling that could be felt more than seen. As it seemed logical to remove the excess, that was tested but without improvement. The original model lines were carefully prepared for the builder, and Bath started work with lofting and the ordering of material.

Starling must have thought more than I did about stability or perhaps the effect of the keel on leeway, as his models had more of a toe on the forward part of the keel, putting the ballast deeper. This gave them more wetted surface which seemed to me a negative factor. The fact that he put more lateral plane where it counted was a plus which I did not fully appreciate then. I think I did more than Starling to pull out the lines above the water, especially aft where I thought he had overlooked the possibility of returned pressure in his designs for *Enterprise* and *Rainbow*, a configuration sometimes called a "wave-rider" stern. In his model which became *Ranger* the after overhang was much lower than his earlier custom, which I took as a nod toward me.

This may be a good place to refer to the fact that in the agreement to collaborate we had mutually promised not to divulge the author of the lines used for the new boat. Starling faithfully followed this agreement, never referring in any way to the fact that the model had been one of his. Much later, after Starling's death, Mike Vanderbilt in a magazine article referred to the model as mine, leading me to feel that I should correct this mistake with letters to the magazine's editor and to Mike.

The yard appointed Sam Wakeman as project engineer to coordinate the work. Sam was a sailor against whom we had raced to England in *Dorade* and in races to Bermuda. I remembered him partly for the heavy black beard he had grown while crossing the Atlantic. The assignment at Bath pleased him and us. His foresight and diligence contributed to the good result. The building was carried through with only one major hitch, which occurred when, despite careful preparation, as the molten lead was being poured for the keel it started to escape from the mold. Quick work limited the damage, but considerable reworking of the keel was needed to correct the shape.

It interested me that Sam, in a junior management position at Bath, was the son of Wiley Wakeman who was head of Bethlehem's Quincy shipyard, where John Newell, son of Bath's president, held a corresponding position.

Further work went smoothly until at 14:00, 11 May 1937, *Ranger* was launched and immediately rigged. I returned home and was preparing the office in New York for my further absence while *Ranger* was under tow of Mike's *Vara* from Bath toward Newport. She was to take sails on board there for the first sail. Excited at the prospect, and about to leave for Newport, I received a phone call from an unhappy Rod. Seeming safe in his hands and under tow with an excellent crew, *Ranger* had lost her mast crossing Massachusetts Bay. It was unbelievable, but it had happened. One of the threaded barrels that joined the upper and lower steel rods to form long turnbuckles had loosened, and then opened to leave no support above the lowest panel on one side. Without support the mast flexed to to the other side as the boat rolled in the ocean swell and then crashed back loosening more joints, one after another. The mast was tough and the crew said that before it went it would bend until the head was horizontal, but despite changes of heading to reduce rolling it broke at the lowest spreader and went over the side.

At the Herreshoff yard in Bristol there was a large ship's locker holding the sails we planned to use, as well as an accumulation of gear from *Rainbow* and other Vanderbilt boats. *Rainbow* had been sold to the Hovey family, but one of the large 1934 masts had been reserved as a spare. Now it was time to divide the offices in Bath and New York into two task forces. Starling went back to Maine with Gil Wyland to arrange the immediate building of a new mast while Rod and I worked in Bristol, with Bob Henry who did rigging and mechanical work in our New York office, to turn the contents of the locker into a working rig. We started to pull out and measure the pieces on May 15th and the mast was stepped on Tuesday the 25th, ten days after the job began.

Opposite, *Ranger*'s afterguard, L to R, are Rod, myself, Zenas Bliss, Gertrude Vanderbilt, Mike Vanderbilt, Arthur Knapp. Duties, in sequence: Rover, organized sail changes and checked the rig, aloft and on deck. Relief helmsman and chairman, tactical committee. Navigator on board and professor at Brown University. Observer and informal controller of mainsheet traveler, while not racing. Skipper and helmsman. Sail trimmer, oil can at the ready to silence squeaking blocks. (Photo: Rosenfeld Collection 81798)

My principal recollection of that time, sixty years ago as I write, is of the tremendous cooperation given by everyone who could help us. The people at Herreshoff's, all of them, but I particularly remember Tom Brightman who did the buying, gave us everything we could ask for. I also recall a nighttime visit to a heat-treating plant in South Boston where the interest and care, despite the late hour, went far beyond any business considerations.

We found in the locker a mast designed for the rod rigging, now non-existent, and a mass of cable-rigging elements which had been used on a different mast. After it had been measured we pieced together a rig that was not up to the strength indicated by *Ranger*'s stability but acceptable for moderate winds. We found wooden spreaders which would do. The heat-treating was on new link plates to join the awkward rigging lengths. It was hard, detailed work with great help from all concerned.

The very first sail was all we had hoped. There were many small pieces in that temporary rig. Rod had been over every one of them to see that all were in place and adjusted to share the loads. The crew were all there — 20 men who lived on *Ranger*, plus hands from *Vara*, all under Willy Carstens, the mate, and the afterguard of six.

Mike was skipper and Mrs. V., Gertrude, was observer. Zenas Bliss, a professor from Brown University, navigated most accurately. Arthur Knapp saw to the trim of the sails. Rod was called "rover," meaning that he watched everything with special attention to organizing sail changes and caring for the rig. I was relief helmsman and head of the tactical committee. This meant that Rod, Knappy and I conferred continuously, away from the skipper, so that I would be ready without a second's delay to answer Mike's tactical questions, such as "Shall we tack or keep going?"...."Hold high or drive?"

It was a great moment for all of us as we filled away and *Ranger* moved ahead. Her balance was ideal, and her trim also. The temporary mast was straight under the loads of a moderate sailing breeze. We were ready to nurse it gently if it started to blow, but we were lucky in facing no hard winds with this rig. As we used it our confidence grew and strain-gauge measurements were consistent with our expectations. The rig would do, as it had to, for our first racing. We knew too that the new mast, now being assembled in Bath, could only be an improvement.

I recall one incident of this first sail, minor but surprising. Rounding Fort Adams in a light southerly breeze, we came on the wind and sailed out toward Castle Hill. *Ranger* heeled slightly, 10 or 12 degrees, and the bow rose and fell gently in what there was of the ocean swell. I was interested in the action of the bow which had been snubbed toward the deck to save the weight of a longer overhang, and going forward I lay down with my face over the water. I was admiring the way the hull met the water when the bow settled. As we sailed into one of the larger swells a wave crest drenched my face and I turned to go aft, realizing that the wave had washed away my glasses. Thinking a little ruefully that a perfectly good pair of glasses was gone I took several steps and steadied myself on the forestay, where, looking up, I saw the glasses caught just within reach high up between the forestay and the luff of the staysail. That was good luck, but more than that it was an example of the energy in a mere splash of water hit by this powerful yacht.

On June 3 1937, 23 days after launching, we started our first race, against *Yankee*. As we reached through her lee along the first leg we realized that we had come a long way. Starling, meanwhile, was receiving complete cooperation in Bath on the new rig. The mast design was there, but also of course there were ways to improve it. New drawings were made while the material, which could not come out of stock, was made by Alcoa. New rods were designed. The material and heat-treatment they required was also a problem which Starling, Gil Wyland, and the Bath office handled in overtime. The right mast was ready to take the place of

the spare on June 15th in time for the second series of trial races. We were ready
for it then, knowing that lightness and strength were bound to make *Ranger* faster
and safer.

There was excitement in sailing a big boat and also an undeniable sense of force
and power. I was sometimes concerned about the consequences of gear or rig failure,
but it would not be right to exaggerate: to me all the boats I have sailed in approach
one size. They meet the expectations. In a short time I felt at home in *Ranger*, with
everything normal except for details like the big forces and spaces everywhere.

The rest of the America's Cup summer of 1937 was like that. The story has been told in other places. We were fortunate in a boat with no weak points. We enjoyed it without letting down our guard. Mike saw to that. Ultimately we had a few new sails. The best was one of the first to use synthetic fabric, offered by DuPont and put together by Prescott Wilson. It was a big quadrilateral single headsail, or Genoa, with two sets of sheets, useful in moderate airs. We studied it, we tried it, we liked it, and we confidently hid it away until the Cup races. We also ordered a larger forestaysail than Mike had used, and a larger quadrilateral jib to set over it.

While racing, *Ranger* made it easy for her afterguard; but to a generation unfamiliar with yachts weighing 165 tons and carrying 7500 square feet of sail it must be said that the forces faced by the crew were unimaginable. Our crew was highly experienced and disciplined, with a careful skipper. We were lucky to get through the summer of racing without serious injury. I felt that every day we returned safely to our mooring was a kind of triumph. The upper quadrilateral sheets were lethal. Flogging in a breeze, their length allowed them to whip across the after deck with the stinging speed of a cobra.

The afterguard lived on *Vara* and followed a certain routine. Mike and Rod usually rose before the rest and worked out on deck. After breakfast weather was considered, and that led to a decision on the mainsail to be used. Even though it weighed more than a ton we never left a sail on the boom overnight, no matter how settled the conditions. That policy required real work for the crew, 16 or more strong Norwegian winter fishermen who went yachting in the summer. Mike felt that it might prejudice the next day's sail selection if the sail was there in the morning. We seldom went out early but the exact time depended on whether we were racing or practicing. When racing we always allowed time to check the weather and the sails we planned to use. Sandwiches were there for lunch, and dinner was on board *Vara*. In the evening there was apt to be bridge with some of the skipper's friends but not the younger afterguard, continuing a custom set earlier on *Lone Star*. In both cases I was careful to admit no knowledge of the game even though I played a little at home. Both the intensity of concentration and, I believed, the stakes were out of my range. There was also a good deal of dinghy sailing in the afternoon and evening.

Ranger did everything we had hoped for and more. During the summer of 1937 she started in 37 races, three of which were not finished due to lack of wind. She won all 12 of her match races, including all the America's Cup races, and all eight of the three-boat races. Checking her record I was reminded, surprisingly, that *Ranger* was selected to defend the Cup after only seven trial races. Against fleets of four and five she won 12 and lost two. She never raced after the 1937 season. In 1942 she was sold and scrapped to use her steel and lead in the war effort.

Summer was not endless. Work needed to be done within a time frame, a great

Blitzen, on page 112, was one of a small series of out-and-out racers designed in the late 1930s. Evidence is in the rig and accommodations. This was in the happy time when the best racers had hulls ideal for cruising. *Blitzen* used the hull lines of the cruising-oriented *Avanti*, of the year earlier, although the interior was stripped and the rig was completely new. *Blitzen* gave up mainsail area for a large foretriangle. She was fast and made a fine reputation in the hands of a good crew, but the big headsails were hard to set and change and the rig was not repeated. On this page is *Nyala*, first out of the S&S Twelves. *Northern Light* followed in a few weeks. She would not be sailing today with that short-hoist Genoa, throwing backwind into the main. Now it would have a longer luff and shorter foot and be called a blade and create less backwind. The jib tack should be right down on the deck, and the foot, too, which was known then. (Photos: Rosenfeld Collection 90677F and 97282F)

deal of it thanks to *Ranger*. In this our office was fortunate in arranging for Gilbert Wyland to join Sparkman & Stephens. As a Webb Institute graduate Gil brought just the engineering background that was needed to complete our office technically. He fitted perfectly into the position of chief engineer, taking the lead in all structural and mechanical work, and in the design of powerboats. His outgoing personality had given him a very wide circle of friends in the field of naval architecture, and this complemented the situation Rod and I had among sailors. His care and manifest sincerity in everything he did brought him the respect of co-workers and clients.

With Gil's help we went into our busiest fall and winter. Four boats in particular bring back to me the summer of 1938. There were the first S&S Twelves, *Nyala* and *Northern Light*, and two good offshore boats, *Baruna* and *Blitzen*. The Twelves and *Blitzen* were built by Nevins at City Island while *Baruna* was built near Boston by the Quincy Adams yard, all to the best specifications. It is no criticism of the great Nevins loftsman, Nils Halvorsen, to say that possibly the two most handsome boats that came out of our office were *Baruna* and, the next year, also at Quincy Adams, *Gesture*. I have always thanked the Quincy loftsman, whose name I recall as Ed Lincoln, for an important assist. Although the lofted design should carefully follow the offsets there are minor fairing options in the expansion from the small-scale drawings, and minor changes that a knowing loftsman can carry out advantageously. Occurring in the sheer and deck lines these can make or break the appearance of a boat. Not only did our designs built in Quincy turn out beautifully, but boats they built to the designs of others, such as Francis Herreshoff's *Ticonderoga*, were among the handsomest of their time. I am tempted to say "all time" because I do not admire the more recent trend; but that would not be fair to the great designs of the Scottish pair G.L.Watson and William Fife, Jr.

Our 1938 designs were clean and conventional except that the two ocean racers were fitted with centerboards extending below their normal draft, while *Blitzen*, about 40′ on the water, carried an extra large foretriangle and a tiny main. The head of the mainsail was below the head of the foretriangle and the main boom was very short. She carried a removable headstay, just inside of the permanent one, following the lead of *Ranger*, to use in changing headsails. With Rod as skipper, *Blitzen* won her class in the Bermuda Race and had a long record of success on Lake Michigan, but probably not because of the extreme rig. It was a lot like that of the Six-Metre *Atrocia*, noted earlier, although *Blitzen* carried overlapping headsails. Handling the big headsails called for an expert crew, and S&S rigs did not continue to follow *Blitzen*'s rig geometry.

Baruna was quite different. She was rigged as a yawl and carried a rather large mainsail with a fractional, although high, foretriangle. She was a maxi of her time in the sense that her length on deck was the full 72′ as limited in the major ocean races. I thought a lot about her rig and reasoned that in such a big boat the relatively small Genoa and other headsails would help handling efficiency. Such efficiency contributed more than the minutes saved making a change. In making sail changes easy the right sail for the conditions would be up there more of the time. *Baruna*'s toughest competitor for first to finish was often the Rhodes-designed *Escapade*. She was a fast boat but with a much bigger foretriangle, and I always thought fighting her big sails was a handicap.

While Rod campaigned *Blitzen* in the 1938 Bermuda Race, I sailed aboard *Baruna*. Ken Davidson navigated. Both boats were winners in class, and *Baruna* overall. The 1938 event was a big-boat race. *Baruna* was a very comfortable cruising boat with a deckhouse amidships, an owner's stateroom aft, and a big cabin forward of the house. Right forward were galley and crew quarters for three. In no

sense was she "skinned out." In contrast, *Blitzen* was a machine. Vastly different from today's type in hull form, relatively heavy, narrow, and deep, she was almost empty below except for pipe berths and a partially enclosed head. She forecast the extremes of today; but because these CCA-Rule designs had more displacement than we find today the cruising amenities did not stand in the way of race-winning potential.

In addition to the larger boats we did two new Sixes. The Sixes and Twelves were much alike in hull form. Possibly because of my close contact with the design I think of them as entirely normal. Each was a long boat for her class with fine, drawn-out ends and near-minimum beam. The Sixes were *Djinn*, for Henry S. Morgan, and *Goose* for his relative George Nichols. Hull models were tested at the Stevens tank, and because of their schedule and ours the Nichols boat was the last one to be run in the tank. As such she became almost a duplicate of the Morgan boat but with one exception that, according to the tank, made a significant improvement in her performance. This was the lowering and consequent sharpening of the concave profile under the mast step. The results reported by the tank were dramatic in racing terms, so much so that one could not avoid concern about the reliability of the tests. Such doubts still remain in my mind, all the more because later tests confirmed the belief that a sharp leading edge increases induced drag, especially when tacking, due to flow separation. Such separation would be most detrimental by increasing induced drag while accelerating out of a tack at the lowered boat speed. In turn this would be most serious while match racing, as in *Goose*'s first series. She lost this series, especially in a sequence of short tacks á la Dennis Conner. *Goose* came out late in the season, and although she was selected to defend the Seawanhaka Cup against a Scottish Six, and lost, her record was outstanding in the worldwide Six-Metre Class. In 1939 she won the One Ton Cup in Oslo, and went on to become the standard for tests of postwar boats. She gave new validation to the small-model tests. The many elements — luck, handling, sails, course conditions and wishful thinking in subjective judgements of a boat's performance — let you hang in mid-air, while the quantitative nature of reliable tests put your feet on the ground

I wish I could clarify the question of *Goose*. She was our star Six Metre in the sense that she was a long step ahead of the earlier boats of the class, while later ones were almost the same and were not enough faster to be worth mentioning. She did lose her first match, but that can happen for so many reasons. It is just another reminder that nothing is certain. And *Goose*'s later record was to win consistently. It is hard to say why this was true because she was not radical in the way our star Twelve, *Intrepid*, was. In her time the art or luck or the happy combination just worked.

She did look excellent in the tank. I interpret the test results to suggest that individual design features must not be weighed in isolation. This is a hard position

The Six-Metre *Goose* (1938), on the opposite page, was the best of the pre-war Sixes. Her test model, incorporating only a small keel change from the preceding Six, promised substantial improvement which was fully realized. Later boats of the class were essentially touch-ups because even with new models such improvements could not be repeated until the advent of the shorter keel.
(Photo: Rosenfeld Collection 118536F)

to justify in these days of more detailed analysis. Seeing a minimal model change make a monumental improvement in comparative performance makes you wonder whether it must not be the combination that counts. This leads to my strong feeling that if a design is based on model tests, even after a systematic study of a series of alternatives, the final combined design should be tested, and if the results are satisfactory the hull should be built in strict accordance with the model. As computer runs are now either supplementing or replacing model tests, I advance the same methodology. If good results are promised it is tempting but dangerous to take a chance in the hope of doing better through the promise of any single feature. To anticipate slightly, the Twelve-Metre *Vim* came out the next year incorporating a similar joining of keel and hull. Her racing record was on a par with that of *Goose*. She was built in strict accordance with a promising model, with features similar to *Goose* that we tested too late to use on the earlier Twelves.

The Twelves of 1938 were both good boats and evenly matched overall. They provided an opportunity to confirm my thoughts on the subject of the prismatic coefficient. They had virtually the same dimensions and above-water shape, but *Northern Light* had the higher prismatic by a small margin. As expected, she was the faster boat on a reach while *Nyala* seemed marginally better in light going, especially upwind — that is, at the lower speeds.

After the design of *Nyala* and *Northern Light*, we designed *Vim* for Mike Vanderbilt. The purpose was to race her in '39 in England where the races were sailed "around the coast" — which meant that day races were held off a chain of ports with the class moving from one port to the next. *Vim* raced as planned in England, and the results were good — first finishes in 21 of 28 starts, with two disqualifications — but the prospect of war was too clear to make it a happy summer of sailing. We all felt that changes were coming and that they would not be good.

Following the thread leading from the early Six Metres and *Dorade* has carried us through *Ranger* to *Goose* and *Vim* as highlights of design experience, and up to the approach of war, bypassing some activities that were interesting, at least to me.

In the early 1930s S&S opened a Boston office directed by Emmons Alexander, a friend and sometime competitor of Drake's. Emmons organized several design projects with clients in New England, and during successive winters new boats were building near Providence and Boston. The happy personal associations stay fresh in my mind, especially visiting with Emmons and his wife Claudia, and getting to know Aage Nielsen and Albert Lemos. Both of these gentlemen came from abroad and both became outstanding American citizens.

With the workload growing we decided that the branch brokerage office in Boston should also have a branch design office. Emmons arranged for Aage, a young Danish naval architect, to work with me. In retrospect I can say that such

an arrangement might have been difficult, but it went very smoothly. Aage made preliminary sketches which he sent to me in New York as interest developed, and I would come back to him with suggestions bearing on both general characteristics and details. I was primarily interested in the lines as they led to sailing performance, and would recommend displacement, prismatic coefficient, sail area or Dellenbaugh coefficient, and sometimes details of shape or arrangement, with thoughts on scantlings. We must have thought along very similar lines, and Aage must have had more respect for my ideas than they may have deserved, for we never disagreed. Aage did all the final plans and took responsibility for inspection when the boats were built. He was a very quick and neat draftsman, had a good eye, and was conscientious in the extreme. I often thought that if I were to sit back and ask someone to provide plans for my new boat, it would be Aage Nielsen. After only a few years the war broke up our direct association, and after the war Aage opened his own office and produced many fine boats. He continued to give S&S a hand if we were busier than he was. Aage did not share my interest in racing, but when the MHS gave real cruisers an opportunity to win his *Holger Danske* took first to Bermuda in 1980.

Albert Lemos was a very different person, although he shared the same characteristics of skill and conscience. He owned a small yard in Barrington, Rhode Island, outside of Providence. Emmons Alexander took me to him in the early 'thirties as a promising builder for the first powerboat for which I was individually responsible. He built the boat, *El Nido*, at a reasonable cost and very well. After that we were able to see that he did one new boat each year until the hurricane of 1938 completely washed out his yard. Then he went to the position of head boatbuilder at the Herreshoff yard in Bristol where he built one more fast powerboat for *El Nido*'s owner, E.E. Dickinson, Jr. I'm afraid that Albert was not an organization man and that he never repeated the satisfaction that I hope he experienced during the short period of work with our office. In later years he built two small boats modeled on *Vim* and *Bolero* which he used himself on Narragansett Bay. As time passed Rod and I saw these little daysailers at Newport, and as Albert grew older we saw him at the home of his daughter nearby. I can only recall him as one of the best citizens I have known. I understood that he had come in a schooner from the Cape Verde Islands, and had set up his own yard without being able to either read or write. He had no trouble following plans. Of his two sons one has retired as an Admiral in the U.S. Navy, and the other has held a senior engineering position with General Motors. I cannot exaggerate the admiration I have always felt for Albert Lemos.

Similar pleasant associations came with the start of our work for foreign clients. The first of these was Guy Rex, of Hobart, Tasmania, whose *Landfall*, has been mentioned. We never met until much later but became good friends by letter. Then in 1935 we heard from Claes Bruynzeel who became the owner of *Zeearend*, one of my favorite designs. She was just under 40′ on the waterline with 11′-6″ beam, a good compromise between the narrow beam of *Dorade* and the swing to a good deal more that followed. She came to Newport from Holland in 1936, along with seven German boats, to sail in the Bermuda Race. The fact that she was first among the invaders did not put her very high in the fleet, but the next year when she won the Fastnet I felt justified in my hopes for her.

Bruynzeel was one of the few clients with whom I have lost my temper. In Newport the night before the start he came to me crying and asking for my support of his demand for a last-minute change in his measurement certificate. We had made, in the office where there was the necessary time, our customary check of all rating certificates against design measurements. Here, without time, no plans and no measurer, with hardly a place to sit down, he was suddenly insistent in a way that got under my skin that a mistake had been made. I don't think I cared one way or the other what he claimed, but I didn't believe that his case had merit. Particularly I considered that the timing was all wrong and the owner was making too much out of too little. So I said "No" and told him to use it and like it.

We had very few arguments with clients, although occasionally there was a feeling that our costs were high or we had not given full support on the subject of a yard bill. I felt keenly one case about which there was no argument. This was a client for whom we had designed several successful racers, and the last was a disappointment. I was disappointed, too, but what hurt was his evident feeling that we had not done the best we knew how. This was not our only performance failure, but it was the only time we were accused of not trying.

Correctly measured or not, *Zeearend* opened the way in Holland and led to two successive designs for Dutch owners. The third was Cornelius Van der Vorm of Rotterdam with whose whole family we became good friends. For him we designed *Zwerver*. The war interrupted her sailing career, but she led to a second *Zwerver* after the war which was built under the direct supervision of his son, Otto, who kept her beautifully for a number of years. In 1951 she won the Fastnet. Otto later was head of a very large shipyard in Rotterdam. The good feelings of Europeans for Americans helped to spread our work overseas in the postwar years. But we are now getting ahead of ourselves, ahead of the war which seemed inevitable for everyone in 1939.

7

AT HOME

The ten years that ended in 1939, with the start of the war in Europe, could not have brought more than I had experienced in the way of luck, success and excitement, so it is hard to explain why there were several months when I wished to hide from the world of sailing. I remember one day when I had an appointment with a prospect in Essex, Connecticut, for dinner and overnight and I asked my secretary to call at the last minute to say that I was sick, though I had no physical symptoms. In my mother's country house in Sheffield, Massachusetts, where I did my best to retreat without making my feelings too obvious, I reviewed finances and discussed with Susie the possibility of retirement until I could find something easier. That wasn't another job as such, although it might have been writing or painting. My malaise was real, and when wartime came the different work was somehow a relief. Serious as was the war it may have been another instance of good luck in saving me from a real problem.

I have never studied psychology and cannot logically explain the reasons for my feelings. They may have been a type of depression brought on by a combination of weariness and too much of one thing. Readers will probably not question my devotion to sailing and sailing boats, but I think I have been lucky in having some other interests in family, travel, painting, music and the architecture of buildings as well as ships. For some time I had been exposed intensely to boats, boats and more boats. All of a sudden it was just too much.

Regardless of the immediate cause, my respite in Mother's country house was natural. The country has always been a happy place for me — almost as much as the sea. There are compensations, balances, in all things. It has seemed to me that physical laws such as Newton's, applying to the conservation of force or momentum, may be able to be applied in a less physical sense as implied by the cliche "there's no such thing as a free lunch," which has a very broad reach. Even now, when I am often congratulated on having made a life work and a good living from something I loved, I agree, and I really do; but I still reflect that it is not quite that simple. The tide runs in and out. I think of Yeats' poem "The Choice" which starts: "The intellect of man is forced to choose/perfection of the life, or of the work." I always wished for more in the perfection of both work and life. It is not cynicism to say that this was impossible.

Something was sacrificed, and there were hard spots, but life has been very good to me. From way back I was lucky in love, which brought me from high-school times, in the form of Susie (Florence Reynolds), the best possible wife. I felt she was the only one for me from our early high-school days. She was smart enough to keep me worried about her feelings for a long time. When it seemed possible for me to earn some kind of living we decided to marry, and we were married in Scarsdale on October 21st, 1930. I know I never regretted it and I hope she didn't. We parted on June 16th, 1993 when she died of cancer in Hanover, New Hampshire. I received generous sympathy, but it was a relief for us both. I'm sure others have found the worst of it is knowing that you have never made appreciation explicit. Could I ever have said how much she meant?

We were lucky to have had two sons who were good to their mother and are good to me now. Their activities have varied and they are very different, but recently they have worked successfully together on the repair and restoration of old houses in southern Vermont and New Hampshire. They influenced our decision to live in that area when we left Scarsdale, although we had long thought of the house in Sheffield, Massachusetts, as a retirement home.

This may be a good place to say a little more about our life together, intertwined as it was with boats. One of the hard spots was the divorce of my parents which followed the 1931 summer of the transAtlantic success. Part of what made it hard were the strong emotions we, the younger generation, had for both parents. My mother was a person of very high ideals in every possible way, but especially on moral grounds. Her standards may have been difficult to meet. My father strayed to a degree, very limited I think, and wanted a divorce.

I don't think that we realized anything was wrong until we were told. We appreciated all that both parents had given us and had strong feelings for both. We were immediately sympathetic to Mother who, sadly, felt she had failed her husband and family in her efforts to be the perfect mother and wife. Both Rod and I talked with Father, and I remember writing him a letter which he evidently showed his lawyer, a family friend, who said to me that he could wish that Father could see it my way. We owed so much to him. Father was and remained identified by his exceptional generosity and confidence in me and my brother Rod. He did everything and more for his family. We knew this and, if not fully, to a degree we appreciated all he had done for us. It was not only sailing. Even though I was less athletic than Rod we were both active in high-school sports and Father was always at the games with his early movie camera. Our grandparents, his father and mother, were often there too. We were a family that played together. We watched the tennis at Forest Hills and the Yankees at the Stadium. It was hard to accept what had happened when they parted. Mother, though she hated every minute of it, had been persuaded to go to Reno and Father went to New York. His parents lived in a comfortable house in the Bronx. I think he moved in with them. It was hard on them too.

Susie and I had, successively, two Scarsdale apartments during about four years after our wedding. Our first son, Olin III, arrived in May 1934, and during that year we built a house in the southern part of the town. By 1936 we decided to build again a little farther afield; this was a somewhat roomier house as Susie was pregnant and we felt we were prospering. That was the year *Ranger* was started. We had made a good friend in our architect, Don DeBogdan, a native of Poland who had fought there at the end of World War One and went into the American army in World War Two. As both architect and friend he did well for us when we could give little attention to the construction of the second house, what with an expected child and *Ranger*. We enjoyed that house and lived in it from 1937 to 1978.

Despite the shiny surface I think of the time in late February and the following March of 1937 as the saddest of my life. After selling one house and starting another, we lived with my grandparents in the city. I spent a lot of time in Maine. Olie was then about three and Susie was pregnant. The grandparents were generous and loving, but Grandmother Stephens was a manager and three-year-old Olie meant everything to her. I am not a woman or a mother, and I can't exactly describe her feelings but I'm afraid that Susie began to feel she could not call her child her

own. There were no outward signs of stress, but Susie was unhappy and eventually
we went back to Scarsdale where her mother had a small apartment with an extra
room which we used. It was not an easy time, and one day the doctor phoned me in
New York and asked me to come out to his office. There he told me that he had
examined Susie and found no sign of life. He assured me that Susie would be okay
but that he felt the baby would be stillborn. That was what happened. It was the
saddest day of my life. I'm sure Susie felt it even more, though I'm not sure I appreciated just how she felt.

We move with time, and in April the new house was ready and a new phase of
our lives began and continued in that house for the next 41 years. Soon after moving
in I went to Bermuda where I sailed with Briggs Cunningham in the Six-Metre
Lulu in a good series. I suppose I should have skipped that trip. Work over life.
Then it was off to Bath, Maine, to launch *Ranger*. It was an impossibly good summer, but I still feel the loss when I think of that spring — and, I'm afraid, selfishly.

There were brighter moments. Mother had moved in 1935 from Scarsdale to a
small farmhouse in Sheffield, Massachusetts. Her sister, my Aunt Julie, lived with her
there and Susie visited frequently. I visited as often as I could. Whether she approved
or not she never interfered with young Olie. She and Susie worked well together.
The house was old and more attractive than liveable. The first winter was pretty
rugged for Mother, but the next summer architect Don made plans to keep it comfortable on a year-round basis and they were put into effect before winter.

Mother enjoyed the country and her garden, and made the place more and more
attractive. She enjoyed her young grandson and was happy to have Susie and Olie
whenever I was away. But none of this kept Mother from what she believed was her
failure. I'm afraid she had little wish to recover from a combination of illnesses that
took her away in the fall of 1941, shortly before the arrival of our second son, Sam.
The house in Sheffield was rented during the war and became a second home for
Susie and me when the war was over and we bought the shares of Rod and my
sister. If the early years in Sheffield were clouded, the place saw some very good
years for our family. These were all the better for the fact that Susie's mother and
Susie's brother's family, his wife and two boys, just about the age of our own, spent
a series of summers in Sheffield. We had a pond for swimming; there was good
trout fishing and even a little sailing at nearby Twin Lakes; and next to us there was
an active dairy farm with a young family of matching ages. We spent wonderful
summers there.

I am often asked about my boys and sailing and can only say that they missed
something that was a great experience for me. It would have been difficult for me to
give them what I had, largely because my sailing was all with clients and much of it
was abroad. Undoubtedly more effort on my part could have given them greater

opportunities, but despite the real joy of my own earliest days on the water my personal sailing became more and more a business with the rewards on the technical side and involved with the work I did on rating rules and later in the development of international offshore racing. It was absorbing and time-consuming work.

In that prewar time we enjoyed activities with friends, both neighbors and those from the sailing world; but beyond boats and sailing our interests had no sharp focus. In the course of visits to Starling in Wiscasset I was usually left alone in the evening with books and an excellent collection of recordings, largely orchestral. We had known music at home in several forms. Father played popular songs on the piano as well as the mandolin. We also had an instrument called a pianola which could be rolled up to the piano keyboard so as to strike the keys as directed by a perforated piano roll so long as the air pressure was maintained by the use of foot pedals. Rod, my brother, played the accordion, which he had learned from sailing friends. One of these was Zenas Bliss, Brown professor and later University Provost, who was navigator aboard *Ranger*. I did not play any instrument, although I am told that I asked for a saxophone and was denied, probably for good reason. I had taken some piano lessons but had given up. Anyway my feelings about music were sharpened by two events: I enjoyed Starling's recordings well enough that I promised myself a good phonograph if the next year was successful, and Rod generously gave our new 1937 house a small spinet-type piano. Susie and I both worked at it and then tried duets. We were serious enough so that when our elbows clashed we acquired a sister unit and continued our duets face-to-face rather than side-by-side.

We were not so serious that we didn't allow a different interest to later take over, but there were times with the two pianos that were times to celebrate. Ken Davidson was distinctly musical. He visited and enjoyed both the phonograph and the piano. He was especially fond of Beethoven's Seventh which I played on the phonograph and he played, not at the same time, in a piano transcription. We had a neighbor who played quite well and we acquired a two-piano arrangement of the Seventh Symphony. Once or twice they both came to the house and pounded away at the Beethoven. Perhaps it was more fun than music. I remember liking it greatly.

The different interest was painting. I had worked with oil paints sporadically, and it may have been the routine of government work during the war that caused me to pick it up again. I became increasingly interested in painting as a weekend activity. My subjects then were landscapes and the attractive or picturesque. Susie and I went out together to find suitable themes. Frequently we had the company of Fred Bradley, an experienced sailor, in business as a photographer, mainly of fashions, but also a Sunday painter. He was a helper with fundamentals. I enjoyed the music, as I still do, but I became much more fully committed to painting. From the early war years until we left New York, as often as we could we spent Saturdays visiting the

Susie poses in Sheffield, Massachusetts, by our Riley, a British sport sedan, circa 1954. We both enjoyed driving and did a lot of it together, both in the USA and Europe. That Riley was fun, but needed a lot of attention to keep in tune.

(Photo: Author's Collection)

galleries and museums in the city.

Early in this time we found and bought a very small painting from the gallery of Antoinette Kraushaar. It was a figure of a clown which we later traded back for a painting we liked more. One we particularly liked, and had to buy, was a Vermont landscape by John Heliker. I told Antoinette that I was trying to paint and could use some help. She spoke of that to Jack Heliker, who was instructing a small group of friends, and he let me join the group one evening a week. This developed into a longtime friendship. I never became a good painter, but it was fun to work at it and to occasionally buy an affordable painting that Susie and I both liked. Jack's advice helped us in that, too. I believe that all of this began to educate my eye.

The gallery visits were best in the 1950s when there were not as many places as there were later. Early on we came to know the gallery owners and to recognize the work of most of the artists. As the galleries multiplied, and the painters also, and as prices rose, there was relatively less incentive to make these weekend trips, but we went on until we left town. The museums were still there and one of our standbys was the Asia Society. Much of Eastern art has a special appeal for me. I have enjoyed none more than the archaic Chinese bronzes, but our tastes, Susie's and mine, have included both the earliest and the most recent painting and sculpture. Painting and music were interests that Susie and I shared. I think of them as always interesting and in the right cases as sources of wonder. Not long ago these feelings were renewed by the Cezannes and Picassos in the Museum of Modern Art where I managed an afternoon before a next-morning, once-a-year meeting at the S&S office, just to keep in touch.

Again recalling how one thing leads to another, it was pleasant to meet some of Jack Heliker's more forcefully avant-garde friends. I am thinking of a group that once spent a few days at our house in Sheffield. There were Jack and his painter friend Bob La Hotan together with John Cage, musician, Merce Cunningham, dancer, and Richard Lippold, the sculptor whose rather chic work hangs in Avery Fisher Hall. I can say for Cage that when we arrived on a Friday evening he had discovered the old-fashioned freezer in our garage which he filled with some of the best ice cream I ever had. Merce said he had left Susie a dance in the garden. I had enjoyed the rhythm and the harpsichord-like sound of John Cage's sonatas for prepared piano, but the haphazard nature of his music, as selected by chance, to which Cunningham later danced, was a little too abstract and intellectual for us to follow into their recent years and we lost contact with all except Jack and Bob.

During these war years and for some time after, I went down to Twelfth Street after work for courses at the New School. I worked first with Yasuo Kuniyoshi, a well-liked Japanese-American painter, and later with Louis Shanker who was committed to abstraction. I also audited classes in literature and art with Heinrich Blucher. I liked his views which I shared with respect to Homer and the appreciation of Byzantine, Romanesque and Gothic art, although Baroque, another of his enthusiasms, continued to be over-ornamental for me. He said I was very wrong when I compared St. Peter's to a gold-plated Cadillac. Blucher, a German refugee, taught also at Bard College and was the husband of Hannah Arendt. He was a voluble and mesmerizing lecturer.

A happy recollection of this period is of going to a nearby Italian restaurant with Shanker and others after his painting class where we stoked up on green pasta, spaghetti al pesto, which incorporated enough garlic so that Susie at home in bed said that her nose announced my return before I reached the house. Later, near the docks in Genoa, we enjoyed pesto at a restaurant called Mario's. We were adventurous with food. Susie was a good cook and we enjoyed good food together, at home and when we traveled, always scanning the *Guide Michelin* for starred restaurants within our budget. We found wonderful meals in France, of course, but in terms of value Italy was our favorite.

European visits became frequent after the war. Sparkman & Stephens not only found good builders but gradually we found European clients. In our European associations I was able to benefit from a combination of circumstances. One of those was that I liked cars, and if they were sport machines so much the better. I liked small cars, too. The first non-American car I owned was a little British Austin. It was handy and easy to park for shopping and visits in New York. Susie liked it in Sheffield in the summer. During the war I had a rather sporty Buick bought from Briggs Cunningham in 1939. In the late 'forties he let me have, reasonably, a Cadillac with high lift valves to boost its power. I was horrified to find that its best gas mileage was about seven miles to the gallon. Briggs referred me to the shop that had changed the camshafts and they put back the original Cadillac cams, roughly doubling the gas mileage. I never really liked so big a car, so I turned it in for a two-litre Riley, an English sports sedan. The Riley was fun to drive and became a learning experience as the removal of carbon from the cylinder heads and valves was needed at frequent intervals. The car was equipped with a good handbook, so I proceeded to do this myself and rather liked the work, learning as I went along. Eventually the Austin was replaced by a second-hand Riley roadster and the first sedan was replaced by a new one. Obviously I liked the Rileys despite their faults, of which there were two in particular. One was a water pump that frequently needed a new carbon ring seal to cure a leak. I became fairly adept at that operation, but more interesting was an air lock in the fuel system that too frequently stopped the delivery of gasoline to the carburetor in hot weather. Of necessity, Susie learned to loosen and then retighten a coupling in the line to relieve pressure. Once when the engine died she pulled to the side of the road where some laborers were digging. They were astonished when she lifted the hood, went through the routine, and drove on, to their applause.

But enough became enough, and I swapped the Riley for a second-hand small Mercedes of prewar design but more recent construction. We called this dignified car Daisy, but as I have explained to others it returned my weekends to me. No more problems with stopped fuel lines or leaking water pumps, no adjusting of brakes. One result of all this was that both sons became car enthusiasts and in the course of time there were VW Beetles and MG TDs parked in our driveway. Just one more car story. Sam announced one morning that he had come home without the VW he had used the night before. He had capsized it and the car had been towed to a shop for repairs. Fortunately no one was hurt. The car was insured for liability but not for such damage as this. I told Sam that if he had been okay I would pay for the repairs but if he had been drinking they were up to him. He said he would pay.

After the war, with building yards and S&S clients in Europe, it was possible to combine business and pleasure, traveling by car. The strong dollar made it relatively easy to buy a new car in Europe, drive it there, then import it with a second-hand valuation for duty. Our first experience was in 1955. I flew to Sweden and sailed at Saltjobaden in a new boat for a member of the Wallenberg family. The builder was Bengt Plym, one of the best-ever builders of wooden yachts. I stayed with him on his cruising boat, which was too small for stored hot water. Moored with bow to the shore we washed by diving over the side in the morning. I recall that cold Baltic water, and I also recall coming in after a race to a lunch of thin Swedish pancakes with brandy and sugar. Not all sailing is tough and hard and cold, although such it can be. After Saltjobaden it was by air to Hamburg where I met a new small Mercedes and drove it to LeHavre to meet Susie and Sam, who had come by sea. Along the road in France I picked up a farmer. I believe he took me, with a new German car, for German. I had a little French, and when I said, undoubtedly with a strange accent, *"Je suis Americain,"* he worked a little harder to communicate.

After meeting Susie and Sam at the pier we spent a night in Rouen, and late the next day went on to Versailles and Paris. That year it was nearly all vacation as we went south through France, visiting the chateaux along the Loire and on to the Dordogne where we had the great experience of going into the cave of Lascaux and seeing the prehistoric paintings with our own eyes, something I will never forget. Continuing we visited Aix and traveled the Riviera coast on an over-ambitious day to the Portofino area, where we stayed and visited the Sangermani yachtbuilding yard nearby. On through Italy we visited Rome and took a more leisurely drive north into Germany to Munich and on to Rotterdam. There we visited with our clients and friends, the Van der Vorm family, and shipped the car to New York.

We repeated this sort of trip several times, generally seeing more yards and clients but still getting in plenty of sightseeing. On the first trip we had made reservations for every night, but later we preferred more flexibility and we never failed to find a place to sleep. My great interest was in Europe's early architecture, particularly the Romanesque churches. Something about that kind of solidity and the individuality of the sculpture had a great attraction. Along the way I took many photographs, usually hanging two cameras around my neck, one for color and one for black-and-white. The routes we took were frequently dictated by the locations of those cathedrals and churches that promised to be the most interesting. I studied books of European architecture as I worked out the itinerary. I had read a recent book on Notre Dame de Paris, and of course *Mont St. Michel and Chartres.* These were two of the greatest we visited, although among my favorites was Autun.

Surely travel is many things to many people. I enjoyed my travel, and I was happy to travel a number of times to Europe and elsewhere, often with Susie and sometimes alone on business. I felt fortunate in circumstances which put me in touch with active and interesting people, and gave me an entrée that fostered collaboration and friendship. I was happy that so often clients became friends. Without criticizing clients and their friendship in this country, I felt that often in Europe the clients were likely to be more appreciative of the artistic element in design and more ready to recognize and accept the element of chance as opposed to calculation as part of a new project. It is dangerous to generalize and difficult to describe, but in Europe the designer-client business relationship seemed more in the background than often seemed the case here at home.

We had few difficulties with clients, in the U.S. or overseas, but one source of conflict is worth mentioning. Probably in common with other types of architectural work there could be a sort of land-mine in the process when some client felt his personal claims of originality had been overlooked. For us this never reached the point of outright or legal claims; but I know there were times when a good client felt in some way injured after a succeeding boat incorporated a feature first used in his boat or suggested by him. This sensitivity might involve any feature from a complete design to some minor detail of trim. Our effort to make our position clear from the beginning was a form letter given to all clients asserting that we offered a license to build to our plans, although the plans and the right to use them remained our property. If two or more boats used the same plans at the same time or in close succession the costs were divided and a stated fee was charged for each use. I don't recall any case when the passage of time made this difficult to apply. Unless instances were simultaneous or close together the design was usually changed or the detail overlooked.

In our dealings with European clients we found the social contrasts interesting and pleasurable, from the relative formality of the north, Sweden and Denmark, through Germany and on south through France and the very welcome informality of Italy, where I most enjoy returning. But over the whole range I felt welcomed. Now remembering former days of sailing, so too I picture an evening in Germany with a prospective client, sitting after dinner with a bottle of good Rhine wine and discussing a possible new boat and both of our memories of sailing. I think it is a libel on the French when it is suggested that some lack of friendly feeling for foreigners may exist there. The French have given me some of my warmest memories. As when Gaston Deferre, mayor of Marseilles, came to his heavily-guarded (Algerian troubles) front door in his bathrobe to greet Susie and me after deciding we would never find his house at the end of a long drive from Spain. His directions had been good and we had reached a tiny tobacco shop where the keeper had only to direct us a hundred metres up the steep and narrow hill and we were there, although we were late. And how his wife, a wartime nurse, had welcomed and cared for me when I had one of the nastiest colds imaginable. Such times are good for the heart and soul, and recalling them is the same.

Although I think of Italy as a favorite — I have found nowhere quite the equal of its people and its food — I must tell of one of the most boring evenings I remember. I was with a good client who was entertaining a friend at dinner. An excellent restaurant helped me to suffer through the evening. It turned out that the friend, all in Italian, of which I knew only a few words, was boasting of his new Ferrari car, and the two argued in vigorous Italian, it seemed all night, about the odds on a bet as to whether the car owner in his Ferrari could beat the time of his friend, by airline, between Milan and Rome.

I was about to write that the small yards were the most welcoming when I recalled my son's army hospitalization in Frankfurt, Germany. I had told him that if he needed something to help him pass the time he might call on Horst Lehnert, manager of the big Abeking and Rasmussen yard in Lemwerder, near Bremen, to whom I had also written. The first thing I knew was that when Horst heard from my letter that Olie was in the hospital he had taken the train, halfway across the country from Bremen to Frankfurt, to visit him, and phoned me at home to report his condition. And in France I think of a small country yard near La Rochelle that afforded another of my warmest memories. Launching became the opportunity for a feast on the lawn of the builder's home, where the designer and the owner became part of the family, sharing food and wine, crusty French bread and cheese, fish and meat and salad, and wine of the village, all set on a long, plain table at the top of a bank of green grass along the road. A most generous reward. It is hard to reciprocate such things, which makes me a little sad — and, anyway, nostalgic.

8

WAR AND POSTWAR

Preparations for war began as the 1938 sailing season passed. S&S felt it as we prepared for a design competition held by the navy. I think they wanted to feel out the yacht-design organizations that seemed qualified to handle wood construction and to do plans of the kind they would be needing in case of mobilization. The call was for contract plans in two categories — fast torpedo boats and medium-speed submarine chasers. All entries would receive something to pay for the cost of the work, and the winners somewhat more. With Gil Wyland taking the lead we went into both classes, and worked hard to produce winners. When the first results were announced S&S had won the torpedo-boat class, and failed on the subchasers.

On page 134 a DUKW maneuvers in rough water. This was Rod's project from the time he took the plans to General Motors until the war ended. There were many small modifications of the first finished vehicles, the most important being the control of tire pressure from the dash. Very low pressure was best across the sand while much more was needed on solid ground. There was also some replacement of plain steel parts by stainless steel or bronze.

(Photo: Rosenfeld Collection ANN4313)

As another step toward bringing yacht designers closer to the navy, a meeting was held in Norfolk, Virginia, in the summer of 1939. I attended with Ken Davidson, and we drove down together with our wives. We had passed through Washington, and I still remember the spot where we were stopped in traffic near a fast-food stand just at the far bank of the Potomac River. As we waited to move, broadcast music was interrupted by the news that Hitler had invaded Poland. We heard the announcement, and as we moved again we knew that our work would be tested in a more serious way.

That first test came with, ironically, subchaser plans. Liking boats that moved fast, and having won the PT-boat class in the competition, I was disappointed not to be making the torpedo-boat drawings. This was soon after the trip to Norfolk, well before Pearl Harbor. We were set up to do the detail work on a navy plan for a 110′ subchaser to be built at the Fisher Boat Works in Detroit. She was to be the test bed for a new lightweight "pancake" diesel being built by General Motors under the eye of an engineer named Rippingill, first assistant to Charles Kettering. The crankshaft was vertical and drove the controllable-pitch propeller through bevel gears. This made it simple to adjust propeller pitch through a hollow shaft and avoided the need for a clutch or reverse gear. The concept was attractive and worked in a considerable number of the 'chasers that were eventually built, although the engines were considered temperamental in service.

I do not wish to libel those engines because as recently as the spring of 1998 a Norwegian colleague, knowing my interest, reported that one of our subchasers from the war period, fitted with those same pancake diesels, was running in regular service from Norway to the Faeroes. Obviously the engines have been well-maintained, but that's not bad for two 50-year-old, and temperamental, machines.

As war became closer we continued with subchasers, and taking the navy's design drawings we did detail plans for nearly all the builders in that class, a minimum of several hundred boats. We never were given a reason for the seemingly irrational switch in design responsibility. I still feel it is the sort of logic to be expected from the government. Yet it may be more or less than governmental misjudgement. Our office had already become actively involved with Fisher Boat Works on some yacht work and, as recently suggested to me, the Englishman, Hubert Scott-Payne, had designed PT boats in Britain and had negotiated an arrangement for promoting his PT-boat design with Elco, a builder with good production facilities that could build in quantity. During World War One Elco had built 550 torpedo boats for the British in 488 working days. So, for whatever reason, we never had the PT-boat work. In terms of business, right through the war we had all the work we could handle, but in terms of wishing and specific

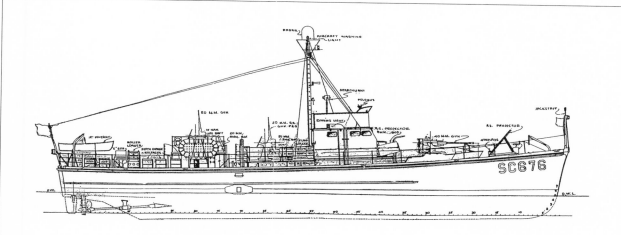

interest we were disappointed not to have been given design responsibility for some fast boats.

These wartime activities took us completely away from yachts for a period of about six years. We had to build up the size of our office to handle navy detail plans for several classes. We were kept busy but often frustrated by many changes. Especially frustrating were those that involved the ripping out of completed work, seemingly at the whim of some inexperienced officer. We were busy doing our best, but our greatest satisfaction came from two truly original projects. The first of these was the design of amphibious vehicles, and the second the development of a "deck-balk" pontoon bridge.

The experience of working for the government and coordinating engine installations with General Motors and other big organizations was entirely different from the independence of our work on smallish yachts. Gil Wyland was like an anchor to windward. He had good training, academic and practical, and being who he was he had innumerable friends involved in war work. These included schoolmates from Webb who were active in the civilian side of the navy's design offices or, in some cases, reserve officers. He had worked on large vessels at the New York Shipbuilding Company and on motor yachts at the Luders yard and the New York Yacht, Launch and Engine Company. He was a sailor at heart but he knew engines and their installation. Through his personal links he knew how to find good people to head departments as the office expanded and was divided into sections. And his experience in larger offices had taught him the fundamentals of organization, all of which was new to me. New to me too was the administration of wartime wage categories and the need to accept the formation of a union.

As I was the nominal head of the firm — that is, the design department — and Gil was my strong right hand, we made frequent trips together, at that time to

The design of 110' subchasers was a continuing project because of the many alterations. These were frustrating to our office, and often seemed unnecessary, frequently reflecting the whims of commissioning officers who had little training or appropriate experience. Some of these are still operating, one between Norway and the Faeroes. They are good seaboats despite heavy rolling.

(Courtesy of Sparkman & Stephens)

Washington, where we discussed contractual arrangements with navy contracting officers and were sometimes advised about the yards that would be building to our plans. The bulk of the work required our office to take design or "contract" plans from Washington and do detailed working drawings for various building yards. Our work was under the direction of a navy office in New York City known as the Supervisor of Shipbuilding, or Supships. The subchaser project, which we had started even before the war, extended through the war. We kept working at it with the navy's many modifications right through it all. But as time passed and one type of work slowed down, new work on other types came along.

Managing all this meant expanding the office to more than a hundred in all. Although this is small by industrial standards, it meant that a more formal organization was needed and, as already noted, Gil was my guide. Through his network of friends in the ship field we found good leaders for the four principal departments: hull, engineering, scientific and purchasing. People with marine training or experience were assistants to the department heads, and to help in getting out the plans we found architects and draftsmen from many fields. A substantial part of the work was in the buying or procurement division which acted for the group of building yards using our plans. Materials and hardware were approved by Supships, and uniform installation plans were made. We ordered what was necessary for the yards, and in this we took a very firm stand against placing an order in our name until we had the money in the bank. This seemed tough and uneconomical to some yards, but the navy accepted our stand and of course it was the navy that financed the procurement.

For me it meant stepping up my ability to communicate. I recollect handling a great deal of correspondence. This combined letters to the yards transmitting and explaining plans and financial arrangements, and letters to the contracting officers and Supships about the scope of the work with many changes. I also communicated with draft boards to explain our status as design agents for the government and our need to hold experienced people. Sometimes I went to the draft boards with a threatened employee, and it is a comment on the times when I report sensing some surprise coupled with approbation when I made such a visit with a highly useful African-American employee whose services we were able to hold.

Most of this work was for the U.S. Navy, but we had some U.S. Army contracts and some from the Office of Scientific Research and Development, OSRD. Virtually all were covered by payments of our cost plus a fixed fee based on estimated costs. Careful accounting was needed to justify fees on the many changes that needed to be made. As the major plans were done the navy fed us a class of harbor oil tankers, really self-propelled barges, and this work went on and on. For the army we did a couple of aircraft rescue boats and, more original

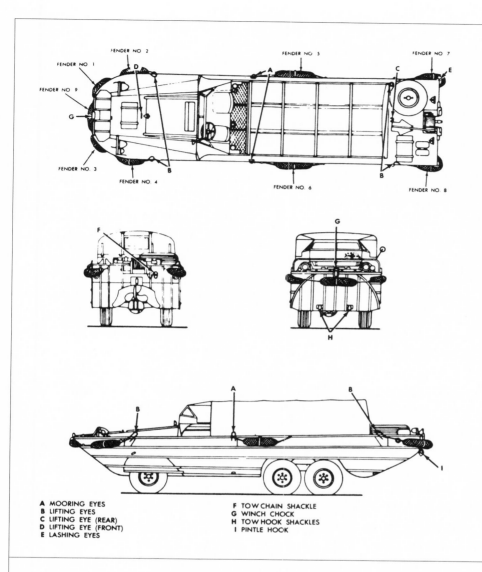

FENDER NO 1
FENDER NO 2
FENDER NO 5
FENDER NO 7
FENDER NO 9
G
FENDER NO 3
FENDER NO 4
FENDER NO 6
FENDER NO 8

A MOORING EYES
B LIFTING EYES
C LIFTING EYE (REAR)
D LIFTING EYE (FRONT)
E LASHING EYES

F TOW CHAIN SHACKLE
G WINCH CHOCK
H TOW HOOK SHACKLES
I PINTLE HOOK

in character, the pontoon bridge. Projects for the OSRD were more interesting and experimental. They called for the development of two amphibious vehicles.

These vehicles were started after a visit from P.C. Putnam, who represented the National Defense Research Committee, a branch of the OSRD. His first request was that we study a small triphibian, by which he meant a vehicle that could fly, swim, or roll on wheels. We immediately questioned the flying, both as a practical matter and as unsuited to our abilities; but Gil and Rod got together and made simple studies of an amphibious Jeep. This was essentially a small light steel barge hull fitted around a conventional military Jeep. Ford was then building Jeeps, although they had been developed by Willys. Rod took our drawings to the Ford plant. The conversion was simple, and an operating amphibian was soon ready for a demonstration which showed that it would work. Even though it worked, it was hardly a triumph in terms of war usefulness. There was a marine propeller in a tunnel aft that was driven by the engine for a low speed of about four knots in the water. The payload was around 500 pounds. A few were ordered for the army, presumably for reconnaissance where water might exist, but the floating Jeep's chief merit was to introduce the larger DUKW.

Our office, led by Rod, did a useful job on the amphibious truck, given the code name DUKW by its builders. It followed the concept of the smaller vehicle, though in this case based on the General Motors 2-1/2-ton truck with six driving wheels. This rather larger vehicle was enveloped in a steel bargelike hull driven through the water by a propeller in a semi-tunnel. Being larger, both capacity and speed were higher. Rough-water behavior was remarkably good. As time passed many DUKWs were built. They were built well enough so that more than 50 years later some DUKWs are still running in sightseeing services catering to tourists who enjoy a ride through the city streets and a run down a ramp for a cruise on the bay or river.

The DUKW project showed what can be done when enthusiasm and the right people are combined. It was in pleasant contrast to much of the war work that seemed overly detailed and frustratingly slow. Very simple drawings and hydrostatic calculations were made in our New York office, which Rod carried to the G.M. Truck and Coach Company in Pontiac, Michigan. I think Ernie Fetske, later independently active in much faster boats, did some of these studies, but the plans were much abbreviated, and it was the carefully studied details that Rod worked out with the GM engineers that made the DUKW a wartime success story. In 32 days of work together in Michigan they laid down the lines on the floor, scaled to fit around the truck, welded the amphibian together, and were ready for successful trials.

In a rather surprising promotional gambit the OSRD arranged a large-scale demonstration at Provincetown on Cape Cod in December, 1942. Several new DUKWs had been taken there to demonstrate to some army brass their ability to handle cargo over the beach from an offshore vessel. At that time there was an offshore patrol of yachts enrolled in the Coast Guard to spot enemy submarines, and one of these yachts returning from patrol managed to ground, on a stormy night, on the bar off Highland Light. When a rescue call came in, Rod at the behest of the local Coast Guard officer, with a small crew including the photographer Stanley Rosenfeld, took a DUKW down along the beach, and then out into a rough sea. They reached the stranded yacht, where they picked off the crew and brought them ashore. Stanley was well equipped and brought back some pretty dramatic nighttime pictures of a real rescue. Sometimes everything clicks. Rod stayed with the DUKWs, traveling to Scotland and the South Pacific, training crews in fast cargo handling, and showing once more what knowledge and enthusiasm can do when the pressure is on. Rod received a letter of commendation from Lord Mountbatten, recognizing the value of DUKWs in the Pacific, and later the thanks of General Eisenhower for the part the DUKWs played in the Normandy invasion.

The deck-balk pontoon bridge was done for the Army Engineers of Fort Belvoir, Virginia. The army's bridge equipment had not been critically examined for years. It was heavy and required large quantities of wood. The engineers contracted with S&S to study the use of aluminum, and I think the first thought was that this would relate to the boat-like design of the floats, or pontoons. However, an able civil engineer (regrettably I have lost his name) who was in our organization then reasoned that the wood decking was redundant. In the old bridging the longitudinal stiffness needed to spread the load over more than one float came from a set of longitudinal members known as balk, which had to be covered with transverse plank decking to make a roadway. This decking did nothing for the strength of the bridge and only increased its weight. He proposed the use of hollow aluminum beams, or balk, with dimensions selected to give the needed stiffness, which would be wide enough to fill out the desired width of flat deck. Thus a single set of structural members could both distribute the load and provide the surface. The beams were staggered by pinning them to alternate gunwales of the floats. The Army Engineers approved the idea for study, initiating an interesting and successful development.

There were still design questions. Today I think that a computer would make their solution much easier, or at least quicker. The floats had to be limited in size and weight, and consequently in waterplane area and flotation. Thus the balk had to be stiff enough to spread heavy loads over several pontoons, and also to bridge the span between them. But if they were stiffer than necessary they would "hog" the load, becoming either fragile or too heavy. The calculations did not seem easy or sure, and so we went to the test tank in Hoboken for confirmation. Using scale models of the pontoons, and wooden balk scaled in stiffness, we checked the distribution of load from the deck to the floats, and the deflection of the balk, to confirm a satisfactory solution. I remember doing a calculation with the object of justifying the test result which seemed pretty complex at the time. It was, at least for me, difficult work.

When prototype equipment was ready Gil and I went out to Yuma, Arizona, for tests where a dam controlled the flow of the lower Colorado River. By varying the flow a bridge could be tested in changing river currents. There we could see just how it worked, from assembly through load-carrying to disassembly. Minor problems at the gunwale attachments were corrected, and we were pleased when the army placed a production order.

I did my best with the general direction of the office, something different from designing yachts. As previously noted, there was a good deal of correspondence as well as a good deal of modification to plans on our drawing boards. Perhaps it helped here to have a certain degree of patience. Previously Drake had relieved me of most of the business side of the yacht work, but details of work for the government were hard for him to accept so I did what had to be done. One of the things that Drake could simply not manage was negotiating with a union that he saw as a major impediment and I accepted as a necessity. It helped to make some order out of the various payroll categories essential to wartime employment regulations, and it also made for orderly and useful communication with a suddenly large group of new people. There were negotiations about some requirements or expectations which might or might not have been reasonable. I figured that this was a good time to use patience, and overall I rather enjoyed this exchange which in another view might have seemed an expensive waste of time. There were frustrating trivialities, but they were part of the job too.

We had been involved in war work for five years before the first postwar yacht work came along. I think the first new yacht design came as we became hopeful that the war was coming to an end in early 1945. It was a 40´ one-design for use in Brazil. The organizer, José Pimental Duarte, had built a larger cruising yacht, *Vendaval*, to our plans just before the war. He was one of our first foreign clients and his two sons were later active sailors in Rio. Rod and I had the unhappy experience later of making lunchtime visits to him at the Memorial Sloan-Kettering Hospital in New York, where he was seriously ill. When he eventually went home to die we knew we were losing a good client who had become a warm friend.

Happier days came with the surrender of Japan and then Germany; but there was winding-up work to be done on our military projects, and some new studies as well. One of these was a PT boat to be built by Bath. This appealed to me not only as a fast-boat project but as something experimental. The purpose was to make the best use of some new Packard engines which had 16 cylinders rather than the 12 cylinders of previous high-performance Packard engines. It was also to test aluminum-alloy hulls. There were four boats built, varying in design and structure. I remember working rather hard to convince the contracting officer to allow funds and authority to test the loads felt in the hull when it hit a wave at high speed. Bath built a short hull section with the proposed scantlings and instrumented it to measure deflections as it was dropped from increasing heights. I think it was a useful exercise. A single boat was built which held up well. I believe it was ultimately sent to Vietnam. Our hull was slightly heavier than an

Elco boat which we thought of as competition. They had used an efficient but complex construction scheme incorporating aircraft materials and light sections. We thought better resistance to corrosion justified the small sacrifice in speed provided by heavier parts of corrosion-resistant alloys.

This was not a big job but it kept some of us busy, and it was not long before, as a firm experienced with wooden hulls, we were put to work on non-magnetic minesweepers to counter the danger of magnetic mines used in the Korean conflict. Eventually we were again distributing plans to builders that were employed on these boats, much as they and we had been in wartime subchaser work. In 1958 this work was finished rather abruptly. That summer while my attention was concentrated on the America's Cup we had our closest shave with financial difficulty: Separation payments to employees we were no longer able to keep busy absorbed nearly everything we had been able to save in the busy years.

Orders for new yachts were still scarce immediately after the war. Inflation made them expensive. For a time there was little excitement. Races were won by prewar boats or very similar designs. Our *Gesture* won the Bermuda Race in 1946. I sailed with Rod in *Mustang*, the NYYC thirty-two he had bought from Harvey Conover for whom we designed a centerboarder of about the same size. Racing *Mustang* in that Bermuda Race, Rod insisted that I was the skipper and one bad tack I called cost us first place in class B.

The late 'forties and the 'fifties became the era of the centerboarder. The reasons are not entirely clear but it seemed likely that service in the navy, in at least some cases, fostered a liking for the sea among young veterans. The weather of the Bahamas was attractively warm and stable and there were many isolated coves and islands accessible to boats of shoal draft. Harvey Conover was one of the first to order and build a centerboarder to replace the deeper-keel NYYC thirty-two. Carleton Mitchell, who later built *Finisterre*, influenced the thinking of many with the publication of books and fine photographs of his Bahamian and Carribean cruising. He first owned the Rhodes-designed centerboarder *Carribee*. The CCA measurement rule treated the type favorably, as demonstrated later when "Mitch" sailed *Finisterre*, our design, to three successive Bermuda Race wins — '56, '58, and '60. In '57 he sailed *Finisterre* to the Mediterranean and back. Such influences resulted in a vogue for shoal-draft cruising and racing boats which S&S met with a growing number of new designs.

Finisterre's record required more than the luck she undoubtedly experienced. Mitch was an experienced sailor and organizer who led a loyal and hard-driving crew who knew the boat. Mitch knew how to make a centerboarder go. Many near-sisterships were built to similar plans which we sold very successfully. Many seemed slow in light weather, as did *Finisterre* after Mitch sold her. Some others sailed well. I think Mitch was exceptional in his ability to keep *Finisterre* going when the wind was light.

Personally I was never enthusiastic about the type despite the work it brought to our office. I never felt free of the recognition that capsize was possible, and I tried always to advise new owners that the beamy shoal hulls could go over and stay over, whereas there was really no possibility that the deeper full-keel type could do the same thing unless it was completely flooded. I am still sensitive to the possibility that this was the cause of *Revonoc*'s loss with Harvey Conover in a Gulf Stream storm. Collision or structural failure could have been the cause, but I might be happier today if Harvey had been in a full-keel boat.

Motorsailers formed another growth category, headed by *Versatile*, a 90-footer for Harold Vanderbilt to replace a larger steel motorsailer that had gone to the navy. There were a number of smaller representatives of the type. There were also a few new out-and-out racers like the Six-Metre *Llanoria*, a two-time Olympic winner. And of course there were Twelve Metres. We will look soon at the Twelve-Metre Class which became active later, after '57, as the class chosen for America's Cup competition.

Relating to construction rather than design, an important postwar trend was toward building abroad. Air travel made it easy to oversee yachts being built in Europe; the strong dollar made it relatively economical; and the German and Scandinavian yards were anxious for work while many American builders were either closing down, lacking the wartime activity, or going on with navy work during the Korean War. The yards overseas became important suppliers of new yachts. As Europe gradually recovered, American yacht designers had the experience and the reputation to be favored by foreign clients. Our office became engaged in activity all around the world, but the new yacht designs, while welcome, were done by a very small force. As discussed previously, the large wartime staff was no longer necessary and the office finances were severely strained by separation payments to the staff we no longer kept busy.

I was amazed by the persistent stability of the European yards through the upsets of war and defeat. The American boatbuilders had changed completely over the war years. This included management in many cases, along with the work force and the layout of the yards. There were exceptions, but generally the builders we knew in the 1930s were no longer prepared to do the kind of work they had done. The Nevins yard at City Island, so dependable through the 'thirties, had changed hands during the war and its yachtbuilding skills had diminished. Gradually others recovered their former skills, and new yards took up the craft, but the European builders had not changed in the same way. Interestingly, I had been assured of this by one of the people who made up our

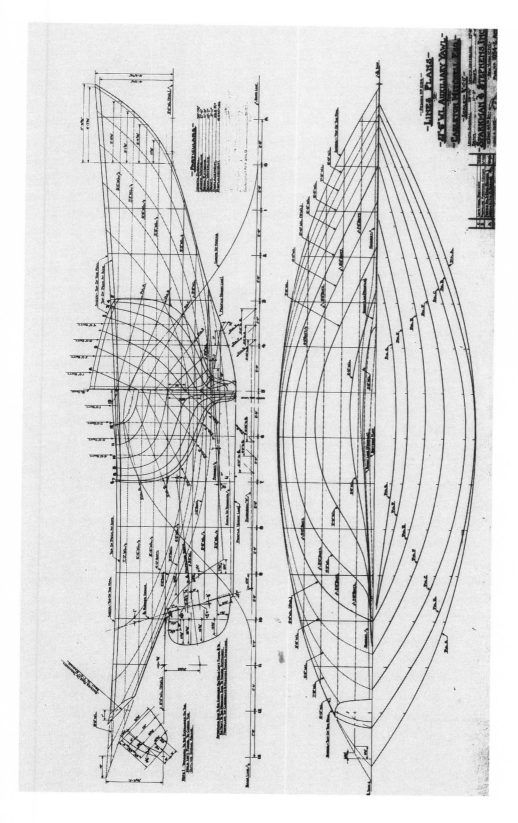

Here are the lines of *Finisterre*, S&S's most successful centerboarder. She won the Bermuda Race in 1954, 1956 and 1958. A good boat, stable due to generous beam, and great in strong winds, *Finisterre* was also campaigned very well. Her owner, Carleton Mitchell, and his crew knew how to keep her going through the light patches. Only a unique combination of skill and luck could have given her three in a row to Bermuda. (Courtesy of Sparkman & Stephens)

wartime staff. He was an elderly German, a loyal U.S. citizen, who assured me that a German builder would surely be ready to continue the kind of work he had done before. This was a personal experience in the battle between continuity and change. Continuity was strong in Europe. I shall leave it to the reader to philosophize on this point. The advice of my German colleague was correct.

The combination of old-world quality and new-world originality gave good results. Rod got back into the yacht work following his wartime contribution training DUKW crews in both the Pacific and European theatres. His interest in detail and his ability to be thorough and quick at the same time in doing a series of European inspections helped enormously in building confidence that our designs would be well-executed abroad. Rod made most of these trips, although I made some, and he planned them in detail before leaving, allocating the necessary time at each of several yards.

One of the builders who regularly, meaning one boat a year, worked to our plans was Bengt Plym of Saltjobaden, Sweden. It was an education to see how he handled wood. The planking was sawn early and stacked overhead to dry. He preferred to use single planking as opposed to the double we tended to specify. Once finished you couldn't tell his single planking from the best of the double. Good boatbuilders tend to be individualists and Bengt had a number of special ways of carrying out details, mostly good. When you inspect the work of such a builder you have to find a thin line between firmness and flexibility. The better the builder the more the inspector can feel confident in letting him use his own details. We, too, had our preferences and the good yards were usually interested in them. Rod had a sort of Bible, a book of type plans or details showing how he liked to see bits of deck work, or joinerwork, or structure, carried out. These small prints helped both the builders and ourselves to complete each boat according to our standards. Rod often supplemented the drawings with photographs of details he liked.

Sometimes there was humor involved in these visits abroad, as when, at a small yard in southern Denmark, I asked one of the boatbuilders for a screw he was using to fasten the planking. When I pocketed the screw, intending to analyze the material, I was conscious of an exchange of glances, no doubt because the builder had been firm with his workers regarding the loss of inventory.

Our foreign activity began in the Scandinavian countries and in Germany and Holland. Soon it spread farther south through France and into Italy. I have mentioned the downside that I have sometimes felt under the pressure of constant effort; but I found as our work spread in Europe the downside diminished as the benefits became clear. I found the opportunity to see new places and new faces to be a clear bonus, and I often felt something very happy in relationships with the new European clients. They seemed to appreciate the work of a competent professional, recognizing fully the presence of an element of art and chance it implied. Even if a principal lesson of this story is the way the early need to guess and take chances was replaced over the years by increasing knowledge and better control over the result, some projects turn out better than others, and in this we recognize the presence of art or luck or both. The other side, of course, is that in aiming high some disappointment may be inevitable.

After the war, the builders were widely varied and so, as discussed, were boats. A great influence was the developing interest in offshore racing, which propelled new thinking about both boats and measurement rules. In the U.S. the Bermuda Race was revived in 1946. In England I think the Fastnet came back in 1947. The Australians, farther from the war, sailed the Sydney-Hobart Race in 1945. It was won by Captain John Illingworth, who became increasingly successful in offshore racing and design working in England with Laurent Giles. He pioneered light and rather extreme designs that did not seem typically British. *Myth of Malham* was the first of these and one of the most successful. She set new standards of performance in offshore racing. The design approach that made Illingworth successful may illustrate contrasting designer's views of the rating rule. The direct aim of *Myth* was speed. She was light, narrow and had a deep keel, rather like the designs of today, none of which favored her rating under the rule formula; but in consideration of the method of length measurement, she was short-ended and the deckline was pinched and narrow at both ends. With a similar aim I might have used the heavier proportions favored by the rule while employing a favorable shape, a sort of envelope fitted around proportions and generally heavier than the Illingworth designs. Later, after I studied the RORC Rule, that approach seemed to work, as S&S designs held their own. True to expectations, when boats of different character meet, race conditions, course and weather, define the result.

At home the offshore boats continued to race under the CCA Rule, and the winners represented a fine seagoing type. Our *Bolero*, designed for John Nicholas Brown, was one of those in the maxi group. She was a development of *Baruna*, and the two were very close in size, rating and speed. They were campaigned hard, with Corny Shields frequently in charge of *Bolero*, and myself a watch captain, Ken Davidson the other. We had some wonderful, close racing. The Newport-Annapolis race of 1951 was one such, in which, beating out of Newport in a slowly freshening sou'wester we stayed within boat lengths, and on the long stretch to the Chesapeake both yachts, carrying spinnakers, were always in sight of each other. We rounded the lightship abreast and ran up Chesapeake Bay together, only to beat again up to the nighttime finish with *Baruna* 24 seconds ahead across the line, and about 15 minutes advantage on corrected time.

The war experience brought nothing new in hull design, but it brought new materials and with them new possibilities. Corrosion-resistant aluminum alloys led to lighter hulls and masts, while fibreglass reinforced synthetic resins prompted the development of standardized boats by providing both production economies and lower maintainance costs. We had done a few aluminum masts in the late 1930s, following the lead of the J-Boats. *Vim* and the latest Sixes had them, but it was only in the 1950s that their use became general. All except the largest spars are made from tubing for which the extrusion die is expensive so that the first masts were costly while subsequent masts made from the tubing of the same size were much less so. As an inventory of dies was built up, alloy masts became increasingly practical, and it was not long before their use was universal. Technically the material has good characteristics; although not as strong as steel, the fact that it is only one third as dense makes possible a thicker wall, less liable to denting or buckling. Relative to spruce its greater density permits the wall material to be concentrated farther from the neutral axis. Additionally, the strong material makes it possible to attach the rigging with small, compact fittings rather than the long, expensive "tangs" required with wooden spars. The general use of aluminum spars came rapidly as yachtbuilding grew after the war. By 1996 we should note that aluminum was being replaced by glass-resin composites reinforced with carbon fibre.

The work at Bath with aluminum convinced Gil Wyland and Geerd Hendel that aluminum alloy could withstand corrosion and would become useful as a yachtbuilding material. Both built small aluminum sailing boats for their own use as soon as they could. Gil's *Windcall*, built at the Jakobson yard in Oyster Bay, was ready for trials on New Year's Day 1946. I remember the day for its weather as I drove from my Scarsdale home to Oyster Bay on roads covered with ice. The freezing rain continued as we went for the first sail. *Windcall* was a great success, and Gil enjoyed her for more than 30 years of cruising and racing, proving that even so early a riveted-aluminum hull could withstand the corrosive properties of salt water. Late in her life some rivets were replaced, and she had extensive deck work done, but she depreciated no more than the best wood construction and less than any but the best. Due more, I'm afraid, to his age than to hers, Gil eventually sold her. By that time she was ready to live out her life in fresh water, where she was sailing when last I heard.

Aluminum-alloy hulls began to arrive after that. They have never taken over the entire field, although their combination of strength and light weight was, and remained into the 'nineties, compelling in larger racing boats, and generally in the case of single units. Aluminum's advantages over steel are the same as those relating to spars. Relative to wood, the hulls are lighter for equal strength, but except for racing boats this is not always important. Nor is concern about corrosion a compelling disadvantage, although it was often assumed to be. The feasibility of welding took over slowly, even though riveting was costly and provided an entry for some corrosion. Aluminum has advantages for certain types of yachts; but wood was and remains an ideally attractive material in its finish and inherent fairness of line, two important aesthetic qualities. Wooden boats are again being built in some numbers after a decline to near zero during the 'sixties and 'seventies. Cold-molded wood employing epoxy adhesives has remained a useful material. Its inherent aesthetic advantage over aluminum or fiberglass is still recognized. And glass-resin composites, fiberglass as it is called in the U.S. and GRP in England, have transformed boatbuilding. Composites have taken the place of aluminum alloy even in many of the largest yachts.

Gil's *Windcall* was the first S&S yacht design done in aluminum alloy. After the early 'fifties, new boats from less than 50′ overall up to the ocean-racing maximum of 72′, including many of our best racing yachts, used that material. One of our best CCA-Rule designs, *Dyna*, a centerboarder for Clayton Ewing in 1956, was built of aluminum. Other successes, such as *Palawan* in 1965 and a bit later *Yankee Girl* in 1970, were aluminum, as was the large power yacht *Aurora* built in Italy in 1961.

Palawan and *Yankee Girl,* along with *Clarionet* and *Roundabout* of 1966, illustrate early use of the separated keel and rudder and served to confirm the speed benefit which accompanies the reduced wetted area and increased keel aspect ratio. This configuration was not new, although American and European recognition of its advantages was in eclipse for some 60 years. Both sides of the Atlantic had examples during the 1890s, some built by Herreshoff in Bristol. New Zealanders must have picked it up then and held on while the rest of the yachting world went back to sleep. I believe it was from New Zealand that the idea of the separated keel and rudder traveled to California. Bill Lapworth's Cal 40s were the first I knew in this country. They came out in the early 'sixties before Dick Carter adopted the idea with his *Rabbit*, and I adopted it with boats to be described in later chapters.

Until they came out, the postwar period seemed to offer little that was new in sailing-yacht design, although new centerboard designs drove much of my activity. In the light of the present, the compromise centerboarder *Sunstone*, with more than conventional draft supplemented by board and separate rudder, appears as a good combination. She has maintained the ability to win frequently under both the IMS and Channel Handicap rules despite a 'sixties design date.

9

AMERICA'S CUP

From some time in 1956, on through the summer of 1980, a great deal of my time and effort went into work related to the defense of the America's Cup. That began after a gap of 20 years between the 1937 Cup season and the renewal of racing following the acceptance by the New York Yacht Club of a challenge from Britain's Royal Yacht Squadron for a match in the summer of 1958. Ranger, of course, was the 1937 defender. Her season led into the Twelve-Metre activity of 1938-39. Vim's season in England marked the end of yachtbuilding and was the prelude to the wartime work that transformed our office. The end of the war brought growing international involvement in offshore racing and renewed interest in the America's Cup.

Columbia, shown on page 150, was the first all-S&S Cup defender. Built at Nevins for the 1958 America's Cup series, the first to be sailed in Twelve Metres, she was a development of *Vim*, launched 19 years earlier. If *Columbia* was better than the older design it was hard to convince *Vim*'s expert young crew, led by Bus Mosbacher and backed by John Matthews. *Vim*'s trials races against *Columbia* were the closest of the long Twelve-Metre era.

(Photo: Rosenfeld Collection 160700F)

I am not sure whether the first move came from England or from the U.S., but both the New York Yacht Club and the Royal Yacht Squadron were interested in a continuation of Cup racing. They recognized that with inflation the cost of a new yacht of at least 65′ on the waterline seemed prohibitive. That was the minimum length required by the Deed of Gift governing the Cup races. That deed had been written in 1857 and rewritten by George Schuyler in the 1870s and 1880s. As it was a binding legal document, the NYYC flag officers, led by Henry Sears, found it appropriate to petition the New York State Supreme Court to approve a change. New requirements were established specifying a minimum waterline length of 44′, and deleting the requirement that the challenger had to sail to the site of the match. Acceptance of the 44′ waterline made the Twelve-Metre Class eligible.

That class had been chosen because the Twelves had long been popular in England and had taken hold in the U.S. just before the war. So the interested clubs agreed to a match in Twelve Metre yachts to be sailed off Newport in the summer of 1958. Harry Sears was Commodore in 1955-56 and he began preparing for the defense by commissioning a new design by our office. Money matters delayed full confirmation of the order but it eventually came through. Then, before 1957 was out, two other new boats had been ordered to designs by Phil Rhodes of New York and Ray Hunt of Boston. The 20-year-old *Vim* had also been recommissioned as a serious contender by removing an engine and other heavy fittings. Beginning in the fall of '57 I recall the weekend trips to Newport to check sails and tune *Vim*'s rig. I was happy to see the old boat back in good racing trim but I never thought she would give our new design the very close racing she presented to *Columbia* during the next summer.

The hull of our new Twelve was tested in the tank at Hoboken. We studied a series of variations on *Vim*, the '39 boat, and settled on a design that was very similar in geometry but was slightly longer and consequently was allowed less sail area under the International Rule that governed the class. I believed, and it ultimately seemed true, although marginally, that the coming of new fabrics and possibly new knowledge about constructing sails would mean a rig with slightly more drive in relation to its area. The longer boat was necessarily heavier under the provisions of the rule, as it required displacement proportional to the cube of the waterline length. Given sufficient power from the rig the longer boat was potentially faster, but because of the greater displacement and wetted area there was some added drag at the low speeds of light-weather sailing. The wind strength at the balance point could be estimated from the tank tests, but that depended on judgement as to the power of the Twelve-Metre type rig, and this had to be projected from the force delivered by the *Gimcrack* rig of 25 years earlier, a rig that lacked the overlapping Genoa jib.

The new boat was built at the Nevins yard in City Island. The Lloyds scantling rules for the Twelve-Metre Class still required wood construction, like the prewar Twelves. It was only later that aluminum alloy and GRP composites were accepted. The yard had changed hands during the war and no longer had the rigorous financial and technical management of Henry Nevins or the fine working group he had put together. Fortunately some of the skilled earlier crew were still there. Rod, being responsible for the building work, and I, too, put special confidence in Nils Halvorsen, the Norwegian loftsman who had earlier laid down many of our drawings. He knew the requirements of the International Rule and the importance attached to the avoidance of most hollows in the upper hull surface while still drawing out the ends to use all possible length above water. He was still there. Rufus Murray, previously the wise yard manager, was no longer on hand, but Ernie Akers, one of City Island's most experienced boatbuilders, was in charge of the shop.

Columbia, as she was to be named, was successfully launched on June 3rd, 1958, though not without problems, of which two were serious. Probably the worst had to do with the lead ballast keel, weighing about 20 tons, which was cast by an outside subcontractor. The molten lead had burst an insufficiently rugged mold and the keel was sent to the yard misshapen and much overweight. Many hours with an adze were needed to restore the designed shape and volume.

The second difficulty had to do with the shaky financial condition of the yard, a result of the postwar cancellations of military contracts. *Columbia*'s framing was glued and laminated rather than steam-bent and the epoxy glue needed warmth to properly cure. When it was discovered by testing samples of framing that the glue was not holding, extra screw fastenings were required through the laminates, costing us weight which might better have been in the keel. We learned that the supplier of heating oil to the Nevins yard had refused to make a needed delivery on credit and the shop temperature had dropped during a cold night.

One of the other two new Twelve Metres was *Easterner*, owned by Boston's Chandler Hovey and designed by Ray Hunt with whom he later shared the helm. The more recent efforts to learn, through almost any means, all the details of opposing boats were not then in fashion so I neither knew nor was I much concerned with her dimensions. Seen in Newport she seemed a heavy boat with rather short, sharp ends, which combined to permit her a fairly generous sailplan. As an opponent she was never able to capitalize on the speed she frequently showed. Generally through the season her record was poor, but when we raced her it took time and careful sailing to gain a lead; she seemed to go well until that happened, but once behind she was seldom able to come back. The other new contender was *Weatherly*, a Phil Rhodes design, owned by Henry Mercer and sailed by Arthur Knapp. She was a consistently tough competitor. Against her we seemed to have a useful edge in stronger winds, but difficulty when the wind was light. Of the three boats we had to beat if we were to defend the Cup, *Vim*, in the end, gave us the hardest battle.

The year 1958 began a new era in America's Cup sailing. The Twelves, in replacing the big J-Boats, sailed with very different crews: 11 in place of 31. The backers of the new defenders and their skippers had, in their own smaller boats, found crews among friends and relatives. Now the Twelve-Metre crews were formed the same way. They were not professionals, but they were giving the full summer to sail together and they expected to be housed and fed. So it was that *Columbia*'s managers found a large and comfortable house known as Beechbound on Brenton's Cove, slightly away from Newport's town center. Our boat hung on a mooring in the cove and we reached her by means of a tender, Briggs Cunningham's *Escort*. There were nine such amateurs in the crew plus two professionals who took care of the boat when we were not racing. The professionals were Fred Lawton, who had worked as Captain for Mike Vanderbilt, and Jim Haslam, a husky younger boatkeeper and winch grinder. Other crews made similar arrangements.

Harry Sears had asked Briggs Cunningham to skipper *Columbia*, and Briggs, who had, I believe, supplied Beechbound as part of his substantial contribution to the syndicate, acted with his wife Lucie as host and hostess. Life there was pleasant and comfortable. With the whole crew living together, it was easy to act as a unit, all on board and ready to sail at the same time and to share projects and work assignments, including care of the sails and other maintenance such as that required by the winches and the then-minimal electronic equipment. In the Twelve-Metre era a crew home more or less like Beechbound became regular practice by most of the America's Cup contestants.

Spares and other pieces of equipment were kept in a large "locker," really a room provided by the Newport Shipyard. The gear used for sail-handling was constantly evolving under Rod's direction as he studied ways to reduce the time lost changing or setting headsails. Each of the competing boats found new ways to do this. Their methods were constantly studied and not infrequently adopted by others. New sail-handling techniques were important byproducts of that summer. Rod, of *Columbia*, Vic Romagna, of *Weatherly*, and Dick Bertram, of *Vim*, were all responsible for innovations that became standard practice.

Of the eleven-man crew four sailed in the cockpit. Briggs was skipper, Harry Sears was observer and shared tactician's duties with me. I was the navigator and Fred Lawton handled the running backstays. Rod, forward, took care of sail-handling, organized the crew, and kept a watchful eye on all details of the rig. With practice under Rod's direction the crew work went well and sails were set and shifted quickly. Rod had laid out a new system of halyards and tack fittings providing for the use of an interim jib of heavy fabric set flying on a strong central halyard while one Genoa was being replaced by another as the wind strengthened or fell. He had also devised a twin-pole spinnaker jibe which effectively kept the sail full and drawing throughout the maneuver. While this worked as planned we soon adopted, as simpler, the dipped-pole method pioneered by *Vim*'s crew. With this a man on the foredeck switches the sheet and guy while he guides the pole under the jibstay. This came into general use at Newport that summer and has become standard practice since.

As navigator I accepted the duty to be ready at any time to know the course and the direction of the wind, and as possibly the most important responsibility to save the helmsman from overstanding a weather mark. I believe a leading boat should not hesitate to split once she can fetch. The rationale is that if you are headed on the new tack you are favored, and if you are lifted you fetch anyway. There can be exceptions if the wind is spotty, and depending on the other boat's position. Though our electronic capability was limited, we knew our speed, our heel angle, and our course. I established a standard according to which I could advise the helmsman whether he was up to the speed expected for the apparent wind angle and its strength as measured by the heel angle. This helped to keep *Columbia* up to her best speed for the conditions. In '58 the boat-for-boat attack and counterattack was less intense than it has become, but there were days when we tacked more than 30 times in the course of a close windward leg.

Rod, who was up on the bow for starts, made his own gadget to see how close to the line we were in starting maneuvers so we could be up close but not over. A mirror allowed him to see both ends of the line at once and to see where we were. It worked well for him. Others have tried it but not liked it.

Though it was nothing new, we were early on impressed by the importance of sails and the need of constant adjustment and repair. Colin Ratsey, of the sailmaking firm, was a *Columbia* crew member. He set up a small shop in the basement of Beechbound and handled countless small details overnight. He also provided an overnight shuttle between Newport and his loft at City Island so that heavier work and new sails or sails requiring heavy repair were quickly completed and delivered. Despite Collie's constant work we found sails worrisome. The late 'fifties were a time of change in sailmaking from the predominance of Egyptian cotton to the reign of the synthetics. The Ratseys, family and firm, had a bottomless well of knowledge in handling the cotton fabric but the value of this resource was dwindling and newcomers like sailmaker Ted Hood, a member of *Vim*'s crew, were ingenious in the use of the new materials. We understood that Ted's father, known as the Professor, had worked with Ted to use looms almost abandoned then in New England to weave a polyester fabric, Dacron, driven up harder than normal on abused but easily replaced equipment. This new sail material was superior to any synthetic sailcloth on the market. To compete we used heavier fabric, meaning heavier-weight mainsails. Colin did well for us, so that we had at least one mainsail that we liked. The finish was a light lavender color and it was named the Purple People Eater. On our better days it ate up the opposition.

Vim worried me, as her success implied that I had learned nothing in 20 years. In the end we had the better boat. *Vim* had a great crew, headed by Bus Mosbacher with Dick Matthews as co-helmsman. Ted Hood made *Vim*'s almost-perfect sails, while Dick Bertram and Brad Noyes were second to none in knowing how to handle them. And ashore they had the owner, Jack Matthews, completely dedicated to the condition of the boat. Although they were opponents, Jack and Rod were early morning companions at the Newport Shipyard as the boats were being prepared to race.

In '58 the New York Yacht Club established a trial pattern that lasted through the years of successful Cup defense in Newport. Three sets of match races gave the club's selection committee a chance to watch each boat against a single opponent, with the pairing changing from day to day. The first series was called "tune-up," the second "preliminary," and the final, just that. If points were counted that was informal; the committee was charged to select the boat which, in their opinion, was the most likely to successfully defend the America's Cup. During the final trials the less-promising yachts were visited by committee members and thanked for their efforts in support of the club and "excused" from further racing. That was a sad moment I experienced twice: in the second *Columbia* season, 1962, and in 1970 when the new *Valiant* was a disappointment. In the end two boats would be left, and it has been the rule that races were continued until the winner was clearly superior or the pressure of time dictated the selection of the winner of the last race.

Our season began with a loss to the older *Vim* in a nice sailing breeze, and I remember the concern that I have felt for so long — failing to learn. Then, after several days of fog and lack of wind absorbed planned racing time, *Columbia* won two three-boat races when *Weatherly* and then *Easterner* were making repairs. The first series was completed happily with a win over *Easterner* while *Weatherly* beat *Vim*.

During the second trial series the wind was light and *Weatherly* had the best record. *Vim* and *Columbia* won their matches against *Easterner*, putting her in trouble. Then the four Twelves sailed as a class on the New York Yacht Club Cruise and *Vim* dominated, winning five of the seven races. In an informal sense, entering the final series of trials *Weatherly* was top boat, but neither the first series nor the cruise were supposed to carry much weight with the selection committee. On *Columbia* we knew that the boat we had to beat was the older *Vim*. We knew it even better when we beat *Weatherly* by four minutes in the first match while *Vim* won over *Easterner*. The next day it was *Vim*'s turn to beat *Weatherly*, though by a small margin, and when the committee again sent us again against *Weatherly* we felt they were setting the scene for a final match between ourselves and *Vim*. When we took *Weatherly* again by six minutes she was excused, as was *Easterner*.

The final series was yacht racing at its closest and best. It is fair to say that *Columbia* was slightly faster to windward, the margin becoming more evident as the wind increased. *Vim* probably was the better sailed, principally around the starting line. Mosbacher was now doing all the steering and he knew that if *Columbia* got ahead of him he could seldom reverse the order. Therefore, and to an extent new to us all, he began the race well before the start, usually finding it possible to place his boat so close on the opponent's stern that he could block the leader's moves to return for a start. He could then freely return when he wished, not concerned about a late start as he was leading by at least a boat length, and his skill in coaxing speed from his boat and his tight cover made it very hard for *Columbia* to break through.

As a designer I have had confidence in the ability of the faster boat to win, but when the margin is small one hates to give away the distance sacrificed by tacking

away and rapping off. Briggs had become concerned by his inability to cope with Bus Mosbacher's tactics and had asked Corny Shields to do the start and continue sailing if he wished. For years Corny had been one of the outstanding sailors in the east. He had organized the International One-Design Class in which he had sailed against Mosbacher, and had been consistently among the leaders. Recently he had been hospitalized with a heart condition. He had sailed several times as skipper on board *Bolero* when Ken Davidson and I had been watch captains. Corny came aboard despite doctor's orders and sailed the boat beautifully; but I have always been impressed with the determination and skill that Briggs showed when he took over the wheel, often out of the lead as the result of *Vim*'s great starts, and managed to come out on top at the finish.

This was demonstrated when in the fifth race, with the series tied two to two, and *Columbia* trailing at the end of the first round, Briggs won the vital race with a perfectly sailed weather leg. The final race was different, a battle of spinnakers which I remember well as I was calling the sails. After a good start on the windward and leeward course we led at the first weather mark, where we set a large spinnaker and lost our lead to *Vim* carrying a smaller chute. In a tight battle in less wind on the second beat *Columbia* passed *Vim* and led at the weather mark by a length, which *Vim* recovered with a perfect spinnaker set as we fumbled slightly when I changed my call from the large spinnaker to the smaller one. Despite the hitch, this time again the smaller sail paid and *Columbia* gradually pulled ahead to win the selection by twelve seconds. Tension and release.

Unfortunately the Cup match was an anticlimax. In four straight races *Columbia* easily beat the British *Sceptre*. Our constant practice and our hard work on sails were undoubted advantages, but *Sceptre* sailed as though she was seriously hindered by the sea conditions off Newport.

The summer had meant both fun and hard work for a number of individuals. It was a busy time for such as the NYYC race committee and the selection committee. Both, with six members each, were on hand for three eight-day periods of trial races that extended from July into September, plus the NYYC Cruise and the final Cup defense; but the real effort was that of the four crews who spent the whole summer, not just sailing but working over the boats. Each crew member kept constantly at the work of improving his boat. To me it was evident that the effort paid off. As previously noted, if Rod was at the shipyard at six-thirty in the morning, who would be there too but *Vim*'s owner Jack Matthews. The effort he made to support his boat and his crew surely had its effect, and we of *Columbia* made it our job to match his effort.

Although I have had the experience during nine summers I cannot even now fully explain the constantly growing list of small yet necessary items that had to be completed and checked off after every day's sailing. The need to save weight aloft contributes to the list because of the way strength and weight play against each other, and the hardware in the upper part of the rig needed constant checking and not infrequent repair or replacement. Masthead cranes are all too vulnerable, and halyard blocks need checking for distortion under load and for lubrication. Sails are high on the list, and a tame sailmaker on or off the boat is an essential in a Cup campaign. *Vim* had the perfect person with Ted Hood as a member of her crew, while we had Collie Ratsey who kept busy at the loft under Beechbound.

Columbia had a large complement of sails, most of them although not all from the Ratsey loft at City Island. It was not easy to get them right and Collie worked hard with an assistant from the home loft. In this period of transition from cotton to synthetic sail fabrics, neither the mills nor the sailmakers had quite learned how to handle the new material. Ted Hood had the best fabrics and the greatest experience with synthetics. After 40 years the process still goes on with new fibers aligned with loads; in 1958 it was completely new. Because stability means driving power I did not like the need to use heavier and heavier fabric that raised the center of gravity. Yet I felt that the right shape and the sail's ability to hold it outweighed the negative effects of weight aloft. Our Purple People Eater, named after the children's television character, did well for us with heavier-than-normal 13-1/2-ounce material. It was the best of a number of mains we tried while looking for the right combination. I believe that Ted's fabric weighed 10 ounces.

I became responsible each day for the sails we carried on board while racing. It is interesting now to consider the fact that our concern with weight was related only to having as much as possible in the keel without putting the boat too deep in the water. The Twelves carried side marks of triangular shape and about two inches high. When measured, stripped of movable weight, the lower point of the triangle just touched the water. When loaded ready to race, the upper edge of the mark could not be immersed. Allowing for other weights, mainly the husky crew of eleven, we were limited by their weight to the number of sails we could carry. This was normally one mainsail, ten spinnakers and seven jibs, but varied according to the weather. This sounds like an ample supply but it was just a part of our total inventory. Finding the best sails individually and in combination was a continuing activity and one of our most important. I kept a looseleaf notebook in which the origin and history of racing results, of alteration and repair, and the present condition of every sail was entered in detail.

The attitude toward weight has changed over the years largely because of new classes and rules, but also because of sailing tactics. If some opinions must be tentative there can be no doubt that weight is detrimental to acceleration. Although tacking duels are not new, the present generation of top helmsmen seem to be more than ever dependent on personal combat. My influence, such as it may have been, was to let the boat do it by emphasis on speed through the water, tending toward a loose cover of the other boat, tacking infrequently. Even today among the ocean-racing fleet with its great variety, the light boats win on short courses but the heavier types can occasionally come through when there is less demand for acceleration.

The *Columbia* match began a period of stability in the Cup series marked by the continuing use of the Twelve-Metre Class. Matches were held at intervals of two to four years. In 1962 Australia made her first challenge, but we had only one new defender, Ted Hood's *Nefertiti*. *Weatherly*, improved by Bill Luders' alterations, won the selection over *Columbia* and, with Mosbacher sailing, beat the Australian boat *Gretel* in a series marked by two very close races. *Gretel* was the winner of one of them. The failure of *Columbia* to repeat was a great disappointment to me. As a rationalization perhaps I have felt that her helmsman of that year had trouble coping with her steering characteristic, of falling away from the wind as her course widened and she gathered speed. While unusual, and even undesirable, this behavior, which had been managed in '58, was so different from the behavior our new helmsman knew best that *Columbia*'s windward performance suffered badly.

In 1964 the new boat from the S&S office, *Constellation*, was selected after a difficult season that saw a change of skippers when the relief helmsman, Bob Bavier, took over and in the end easily beat the English *Sovereign* in straight races.

Every new season had its own triumphs and problems, and 1964 stands out in several ways. It started badly but ended well. The organizers of the *Constellation* syndicate were Walter Gubelman and Eric Ridder of Oyster Bay. Eric was the helmsman. During the first trials in Long Island Sound she did poorly. The observation trials in Newport were about to start when I fell ill and Gerry Driscoll, who had joined our crew, drove me home to Scarsdale. From there I went to the hospital in New York for an operation which kept me down for about two weeks. News from Newport was not good. The Luders-designed *American Eagle* was beating *Constellation*. On the afternoon before the second series of trials ended I had a glimmer of hope when Corny Shields called on the phone to report that on a fair windward leg in a typical Newport sou'wester *Connie* had led around the weather mark and on, though the race had to be canceled when heavy fog drifted in. In this race Eric had given the wheel to Bob Bavier.

Walter and Eric had established a management committee of themselves and me as the independent member. I had been absent through the observation series and the NYYC Cruise was about to start. My first duty back in Newport was a delicate one. I had to confirm the obvious by appointing Bob Bavier the official skipper. Eric, who had voluntarily yielded the wheel before the last promising race, gracefully accepted the change that Walter could have dictated. We found Bob Bavier happy

to be promoted and ready to step in. He steered more often during the NYYC Cruise, and when the match racing resumed after the Cruise he was the official skipper, which he remained throughout he rest of the summer.

But before then, *Connie* had lost her mast on the first Cruise run in a norther as she approached Block Island. Towed that same afternoon to Newport in a big sea, the crew found her spare mast lifted from her trial horse, *Nereus*, and waiting by the sheer legs only for the broken mast to be removed. The spare was in place the same evening and was tuned the next day with Rod spending the day aloft. As the Cruise run had to be canceled due to weather, no racing time was lost. I have always felt that a key player in the quick mast replacement was Rod, my brother, who had been asked along for the NYYC Cruise when the eleven-man crew limit was not in force. Bob Bavier has written that once Rod came aboard he knew he had to keep him, but the crew spirit was such that one of the summer's most difficult duties was to notify the one regular crew member who had to go ashore. As it turned out, with Bob steering and Rod in the cockpit, *Constellation*'s earlier record was completely reversed, making her the major winner in the races run on the Cruise, in the Final

Above is *Constellation*, from aft. The mainsail shows deep draft despite the flattening of the bending boom, an early use of titanium, light and extremely strong to accept the bending loads. Here there is a pulpit but no lifelines, and the winches are located below deck. The Genoa sheet is led aft for reaching and under the end of the main boom.
(Photo: Rosenfeld Collection 177488)

Intrepid, shown here, was the most radical and successful of the S&S Twelves. Her short keel and separate rudder were new in the class. Her titanium masthead was another new feature, and her deck was very clean. The spinnaker is nicely set and powerful. Sailed by Bus Mosbacher, she failed to win only two of her trial races in 1967: one when she lost her mast and the other by sailing to the wrong mark. (Photo: Rosenfeld Collection 183427F)

Trials, and through the America's Cup.

Before the last trial I was still nervous. *Constellation*'s recent record was nearly perfect, but the racing had been in light going and the committee had kept us racing, I felt sure, to see us perform in more wind. There was a little more wind in this last race — maybe, I had said, about twelve knots, and *Connie* was comfortably ahead. On the tender we could listen to the weather-mark boat reporting to the selection committee by radio, saying, I could hardly believe, "sixteen knots." I still don't believe it, but *Connie* was in.

The Cup races turned out well — and were really too easy as the margins were large: twice over fifteen minutes and not in light weather. Newport sea conditions seem always to have been difficult for the British challengers.

Three years elapsed before the next Cup season when the NYYC prepared to meet the second Australian challenge. The effort was satisfying to me because of the superiority of our new *Intrepid*. In the Twelve-Metre Class she marked a departure in design resulting from the separation of the rudder from the keel. This made possible a shorter and more efficient keel; it also reduced the wetted area of the hull. This arrangement was not new, as previously noted. American and British yachts had been successful with it at the turn of the century. More recently it had been current in New Zealand and had been used by the American designers Bill Lapworth and Dick Carter in highly successful boats already mentioned. Applied to a Twelve, control of the wetted surface made it possible to expect the more powerful hull to be adequately driven with less sail than had been used before. Due to *Intrepid*'s power, and good tank-test reports, I early on predicted to Bus Mosbacher, who had agreed to sail the boat, that he should have an easy summer if it blew but that he might have to work harder in light weather. This turned out to be true. Whether it was the helmsman or the boat, undoubtedly a bit of each, *Intrepid* was, all summer, an easy winner. She lost only two of her match races, once when she lost her mast, and in an early race when she went to the wrong mark.

Even in such a season the designer's life was not entirely free and easy. There was a day I called Black Friday when both S&S designs, *Intrepid* and *Constellation*, lost their masts due to a spreader design that failed when the mast was encouraged to bend excessively (my interpretation, but not that of Bus). Permanently bent spars are excluded by the rules, but the ability to bend while sailing allows a given sail to adapt to a wide range of winds by pulling cloth out of the center of the sail when the center of the mast is pushed forward, thus flattening it as appropriate for strong winds. On Black Friday it was blowing hard, both masts were bent to flatten the sails, and the spreaders were twisted off the spars. I saw them both go at almost the same time and knew it was back to the drawing board. I had two unhappy skippers to face later that day.

There was no humor in it for me. I could only fear a black mark on the records of the selection committee. No matter how fast a boat may be, she has to finish a race to win, and so the committee looks hard at reliability. Later it was possible to see a lighter side, and I've been told of a comment that could be apocryphal. Mary Monte-Sano, wife of *Intrepid*'s crew member Bizzy, says it's true. She tells the story that as I examined the seemingly guilty broken spreader fitting back in Newport, she came by and looked at it too, remarking innocently that it looked very light. She says that I replied, "Well, Mary, under any other circumstances I'd consider that a compliment."

Despite such difficulties I felt that Newport was the place for me during a Cup campaign. Not that I could do so much — actually I insisted that the day-to-day work with interminable lists of small items should be assigned to another representative of the S&S office; but I think that my readiness to observe and propose and do a little hand-holding made both a practical and a psychological difference. I felt part of the crew. I was in it as deeply as any crew member and I liked it most of the time; and when it was least enjoyable I was most certain it was the place to be. Like Black Friday. I was always given a good room at the crew house and Susie, my wife, was free to join me and she came or went as she wished. I often steered one of the boats in practice sessions and spent many hours observing and taking pictures from the tender. These were often shown at the crew house in the evening when sails or tactics were under discussion.

Intrepid's Cup match resulted in four easy wins over the Australian boat *Dame Pattie*. There was, however, one incident that almost had serious consequences when *Intrepid*, while sailing her normal course in the lead, was hit by the downwash of a Coast Guard helicopter. It was a breezy day, and the helicopter was on a rescue mission involving a small spectator boat that had capsized. The downwash had the sudden force of much more than the existing wind and knocked *Intrepid* down to a degree that threatened the loss of her rig despite a stronger spreader design.

Up to that time the challengers had been from either England or Australia, but now there was interest from France and other countries. Recognizing this, the NYYC announced a new and successful policy: namely, if the club continued to hold the Cup it would schedule the next match in three years and would consider all challenges received within 30 days of the finish of a match as arriving simultaneously. Under this policy challenges for a match in 1970 were received from Australia, Britain, France and Greece, although the Greek challenge was short-lived. Trial races in Newport were again arranged.

Although new countries challenged, from 1970 on Australia consistently came through the challenger trials in Newport as the best of the foreigners until *Australia II* and her wing keel was finally able to win in '83. Marcel Bich, the French Baron, was an interesting and sympathetic participant. He made four great, though unsuccessful, efforts, challenging in 1970, 1974 and 1977 with *France*, and in 1980 with *France III*. He seemed to be in the competition for the sport and fun, and he was undoubtedly disappointed that he never reached the position of challenger. He also liked some of the formalities of America's Cup racing, taking over the wheel in a white suit with gloves to match. He was upset with the American press when it was

widely reported that he had "abandoned" a race after running into a thick fog. He really had no choice, but the word abandoned had in his language implications of running away that were not intended by its meaning in English. The Baron and NYYC Commodore Bob McCullough got on well, and when Bob and I were working together I sympathized when he came by to get some encouragement from Bob.

British (*Lionheart*, 1980) and Swedish (*Sverige*, '77 and, altered, '80) challengers also participated in trials, bringing boats that incorporated interesting features such as an extremely flexible mast on *Lionheart* and a Swedish hull with unique afterbody lines. Even though neither was successful in winning the right to sail for the Cup, it seemed good for the sport to see the widened field of foreigners using new variations within the rule limits.

The 1970 series was a close call for the Cup. Two new boats were built, one called *Valiant*, of S&S design, and the other designed by the owner, Charles Morgan, who had recently sold his boatbuilding operation in Florida. Both hulls had been thoroughly tested in the Hoboken tank with results that appeared

I*ntrepid*'s crew, Mosbacher with hand on the wheel and Bill Strawbridge, principal backer, near him. I am at far right. (Photo: Rosenfeld Collection 183414-19)

promising, yet neither was a very good boat. Similar disappointment may have been true of *Intrepid*, also altered according to tank-tested lines produced by Britton Chance. Whether *Intrepid* had been improved or not remains to me an open question. Sailed by Bill Ficker from California, she was an easy winner of the selection trials to defend.

Valiant was a great disappointment. It was evident from her first sail that something was very wrong, as the disturbance she created in the water was immediately evident in a glance over the stern. We saw later the distance to which this disturbed wake trailed. She was also extremely hard to steer. We did not have to wait for competition to tell that she was slow, but competition proved it. *Valiant*'s performance, paralleled by Morgan's *Heritage*, led to new concern about the validity of the small models towed through the tank in Hoboken. The result was a general switch to a much larger and more expensive testing program.

The ultimate 1970 challenger was again Australian, *Gretel II*, owned by Sir Frank Packer and designed by Alan Payne. In the two-boat trials between the only challengers that came to Newport, she had beaten *France*, the first challenge of Baron Marcel Bich. *Gretel II* was able to make a strong challenge, and the ensuing match was close and not entirely amiable, due to the decision of the NYYC race committee to disqualify a protest by *Gretel* from the race she had won after starting-line contact. *Intrepid* was the winner in a close contest. Alan Payne deserved better luck than he had in his second narrow loss as the Australian designer.

Activity for the next challenge, planned for 1974, centered on two subjects: tank-testing and aluminum-alloy construction, as that material had just been approved by Lloyds whose scantling rules were used by the class. By that time the use of corrosion-resistant alloys had become customary in offshore racers due to its combination of light weight and strength. It presented no new problems in this case, but it did offer a distinct weight advantage that I had estimated might be as much as 4000 pounds. This made a new boat virtually mandatory. After the disappointment with *Valiant* I felt lucky in receiving a commission backed by Bill Strawbridge.

In a new design study the tank problem had to be met. This was not simple, as questions about the validity of the Hoboken tests were inevitable in light of the disappointing performance of the boats of 1970. These centered on questions of scale. The scale of the models that had been used had been limited by the size of the tank and were very small by the standards of commercial or naval vessel tests. I have described the work of Kenneth Davidson in pioneering the use of small models and the wide acceptance of his work. Ken's tests had been useful for many years and seemed well proven, but three apparent failures had to be worrisome. Some element in the small-scale tests had gone wrong and scaling problems seemed the most likely

V*aliant*, **opposite, was a severe disappointment. Although she could never have won the trials or defended the Cup, I can see now that better thinking in 1970 could have helped her performance. I was too quickly discouraged. Some padding aft would have cost a little sail area and hurt her only in light airs, while a deep rudder would have greatly eased a bad steering problem. In the last year Jim Taylor has laid out such changes and she has been sailing well.** (Photo: Rosenfeld Collection 188138F)

On page 169 are *Intrepid* and, to leeward, *Courageous* in 1974. *Courageous*, the first aluminum Twelve, became defender by the thinnest of margins. *Intrepid*, sailed by Gerry Driscoll who had rebuilt her, had the speed and the handling to carry the new boat, despite the advantage of her lighter hull, into the last possible day before selection. *Intrepid*'s second alteration, preparing her for '74, left her with the 1968 bow and an afterbody almost like *Courageous*. (Photo: Rosenfeld Collection 191163-5CN)

culprit. The option was costly, but tests with big models had to be made in this next campaign.

The scale of the small Twelve-Metre models had been standardized as one-thirteenth full size. The Twelves themselves ran about 45′ in waterline length, which implied a weight of 55,000 pounds so that the one-thirteenth scale model would be 41.5″ on the water with a weight of 25 pounds. The large scale we decided to use was one-third full size, giving the model a 15′ waterline and a weight of over 2,000 pounds. The cost ratio of much of the testing was in rough proportion to the weights, meaning that some of the old costs were multiplied by a factor approaching 80. My feeling is that this escalation of cost, even if exaggerated here, had much to do with our eventual loss of the Cup in 1983.

Such a jump in cost at the time of a big jump in the cost of fuel during the 1970s raised financial concern in the minds of the defenders, including officers of the NYYC and the potential backers of the new boat. For that reason, the usual three-year hiatus was altered to four years so that the date of the next match became 1974. Support by some concerned syndicate members weakened. As it was beginning to fall apart, the syndicate was rescued, much to my relief, with the help of George Coumantaros, Eleanor Radley and Bob McCullough. I particularly appreciated Bob's willingness to take on the syndicate management after his bad season with *Valiant*. The result was *Courageous*. She became a success, though not without hard work.

The 1974 trials to choose a defender were sailed among four boats. Interesting was *Mariner*, the second aluminum hull, representing a group headed by George Hinman but owned for tax reasons by the U.S. Merchant Marine Academy. I believe that this was the first Cup campaign to experience the financial advantage of income-tax deductibility, meaning that contributions toward the cost of building and running the boat were made to an organization having the right to accept tax-deductible contributions. Apparently a West Coast syndicate that had not quite jelled had received a favorable I.R.S ruling on a similar approach. This arrangement was entirely legal and was very useful in raising the needed money. It became an accepted feature of later campaigns, but in my opinion it has had a detrimental effect on the whole sport of sailing. Nothing negative was apparent in specific actions of the competitors, but the sailors, skippers and crew, as I sensed it, became representatives of outsiders rather than participants in their own right.

Mariner was interesting in her radical design; that of Britton Chance, Jr. She was tested in the Hoboken tank, but was disappointing in performance. Her most notable feature was an underwater transom, which is the flat transverse surface, normally above water, at the stern of most boats. In *Mariner*, this was deeply submerged so that her underwater body did not end in a fair, sharp trailing edge,

but rather was cut off in a square flat surface. The tank must have reported good results for a model incorporating this arrangement and when the boat sailed poorly the tank was blamed. Scaling problems presumably distorted the test results, as may have been the case with *Heritage* and *Valiant*. *Mariner*'s aluminum-alloy hull was altered in mid-season but she never became a factor in the racing. One thing she proved was that an alteration could be done more quickly with aluminum than would have been possible with wood.

Four boats took part in the 1974 defense trials. *Intrepid* had been altered again under the direction of our office and was owned by a California group headed by George F. Jewett, Jr. She had been rebuilt in San Diego by Gerry Driscoll after a model tested in California using an afterbody form much like *Courageous*, combined with the original bow which had survived. Gerry was the accomplished helmsman. *Valiant* was the fourth entrant, primarily as a trial horse for *Mariner*. As the trials made clear, neither *Valiant* nor *Mariner* sailed well enough to warrant serious consideration, but *Intrepid* showed surprising speed, splitting wins with the new *Courageous* until, on the final day that trials could be held, the new boat won in a breeze of 20 knots or better with Ted Hood steering. The stability and power resulting from the use of aluminum paid well under the windy conditions, although it was a remarkable tribute to Driscoll's handling and rebuilding that he been able to beat *Courageous* with *Intrepid* just about 50 percent of the time all summer.

That season marked the entry of two new and notable faces into America's Cup competition: Ted Turner and Dennis Conner, both of whom had been brought in by George Hinman to assist on board *Mariner*, Turner at the wheel and Conner as a member of the afterguard. After the alteration Dennis had been steering the boat, and when she was excused he joined *Courageous* to handle starts, which he had been doing in *Mariner* with great success.

The challengers of that year came again from Australia and France represented by Marcel Bich's *France* and *Southern Cross*, owned by Alan Bond. *Southern Cross* won the challenger trials but was easily beaten by *Courageous* in the Cup series.

In 1977 there were three challenging countries, Sweden, France and Australia, and for the defense there were two new boats, *Independence*, designed and sailed by Ted Hood, and the S&S-designed *Enterprise*, sailed by Lowell North who had made most of the sails. As the latest entry from S&S, *Enterprise* might have seemed a disappointment. But *Courageous* was the winner in the defense trials, and the two boats were almost identical due to the scarcity of research funds; because it is always so easy to explain defeat, I could easily be philosophical. As the fourth entrant in the defender's trials *Courageous* had been bought by Hood, primarily, I think, as a trial horse for his new boat. Ted Turner had come back as her skipper. She had been slightly altered, shortening her waterline to correct its relation to her displacement, and she continued, if not bettered, her performance of the 1974 summer to become the defender against *Australia* — and not, as intended, the sparring partner of the new *Independence*. *Australia* had won over the French and Swedish challengers in the trial races. Many of the *Enterprise* backers thought she was faster than *Courageous* but she didn't prove it.

The previous winter when Ted Hood received the lines of *Courageous* he reported to me that her displacement was less than that shown on her measurement certificate, and as required for her length. This was one of the most painful events in all my experience. It was hard for me to believe, but a review confirmed that Ted was correct. I went immediately to Bob McCullough, as the NYYC Commodore, expressing my concern. I found him concerned too, but not seriously upset. He saw how badly I felt and asked whether I was worried about the past or the future, to which I replied "only what has passed." He relieved me greatly by saying that what had happened was history and there could be no going back. He was positive and I felt better despite embarrassment, as I knew that adjustments could be made in the aluminum hull with little difficulty. This proved to be the case and when *Courageous* sailed again it was clear that her speed had not been hurt.

As the head of the office I took full responsibility for the mistake, but when it was first reported it was hard to find the cause. Those in the office who had actually done the calculations insisted they were correct, and the displacement was okay. I discovered later that the computer program, written to integrate the displacement by summing individual section areas, each taken with a planimeter, had overstated a multiplier of one of the small end areas indicating more volume than was really there.

The Cup season of 1977 exemplified the combination of circumstances that led to the loss of the Cup six years later. The cost of testing large models was a big factor in limiting experimental work or exploratory research. That increase coincided with a widespread sense that Twelve-Metre design had reached a limit, or at least a plateau, making the sails and handling more important than differences between boats. Dennis Conner exemplified this opinion; I saw it as a self-fulfilling judgement as, without research, improvement was severely hampered. Sail costs seemed constantly to increase, but the greatest jump in the expenses of the syndicate followed Dennis' decision to start preparing for the 1980 season a year early, thus extending the period during which two boats and two crews were supported. And for 1983 his group built three new boats while the crew costs constantly climbed, discouraging many owners and further limiting budgets for research. Although those who came in made contributions through a tax-exempt entity, it was a very expensive business. And, as previously stated, because the syndicate manager stood between the individual sailors and the support and direction of the crew, this seemed to me detrimental to the effort, diluting personal enthusiasms that had been an appealing feature of America's Cup racing and yacht racing in general.

This was the last of the America's Cup campaigns before my official retirement. I was to come back for more, as will be described later, but only after leaving day-to-day work in the office and moving to the country.

10

My work in the 1960s and 1970s was concentrated on three subjects — the America's Cup, the IOR rating rule, and the transition to the new keel shape. While I was thinking a lot about rules and related technical matters, not to mention the America's Cup, S&S continued actively with designs, mostly intended for offshore racing, both at home and abroad. Welcome recognition had come from several directions, but especially from England in 1960 and '61, where the performance of Hestia, *followed by* Clarion of Wight, *brought new activity and made me feel at home in the British sailing world.*

SOME CLIENTS

Palawan III, shown on page 172, was an early offshore racer with the new separation of keel and rudder. She demonstrated its potential for speed. She was also an early boat with a center cockpit. Here she is carrying a reaching jib. The clew, much higher than it would be on a Genoa, allows the sheet to lead well aft leaving an open leech to give better drive than the lower-clewed sail. Present-day asymmetrical spinnakers are similar but are usually set on a bowsprit, making them much larger.

(Photo: Rosenfeld Collection 181787F)

I think of Harry van Bueningen, *Hestia*'s owner, as the ideal owner. A resident of Rotterdam and member of a prominent family, he built a relatively small boat, 38´ overall, to sail with his two young sons and two or three friends. Sailing her down and across the North Sea they took her to Cowes Week in her first season. With excellent handling they made an outstanding record and sailed back to Holland as, I recall, the winningest non-British entry. That was good, but not the end. Harry knew that I attended yearly fall meetings in London and learned that I stayed then at the Hyde Park Hotel. He made notes all through each season, little things that he thought might improve *Hestia*'s performance, and every year over a period of time he brought these notes to London where we could sit down together to consider the items one by one. They might have to do with balance under sail, the height or length of the boom, the type of propeller, fairing on a water inlet or outlet, new sails — nothing big but many small things which when combined made *Hestia* a consistent winner against newer and larger yachts. I enjoyed and admired this man who could have owned a boat of twice the size, and still spent so much time to get advice on the small things and, by putting them into practice, kept a high place in the racing world.

I have mentioned Dick Carter's *Rabbit* as a highly successful boat of the 1960s in which the keel and rudder had parted company. In contrast, the French *Palynodie*, with her rudder far forward on a short keel, was fast but hard to control. In 1965 I was asked by two English clients, Derek Boyer and Sir Max Aitken, to design one-tonners, around 38´ in length, which raced boat-against-boat in the One Ton Cup. Both accepted my recommendation to separate the rudder from the keel, which would be short. We also decided that the boats would be different, not sisterships. Although the two boats were not built to the same plans they were similar, the Aitken boat, *Roundabout*, being somewhat lighter than Boyer's *Clarionet*. As it turned out they shared the top of the class in 1966. In 1990 *Clarionet* was still winning races.

The performance of these "terrible twins," as they were called after they had demonstrated their speed, despite a series of spectacular broaches, uncontrollable spins, was good enough to encourage me to adopt a similar keel for the Twelve-Metre *Intrepid* and the large American offshore racer *Palawan* during the next winter design cycle. Although we were happy with the speed of the terrible twins, we were less satisfied with their steering. Steering was made more reliable in the new boats by the use of a flap or trim tab on the keel which could be linked to the rudder for best control. I was satisfied that the short keel was the right configuration for speed, and though the longer keel had some advantage in deep-sea work, the short keel was entirely safe with the right rudder, and even more positive when combined with the tab. Good boats of that type could be controlled in any weather

Hestia, shown here, was a happy collaboration between owner and designer. A small, unpretentious boat, she has been sailed and enjoyed for nearly 40 years by one Dutch family, cruising and winning races. One fears that *Hestia* represents a combination of possibilities that some kind of progress has made harder and harder to find. (Photo: Beken of Cowes)

and were quite satisfactory when hove to. This hull geometry was not new, but the performance of the racing boats after '67 suddenly made it almost universal within the next two or three years.

Before '67 our activity in foreign countries had continued to grow. Several new clients were from New Zealand, prompting a visit in 1964. I soon recognized a concentration of skillful and smart sailors down there unmatched anywhere in the world. The three boats built in New Zealand could not have been more different. The last of these, built by her owner, a young man named Chris Bouzaid, was similar to *Roundabout* but much modified to benefit from the RORC scantling allowance which Chris had studied to greater effect than I. The first of our designs to be built in New Zealand, in 1960, was a boat named *Sapphire*, intended for racing in a local open class to an interesting New Zealand rule. With good luck she became a consistent winner. The largest of the three, known as *T'aroa*, was interesting but a shade disappointing, probably due to my own stubborn streak. Visiting New Zealand I had, of course, seen the general use there of the short keel and separate rudder.

In correspondence with Douglas Bremner, *T'aroa*'s owner, I had been advised how well some very light boats were doing locally. These boats were, in type, the forerunners of the Ultra Light Displacement Boats (ULDBs), the California sleds. Perhaps if I had followed Doug's advice I would have introduced that type to the U.S.; but I had been lucky with fairly heavy designs which I liked for their stability and windward ability. This was largely wasted on Auckland courses, although personal experience had persuaded me that most races were won on the wind. So we settled on a compromise which was fine when the course included a decent turn to windward. This seldom occurred. Shoreline spectators were important in Auckland, and the courses paralleled the shore. On those courses *T'aroa* was no match for the local sleds.

Doug invited me to Auckland for the first of three visits I have made, making it possible to see an extremely interesting fleet in which the underwater configuration was of the shape just discussed, and was the rule rather than the exception. I noticed that some of the outstanding fast and attractive smaller boats had been designed by a young Auckland man named Bruce Farr. I probably do not need to point out that Farr has become a blazing star in the firmament of yacht design, and Bouzaid has earned an enviable reputation as a sailor and sailmaker. I have seen them both recently and enjoy the ability to remember when.

The success of Chris Bouzaid's *Rainbow II* in winning the One Ton Cup in '69 was naturally welcome, but the way it was done had much to do with killing the RORC Rule. It also illustrates an approach to yacht design that is hard for me to either condemn or applaud. The British rule incorporated a scantling allowance, intended to give heavily-built boats an even chance against more aggressive and lightly built competitors. In this Chris saw a loophole, because the allowance for the heavy structure was badly judged, offering too generous a bonus. As the result of the increased weight resulting from the installation of a steel deck over the wooden one and replacing a small auxiliary engine with a massive diesel, Chris was able, within the rating limit, to add so much sail area and waterline length to *Rainbow II*'s original dimensions as to be almost unbeatable by the more normally proportioned entries. For similar reasons, at about the same time, S&S had done a winning design for Arthur Slater with a better-proportioned but unmercifully heavy hull. We will soon discuss the replacement of the RORC Rule by the IOR. The unhappy scantling allowance was one indication to the RORC officers that there was need to change.

I should not leave Chris and his *Rainbow II* without saying that I have never been more impressed by sheer racing and sailing ability in a crew than when I went on a race with them in the Solent. With Chris steering and Roy Dickson calling the wind shifts, the crew's ability to take advantage of every slant, beating through the fleet in Cowes roads, was an experience I shall never forget. It was true New Zealand-style sailing, of which we have seen continuing evidence.

It was soon after this that Mr. Edward Heath became an S&S client. Our work in England had led to the design of a 34′ fiberglass cruiser-racer, exhibited at the London Boat Show of 1969 as the S&S 34. I was there one morning and was asked to return to the stand, if possible, at two o'clock to meet Mr. Heath. "Who," I asked, "is Mr. Heath?", only to receive the reply "The next Prime Minister of Britain."

I came back as requested and had a brief chat with the prospective buyer who later placed an order. The sponsor of the class had, I believe, made a very successful bet on a horse called *Morningtown* and had used that name for an S&S design which he liked well enough to decide to launch the S&S 34s. He encouraged the owners to name their boats *Morning this* or *Morning that*, and the soon-to-become Prime Minister named his purchase *Morning Cloud*. As I had not followed all of this in detail it was with considerable surprise that about a year later I heard that Ted Heath's 34-footer, one of the smallest entries, had won Australia's big Sydney-Hobart Race. As most readers may recall, the owner went on to become Prime Minister just as announced.

The 34 was the first of four *Morning Clouds* of our design owned by Mr. Heath, two of which became members of British Admiral's Cup teams sailing under the newly accepted IOR Rule. This led to many interesting meetings, including one dinner at the White House and others at Chequers, and to a feeling of admiration for the P.M.'s ability to organize his sailing. His crews included some of the best sailors in Britain. The high office had its perquisites.

Mr. H. had a great interest in music, which led to the installation of a very fine sound system in Chequers. One evening with considerable pride he let me hear a recording made when he conducted the London Symphony. Perhaps I may include an anecdote about the White House and my wife, Susie. We knew that a model of the second *Morning Cloud* was to be presented to her owner in the course of a Washington visit, but we were taken by surprise when we were invited to the White House presentation, undoubtedly at the instigation of Bus Mosbacher, then Protocol Officer with the rank of ambassador. We opened with some excitement the invitation in the name of President Nixon, but Susie's immediate reaction was "You wouldn't sit down for dinner with that man?" Nevertheless, it wasn't long before she was shopping for a suitable dress. We both sat down and enjoyed the dinner.

It was just before Christmas and the decorations were beautiful. The next morning Patty Mosbacher showed us through the State Department's collection of early-American furniture, but the thing that Susie remembered best happened in the receiving line. As we were introduced and shook hands with the two great men, Mr. Heath turned to the President and, looking at me, said to him "This is the man that counts." I was naturally pleased, and Susie, with me, was happy to hear the complimentary remark; but really what it meant to me was the Prime Minister's commitment to sailing and to the Admiral's Cup in which he was hoping to be on the British team.

S&S was becoming active in designs for standardized building. The *Morning* class of 34-footers in England was an example. Important for S&S was the design of a number of Swan classes. We were especially happy in working with Swan and Nautor to experience the excellence of Finnish yachtbuilding. Pekka Koskenkyla founded the firm and identified his different classes with the name of the national bird of Finland. He started by building a standardized version of a One Ton Cup winner of a year before *Rainbow*. He called it the Swan 36. As this program went on another Finnish client, Ake Lindquist, for whom we were doing a 43′ design, decided to build with Koskenkyla and this design became the Swan 43. These boats were attractive and raced well and sold in good numbers in Europe and the U.S.

As Koskenkyla was just getting established, a fire and a financial squeeze led to the need for new capital, and this brought the eventual takeover by the substantial Finnish firm Nautor, active in the lumber and paper business. Koskenkyla became successful selling Swans in the Mediterranean. The interest of Lindquist, who was an experienced Lloyd's surveyor, was fortunate for both Nautor and our firm as he collaborated with Rod, visiting the yard frequently to help the builders maintain very high standards of strength and finish. The result was that Nautor's Swans developed reputations as the Rolls-Royces of the yacht field. Most sadly, after this valuable work in Nautor's early years, Ake Lindquist lost his life in an automobile accident;

but his presence almost from the beginning, and the work he had done, contributed greatly to the continued and continuing success of the Swans. Rod, in particular, watching the building work, was grateful for his support.

Now, more than 35 years after the first Swans, standardized construction provides the fleets that crowd the marinas. Our office was active in this development, although few of our projects had such success in combining quality and volume as the Swan experience. It was a rocky road, or perhaps we should say a rough sea, and the Swan blend of craftsmanship and production efficiency turned out to be hard to copy despite our constant efforts to find firms with solid financing and knowledge of boatbuilding. During the early days the field seemed most attractive to those who knew least about boats. It seems to take some understanding of a variety of skills to build good boats, but in the early days of fiberglass the seeming ease of duplication and the apparently small capital required tempted many to try plastic boatbuilding without possessing the necessary boat or business sense. The established boatbuilders were on the whole a conservative group; they had learned the hard way to survive through accepting and then overcoming the failures of one detail or another, and they were slow to accept the new. It was, indeed, the fools who rushed into something that looked easy.

The possibilities were certainly tempting to prospective builders and to us as designers. We were all optimists, hoping to find something new and good. Looking back I can see that we suffered more than a few disappointments when the product was not up to snuff or the builder could not pay us or complete his work. We must have accepted as sound the promise of newcomers who had no real idea of their costs. Financing was the immediate problem, and this was brought on by not knowing enough about boatbuilding.

Thinking back, it seems to me that those who survived over time were most often builders with boatbuilding experience, groups that had detailed knowledge of all the components of a sailing yacht. They could simply replace the wood hull with the new material and use existing experience to see to the other installations, accommodations, rigs, engines, electrics and a variety of sailing gear, producing a workable package. With time and experience things were sorted out.

These experiences were played out in both Europe and the U.S. There were some successes in fiberglass sailboat building in England, Italy and to a lesser degree in France and Australia. Possibly there were fewer failures but the successes were mainly small. The Swan project, which almost failed and then was rescued by a substantial and well-capitalized firm, became the great success we have described. A success on these shores was Tartan, which produced stock fiberglass boats to our design. I always felt that we had an important American ally in Charlie Britten, the man behind Tartan Yachts. Various Tartans have made owners happy over many

years. As recently as 1997 I enjoyed a short cruise in a Tartan 34. I will not try to name all the many builders S&S became involved with during the past 40 years of stock boatbuilding, some successful for varied periods, some with designs that changed with rules and styles, others continuing with smaller dinghy-like types. The fibreglass builders that have survived the early, doubtful time have now contributed greatly to boat ownership and to widespread enthusiasm for the pleasure and sport of sailing.

I recall this part of our business as difficult, although I recognize how important it was in a business sense because when it worked it was profitable. Our Lightning-Class design has been used for more than 15,000 units without bringing in a penny over the original small fee. We sold the plans outright in 1937, and as we watched the fleet grow we decided not to do that again. Ever since then we have insisted on royalty payments, usually a small sum for each boat in addition to the net cost of producing the plans. We learned that asking too much was hazardous to the health of the proverbial goose; builders had to make a profit to keep going. So many were new and just starting up that it was hard to predict eventual success. But during my later years the profits that we earned from stock boats and the sale of plans very nearly represented just that to us, as our margin between billings and costs was almost nil on the individual designs. Doing the work of design as I thought it should be done was so expensive that I hated to bill our overhead at its full cost.

Just the same, the one-off designs contributed nicely to our activity, and pleasure too, during the 'fifties, 'sixties and 'seventies. These decades saw a general change from longer to shorter keels with the rudder moving aft as the trailing edge of the keel moved forward. We also designed many centerboarders. In these decades fiberglass and aluminum largely replaced wood in hull construction. Our work became more and more international, and I took what part I could in the international movement toward uniform rating rules. America's Cup summers in Newport seemed to alternate with shorter summers at Cowes in England.

Cowes week and all that goes with it makes for wonderful sailing. This is not an entirely rational thing for a yacht designer to say, because there is no other place where luck and skill play a greater part in the results. Not that it hurts to have a fast boat, but around the Isle of Wight it is easy to slip back in the strong currents and the eddies and shoals. And the wind may be strong during this premier event of British sailing or it may drop out altogether. In 1971 when I sailed there we did several races in *Yankee Girl*, with Dave Steere and Bill Fallon. I remember running before it in a good breeze, doing at least ten knots, with spinnaker and blooper set and on the edge of jibing. A fleet of small one-designs was sailing across close-hauled, seeming to have all the doors closed. The gap we found was tight but we got through. Later in the Channel Race, and well up, our new Kevlar main split right across, just above the boom.

Four years later I sailed at Cowes with Jesse Phillips in *Charisma*. He had a fine crew and it was again fun. Jesse was a client I enjoyed in a rather special way which was not always easy. He drove a hard bargain with the yard when he built, and as the architect I accepted the responsibility of seeing it carried out. We tried to write complete and explicit specifications on which the building contract was based, but even so there were changes and extras which had to be settled in the end, and Jesse was not one to make a broad compromise. I appreciated the fact that, as we went down a long list of small items, he expected detailed consideration of all the circumstances on every item; but after that had been done he put the decision about payment to me, and there was no argument if I said he owed it. As the builder nearly always was willing to agree, it worked; but I did not find that it was easy. Overall, I had to be grateful to Jesse and to respect him for his fairness.

I think it would be a mistake to consider too many personalities. Many of our

clients were people who had been very successful in business as the result of real competence. Those for whom I had great respect were a varied group and included Thomas Watson, Jr. of IBM and Pat Haggerty of Texas Instruments. Lynn Williams was another. May I be frank to say that I found no reason to consider all successful men in the same light? There were those whose success I could not understand.

The IOR Rule was accepted worldwide in 1969, and its first application to international sailing was the Admiral's Cup of the summer of 1971. This meant three short races in the Solent and two longer courses, the Channel Race and the Fastnet. The new boats seemed generally good with reasonable proportions. We at S&S had the good luck to have designed the three boats on the British team which was led by Ted Heath's new *Morning Cloud*. All our designs had short keels, with the rudders well aft on small skegs. Some critics objected to this geometry and called attention to control problems which, indeed, existed. Nevertheless, these problems were surely less than they would have been if the rudders had been further forward and attached to the short keels. The boats were fast and roomy and seemed well-balanced as to hull and rig. I preferred to use a skeg ahead of the rudder. That is seldom used

This looks like *Charisma* sailing a Miami-Nassau race I seem to remember. I don't know how we did, but she had good record, always in the fight. I enjoyed the experience of sailing with many different owners and on a variety of courses and in a procession of changing types. I think I have recently been saved some rough rides as age has kept me away from deep water. (Photo: Rosenfeld Collection 192175F) today. To my mind it improved straight-line steering, although probably not turn-ing, and it provided mechanical support for the rudder.

I always spent as much time as I could on as many new boats as possible. I have mentioned sailing several Admiral's Cup races aboard David Steere's *Yankee Girl*, and there were many others. In the 1960s I had considered our most competitive Cruising Club Rule design to be *Palawan* of 1965. She had something in common with the Twelve-Metre type with the divided keel-rudder of *Intrepid* and less than average beam. The newer design, *Yankee Girl*, focused on the IOR, had more beam and a shoaler midsection, sharper ends and a much shorter keel. The model had been tested at the Davidson Laboratory and I remember the pleasant surprise, and amazement coupled with skepticism, with which I reviewed the test results. They were easily the best I had seen for a boat of that size. Disappointment in the Twelves of 1970 prompted doubts; but *Yankee Girl* was tank-tested the same year, and her performance supported the tank.

For the next season we did the slightly larger but very similar *Dora* for Lynn Williams. She has been fortunate in her owners — first Lynn, followed by Ted Turner who sailed her as *Tenacious* to win the rough Fastnet of 1979. More recently she became *War Baby* when Ted sold her to Warren Brown, who has cruised from the tropics to ice in the highest latitudes, both North and South, and has been awarded the Blue Water Medal of the Cruising Club of America. Warren is an exceptional seaman; but *War Baby*'s capacity to absorb the worst that weather can offer has demonstrated that racing success and seagoing ability can be combined in one vessel. I wish I had similar confidence in the present generation of successful racing yachts. Although the International Measurement System (IMS) is a better rule than IOR, it seems in general to favor a type with less-than-ideal seagoing behavior.

I was pleased that our work remained varied in size and character over the years. Most of our new designs went well and a number of clients gave us repeat commis-sions. In England there were several owners who built new boats for each Admiral's Cup cycle. During the 1960s and later the variety and income potential of our design work was enhanced by the standardized boats well-exemplified by the Swans and Tartans. This work was not always so satisfactory, as previously noted, and whether it was going well or poorly there was a lot of correspondence and time on the phone.

In the effort to get it all said I have to admit that, as younger designers became active, winning grew harder and less frequent. I was impressed by at least three of the younger designers in the persons of German Frers, Doug Peterson and Bruce Farr. German had learned the trade under his father in Argentina, and we were fortunate to have him with us at S&S for some time, although I knew that this would be limited. While with us he had drawn the lines, among others, of *Ragamuffin*, Fastnet winner of 1969. I knew that he had an exceptional eye for form and a lot of boat sense. The others I did not know so well, but I had great respect for Doug Peterson after seeing his *Ganbare*, a new one-tonner that raced in Sardinia in 1974. She should have won that series, and what I admired in addition to her speed was her simplicity and low cost, neither of which had detracted from her effectiveness. Doug was soon producing winners. Bruce Farr, even though he has plenty of competition, is riding high as this is written. He has become the high priest of offshore-racing yacht design. As recent circumstances have thrown us together I can easily understand his success. At the time I am considering he had come into the fight from New Zealand with a lighter type than I could accept as desirable, and this forced me to think about rule provisions that would control tendencies I considered unsound. He might well have found me stepping on his toes, but never took it as personal. Then as now he knew how to make the best use of a rating rule. And I must add that his relatively light boats have survived much hard driving and rough treatment.

New young designers were appearing in England, France, Germany, Holland and Italy. In general they were enough younger than I that I did not sense their impact. If I were active today I would feel their competition. Both too young and too many, I shall not try to characterize any of them. The feature I find most notable in the new generation is their ability with their laptop computers as they bring them to meetings. I can only be amazed by the ability to access unimaginably complete files of data displayed in assorted interpretive plots. Those interested in sails can show a series of draft contours and a record of the effect of each sail on performance. I kept sail books myself on a couple of the Twelves, but I didn't have plots of the sail shape with related, precise notes on the wind speed and angle, the heel angle and the boat speed and the main and Genoa trim. Although the data I have cited is often there, it is too seldom all together. Consistent application remains difficult. But on display in a laptop it has three-decimal-place precision and is in impressive color. I am too dazzled to have absorbed it all, but the plots and the ability to display the data in so many forms make me highly respectful. My impression is that so very many of the youngest generation are similarly prepared. I wonder who among the many is going to be able to digest this feast and apply it effectively. I can hardly say whether or not I mean this critically. I can say that I am impressed by the new tools and the many designers who have the ability to handle them. In itself this does not seem quite sufficient. On a superficial level they are all even, and I must realize that I have seen those who are pretty deeply involved. What I hope to find is just by whom and how this flood of information will be best put to use. That will take some good thinking.

1

ROD AND THE TEAM

ways took both comfort and pride in the team
ity and spirit of the S&S design-office group.
were lucky in the way we worked together. We
de mistakes, and some projects turned out
er than others, but I think it is fair to say that
of us tried to do the best we knew how at any
time, all the time.

here were three of us at the head—myself, Rod
Gil Wyland — each taking a certain share of
work. The value of Rod and Gil is beyond my
ity to describe, and the fit was exceptional.
d my part to guide the broad direction of our
k toward whatever goal, whether business and
tations or the characteristic dimensions and
netry of a specific boat.

I think each of us knew his job, and our common objective was to do it as well as we could. I always felt a certain combination of elation and determination that this one had to be the best when every new project was confirmed. Unfortunately there were few, if any, projects that I felt in the end, down deep, had fully achieved those hopes. I have told something here about most of those that came close, but have reported failures, too. It seemed impossible to reach the goal I had seen at the beginning of a project, even with those that seemed best. The distance between the potential and the actual was something I saw too often.

Gil took care of engineering, including hull structure, mechanical installations and electrics, as well as supervising the checking of drawings. Rod's part was to see that details were right, especially those involving rig and deck layout, and the work as it went forward by the builders. He did all the inspection work that he could possibly fit in, both at home and abroad, and it was a lot. The rest of us filled in.

In 1935 my brother Rod gave up his work at the Nevins yard and joined Sparkman & Stephens. This was our biggest step toward a happy and successful team. Older readers will need no reminder of Rod's importance to our firm or to my life. He enjoyed the recognition that his abilities brought. But it would not be right to think first of his accomplishments, which are a matter of record. I prefer to focus on his attitude as brother and partner. It was, I think, unique.

I fear that he never realized how incomplete we would have been without him. When I think how often siblings' lives turn toward conflict, I know how lucky I was in Rod's partnership. Although I was older by sixteen months, as we grew up there was not much deference on his part. We had our arguments and even fights, but as we became older, although we both took part in school sports, he was a far better athlete than I and in a sense he became my protector, and always my supporter. I know that deference was uncalled for in the light of his accomplishments and his importance in our work. He brought the authority of his knowledge, his accomplishments, and his integrity as a sailor and a person to everything he did.

Rod was the complete seaman in his understanding of the sea and boats and the relation between the two. At work, still in the role of protector, this understanding made him a guide ready to correct errors, whether in concept or detail, that the sea might not welcome. His guidance was often in the details, giving advice as to what would work and what would not. Rod knew that I might be too ready to accept a client's wishful, unrealistic demands, and he did not fail to point out negative factors when the owner's heart had been set on details or structures he could not approve. In such cases there was no compromise.

From our first days at Lake George and on Cape Cod, Rod loved the water and learned everything to do with boats. Yet when we sailed together he left the steering to me and did everything else himself. He took care of setting and trimming sails and, over all his life, he applied these skills to rigs and deck arrangements and sail-handling, from 11′ dinghies to 140′ J-Boats. He liked to go aloft and learned the importance of inspection and the danger of metal fatigue from the failure and repair of *Dorade*'s spinnaker halyard in her first Bermuda Race. That he did not have to learn twice characterized his attitude about and knowledge of construction. During our family treks to City Island in the 1920s, Rod could always understand what he saw in the shop and relate it to what he saw on the water. Over and over as a natural mechanic he applied the lessons of his brief period as a boatbuilder in the Nevins yard. In the wide world of boatbuilding, here and abroad, he was respected, everywhere and always.

An example of this was his work at General Motors during World War Two on the amphibious vehicles, the DUKWs. He immediately took his place in the small group of truck engineers, where his teammates recognized how well he knew what he was doing and, with his guidance, produced a running pilot model in just 30 days — a miracle in Detroit. Later, while the DUKWs were staging a demonstration of cargo-handling on Cape Cod, his seamanship and confidence in his design allowed him to rescue the crew of a wartime patrol yacht that went aground in a storm. Both his patriotism and his wish to see the job through took him away to train DUKW crews, first to Hawaii, then to the war zones of the Pacific islands, and then to Scotland leading up to D-Day.

But he was not all work. When he was in Hawaii he cabled me for a considerable sum of money. What was it for? Was he getting married? It seemed that he had found for sale an excellent piano accordion well-adjusted to the marine environment. He considered it an improvement over the one he had played happily in the early *Dorade* and *Ranger* days. He bought this instrument and played it for years after. On *Mustang*, his NYYC thirty-two, he carried it in a special stowage spot. Rod loved *Mustang*, sailed her often out of the American Yacht Club, and made her a pattern for many good details carried on his inspection visits in drawings and photographs. He cruised and raced with family and friends until he felt the burden of his own success by becoming too busy to take care of her and reluctantly sold her. It was typical that when I sailed with him he insisted that I was skipper. It was no fun for me when, in a Bermuda Race, I called a losing tack and lost a close race to a competitor of the same size.

In the firm, the wide respect our clients had for his ability served us well. It made possible our success abroad, where he visited frequently to inspect new construction. Rod and I agreed that good construction was the only route not only to an owner's satisfaction but to our own. Rod's attention to all the details

Mustang, opposite, was Rod's NYYC thirty-two. He first owned her about 1950 and kept her for nearly 20 years. Early on he used her a lot, racing and cruising, usually with Marge and Betsi, wife and daughter. Later on work interfered, and after she spent several summers lying on a mooring he had to let her go. He was happy to be busy but he missed *Mustang* badly. (Photo: Rosenfeld Collection 170513-8)

assured that good work was routine. I have often wished that a detailed log of one of his European inspection circuits could be published as an example of organized efficiency. It would have made a good *New Yorker* article. After making a long list of items for the office's attention while he was away, he would set off on a complicated journey to six or eight European yards. No scrap of time was wasted. He knew the airline and train schedules and made the best of both. He knew how much time should be taken at each yard he visited, and he adhered to his schedule rigorously. It was office policy to bill each owner for his share of the total time and net travel cost of each trip, taking account of the scale of his project against the others. Very few thought they received less than a bargain, and I can think of no one who could have completed these trips in less than twice Rod's time.

His was a tiring, sometimes relentless routine; but Rod found many good friends among the builders, which I realized when I occasionally filled in for him. I did not try to duplicate his pace, and I have already mentioned some of my pleasure in the travel. There were times when the builder's reports to me were enlightening or amusing. I found that, not infrequently, Rod mouse-trapped himself in his polite expressions of appreciation for the hospitality of the builder or his family. As the nature of the work is to inhabit the shore, so the builders are likely to offer fish for dinner. Though I am lucky to enjoy fish and seafood, Rod never cared for fish, and his high praise brought it constantly back for his visits. Sometimes I was able to enlighten the host — delicately, I hope.

The trial sail was the culmination of every boat-design project. Again Rod was in his element: he was all over the boat, and it was exceptional when he did not come up with another long list of work to be completed. Though essentially a sailor, Rod knew engines and their installation. He had learned, I fear through experience, the danger of water backing into the engine from the exhaust system. Assurance that this could not happen was a major concern of his. Free steering with minimal friction was another. We specified that the wheel should turn with an applied moment of no more than one foot-pound. Rod had a one pound weight ready to hang on a spoke of the wheel one foot from the hub. Many builders struggled to comply after the weight failed to turn the wheel. Steering usually required cables and a quadrant, for Rod would not use hydraulic steering with its lack of "feel." His policy was to be certain that the cable could never drop off the quadrant at the farthest tangent point. It was not always easy to crawl under the cockpit or into the lazarette to check this. It was less difficult to be sure the emergency tiller was handy and workable. For one more detail, the bilge was checked to be clean, and limbers were required to be large and open, preferably with a flare toward the sump. The bilge pumps, with a hand pump as an essential, plus electric or engine-driven, were all tested and assured to be ready to run.

The rig was Rod's special concern and the area where his lifelong skill and experience were most valuable. I will not go into more detail except to mention his inevitable concern with cotter pins which were checked for length, end finish, and spread. Flotation, balance under sail, stability, and performance under power, were also tried out. Too many boats are never finished, but when Rod agreed that a boat was done she was ready to go.

Some builders found his demands onerous or finicky. Others were glad to learn and engaged in a constructive give-and-take over method or detail. There were good builders, and there were some even better ones. Abroad, the big yard that set a high standard was Abeking and Rasmussen of Lemwerder, near Bremen in Germany. More recently they have been challenged by Walter Huisman in Holland. Both were and are yards well and highly organized, able to handle the largest projects. From our designs A&R built yachts for many owners, among them Tom Watson and the Aga Kahn, along with some later mega-yachts. Huisman's first use of our plans was to build the very successful ocean racer *Running Tide*. Among the smaller yards, Rod's favorites were those of Bengt Plym of Saltsjobaden in Sweden and Aage Walsted in Denmark. Plym especially had excellent special practices to which we were generally ready to adapt. Each of these Scandinavian builders did several of our best boats, and Rod and I both learned from them.

Boats and the office meant everything to Rod, even more to him than to me. I was happy and relieved when I considered my work done between my 70th and 72nd birthdays. Rod worked on until he suffered a stroke in his 83rd year. I don't think he remained happy, as the business changed in the 1980s and 1990s. Rather than a relatively large number of small or medium-size boats of a conservative type, S&S was designing just a few big ones with characteristics he could not like. He was out of sympathy with the complex machinery, hydraulic winches, roller-furling sails, air conditioning and big electric generators. Nor did he like the straight sheerlines and large expanses of glass that newer clients demanded. And the business had become less personal; so much was done through representatives, decorators for example, rather than the owners themselves.

In a way I think Rod was happier after the stroke stopped his work in New York. Old friends were kind and helpful to him, but above all were a doctor couple, the Drs. Susan and Edward Kline, husband and wife of Pequot Yacht Club, who owned one of the Swans that had been close to Rod's heart. They were helpful to him in matters relating to his health, but even more so when they asked for his help on their boat. He was happy when he was hoisted aloft in a bosun's chair, and on his 85th birthday, as Dr. Susan Kline tells the story, he went to the top of the mast of a friend's Tartan 31 and typically found something that

On the opposite page is Rod where he liked to be. Here he's up on *Rainbow*'s jib stay in 1934 when he first sailed with Mike Vanderbilt. Rod enjoyed going aloft, something I did only when absolutely necessary. He liked the activity of climbing all over a boat, and both sailing and work gave him many opportunities. These included inspecting spar and rigging details on the new boats, or managing sail-handling when racing. (Photo: Rosenfeld Collection 77088F) needed attention. When he was back again on deck, he told Dr. Kline, "That's the first time I've felt normal since I had the stroke." He loved to teach and to advise in the most detailed fashion, and the Klines gave him a new opportunity to do that. For their part, as doctors, the Klines were able to help him cope with his physical limitations, and this included taking him sailing again. He also made a fast friend of one of the Klines' regular crew, Lew Meyer, an airline pilot, who absorbed Rod's ways on a boat.

After hospitalization and therapy following the stroke, and the loss of his wife, Marge, Rod continued to live in his house in Scarsdale with the help of practical nurses through the day, while spending the night alone. His daughter, Betsi, who lives in Washington, D.C., visited him frequently on weekends and I drove down from Hanover from time to time. On the morning of January 10, 1995, when the nurse came to help him dress and make his breakfast she found him in bed as though sleeping, but life had gone. A few days later many of his many friends gathered for a memorial service at the American Yacht Club.

I was proud of the depth and loyalty of our small team of maybe eight or nine technical people. We were lucky to have had the help of more than a few younger designers who have gone out on their own to make individual reputations. Our benefit was temporary, but for a time all were ready to fit in and their contributions were real. I can understand why they left, as the organization was too small to justify hopes of steady advancement. I think there was mutual benefit in these associations and mutual respect and friendship has lasted. Others of similar ability stayed with us for years. To them I remain indebted and appreciative. I think they felt good about their work. I hope it is not invidious to name a few real bulwarks of the office.

Anticipating the way the office was changed by the war which came soon after Gil Wyland joined us, I want to bow to four men who took on responsibility in those early days.

I think Jim Merrill was our first paid draftsman. Although his time with S&S was short, he helped us make a good start. We met Jim when my father bought our first little yawl, *Trad*, from Jim's father, who had built her with Jim's help. So he knew something about boats and he made neater drawings than I could ever do. During the first years of *Dorade*, Jim was a member of our crew. Due to a disagreement with Drake he left the office in 1932 while I was sailing in England. He became a sailmaker in his hometown of Riverton, New Jersey.

Fred Huntington came in after Jim left and did the lines of some of our best boats, including *Stormy Weather*. Fred came from Martha's Vineyard and seemed to have grown up in boats. He had a good eye and the same general views of design as I had. He wanted to win and was tough and thorough in his analysis of those factors that made for speed.

Alexander George worked mainly on powerboats. He was the oldest in our group, and came to us after long experience at the office of Henry J. Gielow, where I had first met him. He concentrated on powerboat design, doing lines with a special type of diagonal which he learned from Mr. Gielow. Rather than representing a plane intersecting the hull they referred to distances between hull sections normal to the surface. His background qualified him to take a leading part in the design of several early S&S motorboats. He stayed with us until well after the war. Older than I, he left us to go south some years before I retired.

Bob Henry, who had studied ocean engineering at MIT, had the best technical education of our small group and was the most versatile. He came to us just when good mechanical design was becoming essential for the firm, and he did two major, helpful projects. One of these was to design a family of geared winches and the other was to do tang fittings for wooden spars that were supported either by 1 x 19 stainless-steel wire or the streamlined stainless rods that came into use as shrouds in the early 1930s. Splicing was difficult in the first and impossible with the rods. The tangs were tapered metal straps attached to the wooden spars by multiple screws. They held the rigging, which now can be pinned directly to the aluminum or composite spars that have replaced the softer wood.

Bob also helped to break new ground in the winch designs. The smaller open-class racing boats, such as Six Metres, were using Genoa jibs but the available sheet winches were single-acting, with cranks on the same shafts as the drums. We needed more power to get the sails in fast, and this was provided through gearing and anti-friction bearings. With Bob's winches, the big Genoas came in much faster. George Crouch, who was then at Nevins, gave us the name of an excellent mechanical job shop on upper Park Avenue in New York, Mantle and Company. They executed our drawings well and reasonably, considering the complication and the limited quantities. I suppose the cost of these winches had a lot to do with the reputation for "gold-platers" that S&S was acquiring. We always tried to specify the best materials in every part of a boat, including Everdur fastenings, bent white-oak frames, and mahogany planking, since we believed that it was right that a boat should be built to last. A little later Bob designed the pedestal "coffee-grinder" winches built by Nevins and used on the prewar Twelve-Metres. Bob and Gil Wyland also worked on a pair of reduction gearboxes to transmit the power of two Curtiss airplane engines in a fast motorboat. We were lucky in the ability of Bob and Gil to do such detailed engineering work.

The group I have described was directly responsible for bringing S&S a fine reputation before World War Two. Unfortunately the war saw the breakup of this small but able team. Bob Henry left early to accept the job of running the Oxford

Shipyard in his home state of Maryland and later went into the navy. Fred left to take a tempting war-related offer–feeling, I think, that our prospects were uncertain. Al George stayed and Gil Wyland was responsible for organizing the large office that developed during the war.

Later, several accomplished people joined the team and played important roles in it. As I write I have been away from New York for nearly 20 years but still at S&S is Howard Pierce. It is a wonder that he has stayed on, but everyone who wishes prints or information about the office or its work has known and appreciated Howie's patience and readiness to find what is needed, by searching the files or calling on his memory. Another long-time helper who headed up hull drafting during our most active period was Bill Mavrogiannis. He was able to beat a difficult personal problem that caused me real anguish at the time, and it was a great pleasure to see him at a drafting board when I made a visit to S&S. Two who retired at about the time I did were Hank Uhle and Mario Tarabocchia, both expert marine draftsmen and especially good at lines. Hank did a great deal of checking during the war years, helping building architects become marine draftsmen, and later he drew the lines of a number of our best ocean racers. Mario did most of the Twelve Metre lines for the America's Cup, along with many others. The ability of both of these men, and their loyalty to the office, meant a lot to S&S and to me personally.

Another helpful employee was Frank Kinney. A Princeton graduate, though not an engineer, he was a sailor with some shipyard background and did independent design work. Irving Jakobson of the Oyster Bay yard introduced him to me, and Frank used a board in the office starting sometime after the war. He had already produced a new edition of Norman L. Skene's *Elements of Yacht Design* and knew the ropes. He could do plans of all types, although he preferred cruising boats to racers. He was on our payroll when not working on his own and was very loyal to the office. Frank wrote a history of S&S titled *You Are First*, and later compiled a sort of catalog of our designs entitled *The Best of the Best*. He was embarrassingly inclined to praise all we did, but it was nice to have such support. It was regrettable that the onset of Alzheimers ended his work for S&S.

Helpful as a jack of all trades was Bill Stiger whose sailing interest and experience, not to mention his unfailing good nature, served the office well. He knew boats and equipment and worked mainly on the writing of specifications and electrical plans.

Last of the closest group was my father, Rod, Sr. He came back late in life and took care of public relations to just the degree we needed. That amounted to following the progress of plans as they became available for publication in one or another of the sailing magazines, finding which would use what, clearing with the owner and all related detail. He was always ready, as a Stephens, to answer general letters, frequently on the subject of education for yacht design, and also show visitors around the office and entertain with conversation and answers to questions. This gave the rest of us freedom for the more technical work.

These were a just few of a larger group, most of whom played a very useful part. There were those who came and went, but few who did not contribute to a feeling of team or family. I felt that we had a common purpose, and that there was no one whose time or effort was measured out by coffee spoons. A number of this group regularly lunched at a round table in the old Prince George Hotel, just across the street. It was a good way to meet informally and we often enjoyed the company of clients or friends who felt like talking boats or liked to meet the people who drew the plans. I was sometimes questioned at home about the advisability of taking clients to a very plain hotel restaurant, rather than, perhaps, the New York Yacht Club or one of New York's fashionable luncheon places. There were some fancier lunches, of course, but on the whole I thought that clients and owners liked to get acquainted with the team they were taking on faith, and our gatherings at the Prince George seemed just right.

12

THE PAST AND PRESENT OF YACHT DESIGN

As I write this, my thoughts keep returning to the changes in yacht design that I have seen. Today I sense that I am in the center of a span between the design and engineering absolutes intuitive and scientific. I can recall how little of the scientific I had to start with, how much I have learned, and how much I still lack. Technical developments during my lifetime have transformed sailing boats of all types and sizes, and it has been interesting to follow the course of scientific developments in some detail.

199

I started my career with the tools of observation and intuition, to which quantitative analysis has been gradually added. Observation included reading, and also the study of photographs. Whenever possible I studied lines and tried to see the way shape was coupled to performance. Norman L. Skene's book *Elements of Yacht Design* gave me a degree of technical instruction, though it is more empirical than scientific. It did provide easily understood instruction on the "elements," with descriptions of the calculations to find areas, volumes and centers, Simpson's and the trapezoidal rules and the use of moments. Looking again at my 1925 edition I see how complete it is with practical advice and yet how limited it is on theory. I never met Norman Skene, but I recently met his daughter at dinner at the Lake Sunapee Yacht Club. It's a pleasant surprise to find such a connection.

It was Ken Davidson who taught me how some of the most important quantities could be measured. It is the constant growth in our ability to measure the forces that propel or retard a sailing yacht, and to understand the way they interact, that has revolutionized the boats and their designs. Ken, by testing models and evaluating sail forces, gave ambitious yacht designers the first numerical performance tools and pointed us in the right direction, but it was the computer with its quick and accurate arithmetic and long memory that gave us a completely new ability to combine the results of the many forces.

I have suggested that Froude's ability to quantify separately the elements of the drag of a yacht hull, combined with Davidson's ability to understand similarly the driving forces, created a new approach to yacht design, now reinforced by the coming of the computer. If you have the means to predict the boat's speed, as influenced by known design characteristics, you can do sensitivity studies by altering individual parameters so as to learn the relation of each to speed. Thus the VPP is used in every competitive design office. Fortunately, in a philosophic sense, the results are not perfect, although they are close. There is still some mystery in sailboat design.

VPP stands for "velocity prediction program" and is applied to computer code that predicts the performance of a sailboat of given characteristics over a range of wind strengths and directions. The Pratt Project at MIT in the 1970s set the pattern for such programs, and now, in various degrees of refinement, a VPP has become a necessity throughout the field of racing-yacht design and in the design of rating rules.

To start, a VPP specifies wind conditions with an assumed boat speed. The computer independently determines the driving and heeling forces and the resistance of the specified hull and finds the boat speed where they are equal. This replaces the initial assumption as the computer loops to bring the assumed and predicted speeds into convergence. Repetition at relative wind directions from close-hauled to running and at a series of wind strengths provides a complete profile of boat performance. It is hardly necessary to say that such information is extremely valuable, but despite the scientific approach and high degrees of refinement, the perfectly accurate VPP is yet to be written.

I feel certain that improved understanding of the mechanics of sailing has been powerfully cumulative and that this accounts for rapid acceptance of certain elements making for speed. Well before Froude it was assumed that friction contributed to hull resistance but no one knew how much or under what conditions. Now, knowing that friction increases just slightly less rapidly than the square of speed, while wave-making drag, once it begins, climbs at an increasingly steep rate to a given level and then begins to flatten, the designer can tailor the proportions to the conditions he expects.

At the Davidson level of scientific analysis before the war we were suddenly able to measure the effects of wetted area and displacement and sail area — not exactly, but within limits, and how each influenced performance. We also learned the value of stability in making use of the rig's power. We found, at the same time, the point on the hull where the forces balanced. And we knew the amount of each force over the range of wind strength and boat speed. I often accuse myself of being slow and stupid in not taking greater advantage of this early revelation. Induced drag, due to side force and leeway, is an example. The tank gave the amount but I never tried to find the parameters that determined how much. It has taken time to find the right combination despite the obvious fact that the way to sailing speed lies in the difficult combination of great stability with small displacement and big sail area. Stronger and lighter materials have been important. It is no wonder that today we see great beam with shifting ballast in the form of crew, water, keel, or all three, accompanied by big rigs. Unfortunately, in my opinion, this is not a formula for seagoing safety or comfort.

As this trend toward light weight and great stability was increasingly adopted, the combined effects were made measurable by the VPP, computer-adapted from Davidson's work, readily displayed as a polar diagram or table on an International Measurement System (IMS) rating certificate. Most sailors are now familiar with both. The drive continued for greater accuracy and the ability to check and explore with the computer the question, "what if?" To find answers we can go back to Newton, Bouguer, and the eighteenth-century scientists because, although the equations they wrote in their day were arithmetically cumbersome, they are now capable of solution by computer, and more quickly and cheaply as speed and memory have grown. The work of such figures has come into new and practical use — essentially in what is now called CFD, computerized fluid dynamics, still a developing art.

In the 1970s Nick Newman, a sailor and professor of naval architecture at MIT, was writing the papers that pointedly criticized the prevailing International Offshore Rule (IOR) and that forecast the VPP. With him a group at MIT were studying the details. These criticisms at first generated my antagonism, but his proposals to incorporate available quantitative knowledge of yacht performance into the analysis and improvement of the IOR nevertheless had to be recognized as truly constructive. It was clear that both Newman and John Letcher, of whom more will be said, independently were on the same tack. They were both pointing the way to a new phase in yacht design extending even beyond the application to rating rules.

Newman's purpose was to show how scientific methods could improve the empirically formulated IOR as a rating rule, replacing it with such good knowledge of performance that a disparate fleet could race with no one preselected to win. This would be doubly true because a better assessment of speed would improve the chances of the more seagoing types, while by evaluating the effects of wind direction and strength on each boat the need to build for specific conditions would be greatly reduced.

This was just what a number of Americans also wanted, so a group of supporters came together to raise a fund sufficient to bring the MIT study to a conclusion in the form of a workable rule. H. Irving Pratt was not only a contributor but he was also able to play a major part in raising the considerable sum needed to do the job. As he died soon after that goal was reached the project was given his name. The Pratt Project provided the backbone of the present international rule, the IMS, but the study also provided an essential tool, the VPP, for present-day competitive yacht design.

The Pratt studies came together as a braid of three parts. The need for as-built hull lines was recognized and a task force designed a machine to take off lines and record them in a form that could be accessed and manipulated by a computer. Second, sail forces were investigated for application to the hull geometry to predict a boat's performance in a wide range of wind directions and velocities. The third component was the writing of the computer code to do this in the form of the VPP.

The estimation of sail forces required the extension of Davidson's work, and throughout the matrix of direction called for the use of revised aerodynamic-type sail coefficients. These were supplied by a data set combining results of sailing trials supplemented by aerodynamic theory. Hull resistance was derived from model-test data and made input to the VPP, to balance the sail forces and set the boat speed. This describes the bare bones of the computer program known as the VPP. It is a newly sophisticated adaptation of the windward speed predictive methods pioneered by Davidson in 1935. A fourth study went deeply into the way existing time allowances had worked and how they might be applied with the improved data on performance related to weather and course influences.

In the MIT program the sail forces were predicted by generalizing the results measured on the yacht *Bay Bea* during a series of Southern Ocean Racing Circuit races. Her owner and navigator, Patrick Haggerty, conscientiously recorded data on her speed, heading, wind strength, and wind direction. As her hull characteristics were known from model tests it was possible to deduce the driving and heeling forces, as Davidson had done with *Gimcrack*, and from those derive the aerodynamic sail coefficients in terms of lift and drag. These coefficients were considered serviceable approximations in the beginning, although it was clear that they were rather inflexible, and the MHS Committee soon developed, with the help of George Hazen's study of applied aerodynamic theory, supported by the full-scale tests, a formula to compute coefficients that could be applied to all sizes, all wind conditions, and many rig types.

With the hull out of water, the lines machine can be located along a base line from which it measures and records on a tape the distances and angles to, say, a hundred selected points on the hull surface. These measurements are fed into a computer to produce hull lines and compute the necessary parameters, approximately 20 numbers, from which the VPP does the hull calculation.

To supplement the hull measurements, flotation, righting moment, and rig dimensions are taken in the water. Similar information can, of course, be lifted from the plans in the course of design, but for rating purposes direct in and out of water measurements are used. The hull and rig measurements are combined in the VPP.

The 1979 Fastnet Race is only too well known to sailors for its tragic cost in the lives of 15 sailors and five boats. Beyond that, many boats rolled, and some remained inverted. This not only resulted in doubts about the effect of the IOR but caused the organization of two study groups, one in England, based at the University of Southhampton, and one in this country, sponsored jointly by the Society of Naval Architects and Marine Engineers (SNAME) and US Sailing. Dick McCurdy, Karl Kirkman, Dan Strohmeier, and I were made directors. Dick became our conscientious and generous chairman while Karl Kirkman played a major part by planning the technical studies. These were intended to explain the reasons for the many failures and frequent capsizes, and to offer corrective recommendations. Robert Peterson, a meteorologist, not a director, joined Karl and me in writing a paper for the '81 Chesapeake symposium confirming the reported sea conditions in the 1979 Fastnet Race. We suggested that it was primarily the steep breaking seas, acting like a powerful jet against the topsides, that caused the boats to roll over while the wide, shallow hull form and high center of gravity encouraged by the IOR delayed or prevented the return to upright. Model tests done in the Naval Academy tank supported this supposition while clarifying the importance of the transverse gyradius in resisting that type of capsize.

Above, Robert
McCullough, New York
Yacht Club Commodore
and syndicate head, looks
on with the designer
while a model of *Valiant*
is tested at Stevens
Institute. The rail near the
top of the photo carries
the instrumentation. In
this test the model was
one-thirteenth full size.

(Photo: Rosenfeld Collection
187634-8)

Our study, begun in 1980, issued two interim reports and a final one in 1985. I think they provided guidance to rule-makers and designers in setting safety standards relating to stability, such as the IMS requirement for a minimum positive range. Guidance was also offered regarding acceptable relations among beam, hull depth, displacement and length for boats lacking inclining data.

Both studies recognized the positive role of generous displacement and a low center of gravity and the negative role of much beam in resisting capsize or the return to upright. The height of freeboard was hard to quantify as it could work in either direction. Our American study saw a large place taken by transverse gyradius in resisting an abrupt roll, probably because our tests clarified the important part played by the force of the breaking seas in causing the Fastnet incidents. As a major contributor to the gyradius, the great importance of rig weight was apparent.

In the 1980s I shared with the other members of the CCA Technical Committee the writing of a book entitled *Desirable and Undesirable Characteristics of Offshore Yachts.* My chapters and those of Dick McCurdy and Karl Kirkman relied heavily on

the research done by the joint SNAME and US Sailing committee, disseminating that work beyond the reach of the earlier reports.

By the 1970s, computers were developing fast and becoming more easily available. In the S&S office we were making frequent use of the towing tank and we often used both the up and downwind coefficients to estimate and compare sailing speeds. We also made the effort to record data on sailing performance which we displayed in polar form. Before we had our own computer, we rented computer time from the New York Stock Exchange where Diana Russell and others of our office, following the Pratt Project's lead, analyzed the sailing reports in order to find sail coefficients by relating tank-test results to full-scale performance.

As this was going on another one of our people, Bruce McPherson, a Princeton graduate, introduced me to another Princeton student, George Hazen, who was soon to play a major role in the formulation of the VPP. George is now well-known for his computer software and as a consultant to yachtsmen and designers; back then he was working on a thesis he titled "The Computer as a Towing Tank." Although

A model of the *Ranger* series is shown heeled in the photo above; the lee side is toward the underwater camera. The lengthened waterline can be seen at both ends. The telltales indicate the direction of water flow and show some separation (eddying) at the stern and some flow toward or under the keel. (Photo: Stevens Institute of Technology) this was not much more a VPP than was our study of sails, George's work, using the computer to study the hull drag by means of a panel program, integrating pressures on the hull surface, was an early use of CFD and the logic of putting computed sail and hull together to forecast performance. In 1976, as part of the design program for the Twelve-Metre *Enterprise*, Bill Langan, then a student at the Webb Institute of Naval Architecture, spent several of his work periods as an assistant in our office. Along with David Pedrick he wrote a speed prediction program utilizing model-test data combined with sail forces derived from the earlier full-scale records. Toward the completion of his work at Webb, where he graduated in '78, Bill did a thesis that put the sails and hulls together to compute speed. In this he followed methods outlined in a Pratt Project report written by Jake Kerwin. Both supported analytic studies of yacht performance to provide rational bases for the design of rating rules. One must be diffident in assigning priorities, but I can say that a paper by John Letcher first showed me a polar diagram as used to exhibit the results of predicting a yacht's speed. In looking back at this paper I have to say that the liberal way it is filled with integral signs may have detracted from one's recognition of its importance.

Although the VPP was produced as a handicapping device, it has become an essential design tool. It is the yardstick of performance. We again have Pat Haggerty to thank for his forethought. In the spring of 1979 he invited a group of Offshore Racing Council representatives to his vacation home on the Gulf Coast of Florida. The objective was to study ways to improve the IOR, particularly with respect to the division known as III-A, a modified version of the rule designed to improve the chances of older or heavier boats which could not race successfully against the extreme newer boats. We accepted at that meeting Nick Newman's belief that in order to make a better rule we had to quantify the factors that produced speed and apply that knowledge to correctly adjust the weight of the various parameters. We further agreed that an effective way to increase that knowledge would be to make a VPP generally available to committee members and advisors. The group recommended that an Offshore Racing Council research committee be formed and that at the top of its agenda would be the formulation of a VPP suitable for use on the type of small personal computer that was just becoming available. John Roome, Chairman of the ORC, the international body overseeing ocean racing, asked Pat Haggerty to become chairman of the research committee. He in turn asked John Letcher to act as consultant to the new committee, with his first assignment to write a Basic-language VPP that required no more computer memory than was provided by the small machine that Texas Instruments was producing.

Those actions became my introduction to the personal computer. I was at first an advisor to the research committee, but after Pat's unfortunate death I became chairman. I had never felt close to the computer work in our office as I had to spend so much time with correspondence and the details of specific designs. My weakness in mathematics also made the programming work hard for me to follow. But I had enthusiastically accepted and used the small hand calculators that had been introduced not so much earlier. It is hard to say why the electronic method seems so much better than the slide rule I had always used, but when Pat Haggerty sent me an early four-function Texas Instruments calculator I wrote him that I felt as though I had been able to take charge once again. This was because it seemed so quick and easy to project dimensional relationships, including weight and stability, beam, displacement, midsection area, sail area and all the important measurements, and to pass them to the drafting room. When Hewlett-Packard produced their Model 65, the first programmable calculator I had seen, I was quick to put it to work, feeling just a little disloyal to Pat, who was a high officer at Texas Instruments. So it was not too long a step to a small computer.

To back up a little, I have mentioned how our office used a big computer belonging to the New York Stock Exchange. This was powerful but cumbersome in that all work was done out of the office. We soon supplemented this in the office with a small Olivetti machine. It was not much more than a glorified calculator, but with longer memory strips it could do longer calculations such as major sections of the IOR. We used it for ratings and for studying the effect of proposed rule changes. In time we added a Hewlett-Packard machine, somewhat more powerful, but generally similar. In 1976, about two years before I retired, we bought an IBM 5100, a Basic-language computer for which we wrote, in house, many useful programs. Although superseded it continued in use for routine office work and accounting. Shortly after the office took on this machine I borrowed one to try out at home, and I realized how far it could go beyond the hand calculator. In fact I remember the feeling of reach and power it gave me despite my inexperience. But my time was filled with necessary work, and I could neither take the time at the office to learn its use or afford the cost of having my own at home. Soon after I retired in 1978 the office bought an HP-9845, and later again, having more time for study and research, I bought an HP-85, a Basic-language semi-portable machine with its own built-in small monitor and printer.

Even before I used a computer myself, I was suspicious of programs that I did not understand fully. While improving with time, I am still convinced that because of a slip or combination of algorithms which may save run time, or just a "bug," there are programs that do not deliver the exact intended results. As good software has proliferated such bugs may not be as much of a problem as the danger of applying quick and easy programs, not fully understood, in ways that are not appropriate. For some time on my machine I used almost exclusively my own programs and those of fellow committee members or from my office. I have still felt handicapped by my lack of mathematical training, and in the years since I have used a personal computer I have looked often for help, some of which has been very valuable. As time has passed new software has become available to take the place of personal programs. This has been helpful, but I believe the discipline of programming is a great help toward understanding the objectives of a program and the information required for a solution.

Everyone realizes how rapidly computers have been improving in speed and power and the important place they have taken in so many fields. This is more than ever true in yacht design, where they are essential and will continue as the source of new understanding and continuing improvement. Obviously there are many calculations that require only simple arithmetic, as for the summation of weights, where computers are accurate and quick and especially useful, for repetitive calculations. The spreadsheet can be a valuable form. Early on, the computer's use in drawing lines was appreciated. Again their accuracy made them useful as there can be no error or doubt about the exact point where planes intersect. Curves can be tested for fairness by analyzing their derivitives as they simulate earlier methods by so-called cubic splines, using the calculated curvature of beams as paralleling the wooden splines once held at fixed points with weighted "ducks." The completed hull form can be viewed on the computer screen or printed as though from any chosen viewpoint and rotated, spun, and rolled to confirm its appearance. Several pioneers of the making and viewing of lines now market fully developed software for that purpose. The complete set of static calculations is part of the package, as is the ability to make full-scale templates. The complete data set can be communicated to a builder by e-mail or by sending a disk. Or full-scale patterns can be sent, bypassing the mold loft.

While I remained in the office we never used the computer for lines drawings, but after Bill Langan took charge a new face, Jim Teeters, joined the firm. From that time on, much and eventually all lines work was done by computer. Today, at every spot where there was a drawing board at S&S there is a computer. Drafting is done by plotter, and such boards as remain are used only to display the prints. Jim had the skill to do all his own programs. Since he has left the office, drawings are made with software produced commercially for that purpose.

Communication, of course, is one of the prime uses of a computer. Flexibility provides the user with simple and quick exchange of text by e-mail, but the transmission of data of all kinds, including graphics, is also possible, along with the ability to research innumerable data sources.

In yacht design, computers are useful for all kinds of strength calculations on hulls and spars, and they can make almost routine the use of finite element and other analytical methods in which the mathematical treatment may be extremely difficult or practically impossible without the computer. Care again seems necessary, however, to escape the trap of using the ready-made programs with insufficient understanding and too much confidence. Sure to come will be the improved treatment of CFD flow codes, such as those measuring water forces on the hull and air on the sails. These require the solution of massive sets of simultaneous equations in a series of unknowns, and powerful computers doing this work today can run for hours to reach convergence. As this is written, precision cannot be assured for either hull or rig, but it is getting close. As both the hardware and the software will surely improve, and as more study makes routine the calculation of hull drag and sail drive, these calculations will be applied on every design to test its performance and will ultimately be a part of many VPPs. Yet all coins have two sides: Becoming apparent is the fact that computer speed does not assure speedy design process. I think the computer so widens design options that the search for the best combination can extend to infinity. Careful preliminary studies should minimize the need for late change and allow linear development.

The graphics capabilities of computers add to their usefulness, as in the arrangement of deck and accommodation plans and in the way these can be done in either 2-D or 3-D form so that the space with furniture or equipment can be viewed as it would look in perspective. Systems such as plumbing or wiring or machinery can be placed on separate transparencies and compared to check interferences.

All in all, yacht design is only one example of the ways computers have changed the work place; but it seems a good example of the extent of that change, which in our case is not just a simpler or quicker way to do our work, but one that is absolutely fundamental to improvements in the result.

13

RATING RULES FOR YACHTS

his section I will discuss rating rules, a specialized

somewhat technical subject, and one in which

ve taken a great interest. The attention a

ng-yacht designer pays to rating rules is due to the

d for a successful racing yacht to "fit" the

ailing rule, coupled with hope that the rule will

ourage the development of a good type as well.

rating rules and the yachts they produce have

sequences beyond the race course. The winning

rs exert a powerful, though uncalled-for, influence

he current fleets of daysailing and cruising

boats.

By generating controversy, rules have been the subject of much fuzzy thinking, and the subject may seem better ignored. Sailboat racing is for fun, yet as a game we see wide differences in intensity between the weekday-evening sailors and those who are out for blood. That difference must define the complexity of the governing rules. Simple rules suffice for the more casual group until they are exploited by designers or owners over-anxious to win. These differences cause friction when they occur within a single class and point up the need for rules appropriate to the objectives of the group involved in the racing.

Rating rules are the formulas that attempt to define a boat's speed in such a way as to effectively predict differences in the time required to complete a course of known length. In the U.S., predicted time is normally computed in seconds per mile. Differences between the predicted and actual times for each boat are compared, and the boats are ranked in the order by which each boat's actual time relates to its prediction. Comparison with a scratch boat results in a corrected time. A different application of rating is in a fixed-rating class in which the entrants are all built within a maximum established class rating and, as in one-design classes, there are no time allowances.

I hope it will clarify the discussion if I refer to a semantic distinction that seems fundamental to the consideration of rating rules, yet is usually blurred. I refer to the difference between *handicapping* and *rating* rules. To me the first is that type of rule in which the historic performance of the boat influences the speed estimate or time allowance. The second, the rating rule, depends solely on the boat's characteristics. It is common usage to speak of time allowances as handicaps, but I will try to avoid that as leading to confusion.

There is a second distinction to remember, namely that which exists between the rating formula — essentially a formularized speed estimate or VPP — and the way the input parameters are taken. An example can be length, the most important influence on speed, which has been measured on deck, at or above the waterline, or between girths, or in more complex or sophisticated ways. Displacement, another important parameter, may be simply weighed, but it has had many surrogates, such as volume taken from the measured hull or from the designer's lines. Each formula of such measurements has its good and bad points, but each results in a different time allowance.

It is also well to recognize that methods of turning the rating into a time allowance can vary widely; witness the choice between time on distance and time on time, according to whether course distance or time on course is used as the preferred system. Opinions are divided today between the new use of multiple ratings, weather and course dependent, and the more common single numbers that remain the same whatever the weather or course conditions may be. Single-number ratings are normally expressed as length, from which speed is determined by varied formulas.

A boat's rating has so much to do with her winning or losing performance that among competitors the broad subject has attracted much thought, effort, and controversy, which can be seen in the conflicting positions of those who devise rating rules. Those positions may be technical, political, national, and often reflect the ever-present war between the pure racing point of view and the point of view that values safety and comfort, and supports the "dual-purpose" yacht. As none of these positions stands alone, the best analogy is to the well-known can of worms. And of course there are sub-categories such as simplicity vs. difficulty of accurate measurement and considerations of application. Cost of measurement and of rule formulation and modification are also necessary parts of the discussion.

At the start of the nineteenth century, the need was seen for a means to provide each individual boat of a diverse fleet some hope of winning. We read of a man named Acker, apparently handicapper of England's Royal Yacht Squadron, who made a table of time allowances for a race across the English Channel based on his judgment of each boat's speed under average conditions. His table was soon extended, dividing the time by the distance, to show time per mile, applied to each boat as an allowance against elapsed time, according to the length of the course. Even before the understanding of how length and speed are related it was realized that big boats sailed faster than smaller ones, leading to the assumption that bulk was the principal criterion of speed and the convenient selection of Thames Tonnage as the ready-made rule.

The reasons why Thames Tonnage did not make a good rating rule can stand as a lesson which has had to be learned over and over from that day to this. For the sake of easy depth measurement, the cargo capacity (bulk) — essentially the product of length, beam and depth — was assumed as the product of an adjusted length, times beam, times $1/2$ beam, which last was used because half the beam was considered an average depth for a cargo ship's hold. The substitution of beam for depth resulted in the fact that less beam produced a lesser rating and a greater time allowance. As a result of the Thames Tonnage Rule, British yachts were cursed with less and less beam for most of the nineteenth century. Reserve buoyancy was badly lacking as typical yachts were described as "planks on edge."

America also felt the burden of the bad use of a bulk rule in which low freeboard rather than small beam reduced ratings. Significant loss of life eventually was blamed on the rules in both countries, and in 1880 the English yachting student and writer Dixon Kemp offered a rule based on length and sail area. Kemp, applying Froude, led in breaking an old pattern so that a number of rules were tested by including length and sail area and, soon after the turn of the century, Nathanael Herreshoff's Universal Rule, sponsored by the New York Yacht Club, was adopted for use throughout North America. This was the first rule to balance the favorable effects of length and sail area by the principal drag factor: displacement. Later rules have applied many refinements while maintaining this principle. The International Rule, already mentioned, was formulated in Europe at about this time. It accepted the same principle.

It must be clear that in a class governed by a rating rule, the objective of the designer is not simply to make the boat as fast as possible but equally to minimize rating — that is, to search for the best relationship of speed to rating that he can find. Points where this occurs are often found and can be characterized as "sweet spots." Ability to "beat the rule" is similar but greater in degree and is more likely due to some omission or poorly judged parameter demanding a change in the rule. The rulemaker is often in the difficult position of advocating the smoothing out of the sweet spot or eliminating an opening for beating the rule, but then must battle the owners of boats that gain through the very provision calling for revision. Small openings can be handled by grandfathering but are difficult when the gains are large.

It may be unnecessary to point out that it has been the objective of all racing-yacht designers to search for "sweet spots" where the incorporation or omission of some feature or some change in measurement will improve a boat's performance or reduce her rating and so "beat" the rule by optimizing speed versus rating. Serious designers have always sooner or later found such spots or combinations, with the result that new provisions to balance the rule have been added, making rules progressively more complex. Semantics may intrude here as "beating a rule" has much similarity to exploiting a sweet spot. The difference seems one of degree, hard to define, but with respect to the rule sweet spots may be mere ripples in continuity, while ways in which a rule can be beaten may be due to some accidental provision or omission — or a poorly founded assumption with an important effect that must be corrected.

Noted earlier was the American acceptance in the 1920s of the European International Rule in place of our Universal Rule for short-course racing. My own experience centered at first on the metre classes, so designated under the International Rule, which found support in New York before its acceptance in Boston. In designing for International-Rule classes, I sensed an advantage in a high foretriangle and, as a "sweet spot," gained by exploiting the opening. Soon this opening was closed by limiting that height to 75% of the allowed mast height. Similarly, in the early days of the Universal Rule, displacement received too much credit, offering another sweet spot, later closed by a limit on the ratio of displacement to length that could be taken as credit.

My interest soon began to develop in the newer field of rules for offshore racing. In this country that meant the Cruising Club of America (CCA) Rule which had been rewritten in 1934. Due to the important influence of stability on speed, for which ballast ratio was used as an indicator, it became advantageous to use heavy elements in the lower hull for the purpose of lowering the center of gravity, while at the same time improving the rating. This was a way to "beat" the rule. I put it that way because the opening was at first overlooked, rather than misjudged, by the rulemakers. This discussion is pertinent to the recent International Measurement System, the IMS Rule, where benefit had been found in two parameters, center of buoyancy location and prismatic coefficient if altered from the conventional values. Finding this advantage, a sweet spot, has led to expensive hull padding and design alteration, followed by changes in the rule.

In 1931, design competitions were organized on both sides of the ocean with the hope of giving ocean racers better measurements of speed, by using the principal speed-related parameters and giving them a new, and more equitable, balance. The next year the Royal Corinthian Yacht Club of Cowes, England, printed a collection of the more interesting designs, many of which were moderate and attractive. The American competition was less successful. As a sidelight on the British competition, I entered a design which, though not a prize-winner, was published in the printed collection. I am happy to still hold a copy of the book. In 1934 I received a slightly accusatory letter about this design. It was from a Scottish owner who had built to my plans and was disappointed in the boat due to the fact that she seemed tender. Questioning, I found that this yacht, named *Trenchemer*, was built of iron in place of much lighter wood as designed, was short of ballast, and even so was floating deep in the water. I might have washed my hands of the affair, as the use of the drawings was totally unauthorized, but I'm glad I tried to help. I suggested re-ballasting and cutting sail area, so that *Trenchemer* became well-known and successful and eventually came into the hands of her later owner, Bobby Somerset, the great British seaman and Commodore of the Royal Ocean Racing Club. A good deal later, due to a light that had been moved, *Trenchemer* was destroyed by sailing onto a breakwater on the island of Rhodes, costing Bobby his life.

That loss was sad for me as I had been acquainted with Bobby for many years. He was a great sailor and great friend to many. He was the first person to greet *Dorade* when we finished the race to Plymouth in 1931. It was a time not to be forgotten — such an experience for innocents abroad. A later experience with Bobby was strictly business. He had bought the ocean racer *Niña*, and for some legal reason I became her owner of record for an interim period. This was another case of disappointment because, as I recall, the transition from the solid *Jolie Brise* to *Niña*, the quick, heavily ballasted modern ocean racer, caused Bobby to regret the purchase as he sailed into the rough autumn Gulf Stream. So the boat returned quickly to the market. *Niña* was acquired by DeCoursey Fales, in whose ownership she had a long, distinguished life that included, adding to the earlier transAtlantic and Fastnet victories of 1928, a popular Bermuda Race win in 1962. One can ask "What progress in 30-odd years?" or perhaps comment "not a bad rule."

The American design competition in 1931 produced some extreme designs, requiring a further search. My recollection is that the proposed rule was insensitive to length at least if the displacement was generous, as in the early Universal-Rule period, so that some large and potentially powerful and fast boats received low ratings. Today a similar mistake could be made, but would not possibly be so flagrant. Preparing for the Bermuda Race of 1934, the CCA then found a good solution proposed by Wells Lippincott, originally to the Lake Michigan Yacht Racing Association. This introduced a useful organizing principal by defining the proportions of a good all-around boat and then giving penalties and bonuses, estimated to balance departures from the standard according to their influence on speed. The CCA Rule had some good qualities that are tempting today. It was abandoned in favor of the International Offshore Rule (IOR) in 1969, and the IOR was followed by the International Measurement System (IMS).

I sat with the CCA's rules committee either as a member or a technical advisor, a group that consisted at various times of Herbert L. Stone of *Yachting* magazine, Clinton Crane, Wells Lippincott of Chicago, John Alden, Ken Davidson of the towing tank, Arthur Homer and Dan Strohmeier, sailors and shipbuilders, and Bill Lapworth, then a West Coast designer known for his fast Cal 40s. It was a compact group of active sailors and designers who were always ready to make small changes if the premium or penalty needed adjustment. It did not have to deal with the pressures of international involvement. Technical decisions at the time centered on the treatment of displacement. (Surprise?) The Cal 40 with a displacement/length ratio of about 200 was considered light, indicating the narrower range in decision-making that made that period different from today. And decisions were made by the members of a single club with a common image of a good boat. There was no need of wider consultation.

Leading up to the change that came in the late 1960s is the story of several areas of dissatisfaction. Despite broad success there were difficulties in measuring certain values — displacement, for one, and stability. Weighing was logically the way to find displacement, although it troubled me because of the too-frequent, and often substantial, differences I saw, knowing the boats, between floated and weighed displacement. Whether it was the length that was off, or the displacement, the problem was the critical relation between the two.

In some areas it was considered impractical to float for length and immediately weigh a boat. Often delay resulted in weight that changed materially between floating and weighing. How the two relate is an important speed factor. Generally the weight increased after the length was measured, lowering the rating. Stability was even more difficult. Already mentioned was a short time when the ratio of lead ballast to measured displacement was used as an index of stability. Boats with heavy structural parts, contributing to a heavy hull, like the centerboarder *Finisterre*, winner of the 1956 Bermuda Race, with bronze floor timbers, mast step and centerboard trunk, received unrealistically low ratings. Recognizing that ballast ratio was unfair, the use of inclining was substituted. The measured inclination under a known heeling weight gave the righting moment needed by the rule. In this, a theoretically correct method was applied despite possible discrepancies in weight and the difficulty of accurate measurement in anything more than the lightest breeze. Inclining is still used and is still difficult to do accurately. It normally means rising in the very early morning, a quiet time on the water, and this is not always enthusiastically accepted by owners and measurers. A very small angle of inclination can be projected to angles in the sailing range, though hull geometry is increasingly important at wide heel angles.

Sometimes the CCA Rule's base-boat concept seemed restrictive, although it still permitted designers some freedom. If extremes were avoided winners could vary a good deal. Winning S&S designs included *Bolero* among the larger boats and *Finisterre* among smaller ocean racers. The aluminum *Palawan*, one of the best, with her separated keel and rudder and rather narrow beam, was very different, and *Running Tide* was different again. *Finisterre* in '56 was a special case due to the low rating resulting from her heavy backbone structure and extremely low ballast ratio. Yet it is fair to point out that in winning the Bermuda Race for the second and third times in '58 and '60 her stability factor was the realistic result of inclining. Other centerboarders did well, surprisingly well to windward, and various keelboats were winners too. But *Finisterre* had the luck that so often follows good handling.

These conditions continued into the 1960s, during which time the other widely used offshore rule was that of the British Royal Ocean Racing Club. Narrower and deeper, the RORC boats were well-liked until the discovery of a big loophole in the overcompensation for heavy scantlings, the structural elements that assure hull strength. Because of the emergence of GRP (fiberglass) construction with its many variants in density, it was more than ever difficult to frame specific scantling requirements which now called for more than the simple dimensions of structural members. This difficulty gave added impetus to thoughts of change toward a new international offshore-racing rule.

The story of the offshore rules and the eventual adoption of the International Offshore Rule (IOR) and the International Measurement System (IMS) illustrates both the possibilities and the problems that have followed advances in the technical side of yacht design. In the 1960s both the CCA and the RORC were applying well-developed rules for offshore racing. Although good racing had occurred under both rules, undesirable details were recognized in both, and the differences between the two rules had put visitors at a disadvantage in international competition. As that continued to grow in the 'sixties, there were several limited efforts toward unity. The first active move was by a group called to Bremen at the initiative of German and Swedish sailors who invited their British and American counterparts to discuss a common rule in the early summer of 1961. The first simple objective was toward uniform sail measurement so that visitors could avoid the need to recut sails, as was often required by trivial differences in otherwise similar measurement requirements.

In 1965 Dick Carter and his family raced their small *Rabbit* in Europe. Their happy summer was climaxed when they won the Fastnet with the smallest boat of the fleet, and Dick came back to the U.S. to boost international racing with all the enthusiasm of a religious convert. He was completely sold on the newly experienced pleasures of competition in new countries. Evidently Dick had heard that I was working at the same cause, and when we finished a phone conversation I had agreed to set up a lunch at the NYYC, when I could arrange it with Fred Adams, then the CCA Commodore. We duly met only to hear Fred confirm that the idea of a common rule was very much in the wind. It seemed that the International Yacht Racing Union (IYRU) had some thoughts about an offshore class in the Olympics and had asked the RORC and the CCA to try to frame a suitable rule. I don't think Fred mentioned the Olympics at our lunch, and I'm not sure when the subject came up, but when it did Dick's enthusiasm, combined with mine, gave extra support to the idea of developing a new rule. We both thought that the Offshore Rules Coordinating Committee (ORCC), a more formally organized outgrowth of the Bremen group, had the essential international representation and technical expertise to write a good rule.

Whatever the immediate cause, the ORCC became the Offshore Rating Committee (ORC) and in early 1967 accepted the assignment to write the new rule. The CCA appointed Dick and myself as representatives and the ORC made me chairman of the International Technical Committee (ITC) and appointed the two RORC measurers, David Fayle and Robin Glover, as British members. Gustav Plym of Sweden and Ricus van de Stadt of Holland completed the group. We were directed to frame a new rule, combining provisions of the CCA Rule for rig measurement with the RORC Rule for hulls. The efforts of the ITC culminated in the acceptance of a rule known as the International Offshore Rule (IOR).

The ITC members, with the exception of Plym, were active yacht designers or measurers who went about the framing of a new rule much as they would have gone about a new design. Their method can best be described as a combination of comparison and intuition guided by experience. Numerical work had to do with comparing ratings as they might come out under one formula or another and intuitive estimates of a boat's probable speed according to variations among the test parameters. Existing rules offered guidance. After an initial stint of writing while I stayed at the Masters House at Beaulieu in England for frequent meetings with David Fayle, the committee met twice a year, making frequent changes which I will not try to detail. The form of the rule followed that of the RORC with many changes of varying import. Over time many boats were built under the IOR formula and there was good racing. And yet — no surprise — there were increasing concerns about the suitability of winning types for offshore sailing and the matter of stability as the boats became more and more dependent on big, heavy crews on the weather rail.

As the rule approached a workable form, Ricus van de Stadt resigned from the committee to drive home his feeling that the rule was too greatly favoring heavy boats at the expense of those that were lighter. Ironically, as weaknesses developed later, the light boats appeared as the true Achilles heel. Aside from this matter there was little dissension within the committee. However, the by-laws of the ORC require approval of the rule as written or changed by a majority of the council. This came easily at first, but the downside of democracy showed up as faults were found. As chairman, I felt good support in the smaller additions, but changes that seemed radical, or likely to cause boats to change their relative ratings, grew difficult to get through the council, which I felt was overprotective of owners who had found advantage in some provision that might be hurting the fleet from a seagoing view. The complications of a democratically controlled international rule were becoming apparent.

Fleets grew. The Admiral's Cup, sailed in alternate years in the Solent under the IOR, was a showcase of international racing. But, as the fleets matured, vulnerability appeared. From the start the advantage of crew weight on the weather rail was clear. The dependence on point measurement generated unattractive bumps and hollows, leading to unfortunate characteristics. The beamy, shoal hull sections of the winning boats limited the range of positive stability — a dangerous tendency.

Among other hard questions was the matter of scantlings to provide hull strength. The relatively new element, GRP construction, complicated the problem because separate hull parts such as frames and planking were nonexistent in that sort of construction, or well-hidden in one-piece hull moldings and hard to define. Directly coupled to scantlings was stability. Under my own lead we picked a disastrous solution. Hope led to a belief that, if stability were penalized, heavy keels would be discouraged and the weight that might have been ballast would go into hull structure, assuring strength. Where much ballast really went was inside the middle of the boat, to minimize gyradius, presumably improving speed by reducing pitching, and often high up to minimize stability and thus favor rating. I thought this needed change, but the ORC as a group was unwilling to agree to any solution I could suggest because of the inevitable rating changes. Displacement grew lighter than ever, an example of the short-sighted power of those opposed to corrective change. When the danger was first seen, correct action could have been taken to reduce the rating advantage of low stability, and this could have saved lives.

The Fastnet Race of 1979, previously described, had a negative impact on support for the IOR. The weather was severe, especially the steep, breaking seas that hit the smaller boats. This focused attention on the lack of seagoing ability, evidently characteristic of the IOR type, and particularly on the way that yachts with reasonable initial stability might have an inadequate positive stability range to prevent capsize. The smallest boats were the hardest hit. The studies that followed in the U.S. and England resulted in better understanding of what happened and why. In this instance, the roll-overs were evidently caused by the steepness and impact of the seas more than the force of the wind. Even though small changes were made in the rule regarding stability, the beamy, shoal-bodied type continued to characterize the winners. The need for scantling rules was felt with new urgency.

I had come back a short time before to head the ITC and was in the process of turning over the chair to Gary Mull. An American yacht designer, based in the San Francisco Bay area, Gary had a quick intelligence and a good engineering background. He had been on the ITC for several years and knew the problems. I felt unable to convince the "no big change" group that new hull-form parameters were needed in the area of stability, but the need for some new control of scantlings was recognized by the council members.

For a short time I was on the visiting board of the American Bureau of Shipping (ABS) and had friends there who were interested in sailing and would support the study of our needs, primarily regulating GRP hulls. On this Gary made a breakthrough when he suggested that strength could be assured by simply requiring strength itself rather than specifying dimensions for framing, planking or decking. Gary suggested requiring that specified hull areas should be able to withstand specified loads, related to boat size and potential speed. Suitable engineering formulas could be entered with the tested physical characteristics of the construction material, to determine the ability of that material as formulated to support the required loads. Thus, any one of a wide range of possible materials could be used as long as they had the strength. That could be found by test. We had the full cooperation of the ABS, particularly in the person of Bob Curry, in writing, checking, and applying this principle. ABS guidance has been an important, healthy influence on the construction of yachts, although my opinion is that the specified strength is marginal. Now, regrettably, after nearly 20 years of plan approval, and stronger boats, the expense has become too great and the Bureau has had to withdraw from covering boats of less than 80′ in length.

I have pointed to the fact that many, especially in America, and including myself, found the newer IOR boats poorly suited to offshore racing. Criticism on that score had force, and the search for improvement centered on a study at MIT concerning computer methods of applying sailing theory. Nick Newman's papers of 1973 and 1975, previously mentioned, coming as they did from an active offshore sailor who was an MIT professor of naval architecture, were persuasive in pointing out the possibility of applying these newly developed scientific methods to rating-rule formulation. This study, which had been independently begun at MIT, grew into the Pratt Project previously discussed. VPP application was its most radical feature and its most valuable.

The VPP-based multi-rating IMS administered by the ORC is current as this is written. It has generated controversy, and its future is in doubt, as is the nature of a possible replacement. I think we should look at some of the reasons why, and some of the possibilities. There is a strong trend toward one-design sailing. This has a lot to recommend it to the sailors, but as the classes grow and multiply there will be inter-class competition, and this will require some rule to recognize the potential of each and to level the competition.

When the MIT suggestions were first made, the Americans were quick and confident in the new, while the British held back with well-justified doubts. I still feel "nothing ventured, nothing gained." Over time in the U.S. (1978) and eventually around the world (1985) the variable rating, which matches course and weather, came into being and was tried with results that are still controversial. It was hoped that by giving owners a wide option in boat type, and by providing an unbiased speed prediction, every owner could race the all-purpose boat he liked best without diminishing his chance of winning.

The Measurement Handicap System (MHS, later named IMS) with its dependence on the VPP, was indeed a new and radical rating system. The time required by any boat around any course under any conditions could be predicted. Maybe. Although it was anticipated as an important forward step, that promise has backfired. This is multi-rating, meaning a different rating (speed) to match each boat's ability with the day's course and wind. That sounds ideal, but there is a catch in the dependence of the speed prediction on the predictability of the weather. An example occurred in an early test of the rule: the 1980 race to Bermuda. Allowances were determined for the expected close reach with some windward work. The race was a broad reach all the way, and the easy winner was strictly a non-racer, good for the reaching course and an excellent cruiser. There were howls of objection because the winner was not a winning type and "should not" have won. But wasn't the rule intended to give everyone a chance, and hadn't that happened? True enough, except that the results were not even close.

The uncertainties of wind strength presented a problem fundamental to a multi-rating system, and this was largely solved by the application of Alan McIlhenny's PCS scoring system in which the wind strength is found through boat speed. Many sailors felt this made it difficult to find their boat's position during the race. More recently, a closely related system to do that, easily applied, has been worked out in the form of PLS.

Wind direction relative to course remains a troublesome problem. My response is twofold: In long races geography will provide clues to prevailing or average winds. As an alternative there is a broadly average ocean-racing course on each certificate. This is safe to use when in doubt. In short races it is usually possible to lay courses to match the wind. If such possibilities do not exist, I'd take a single number, using expected average conditions, with full confidence that the VPP-based rule was fairer than any rule of the past. I intend to return to a more esoteric discussion of multi-rating.

The Performance Handicap Rating Fleet (PHRF) and Channel Handicap (now IR 2000) are handicap systems which reflect actual recorded performance, and they please the majority of racing sailors. Measured by the number of new classes, one-design racing seems to be meeting the needs of many owners. Either PHRF or IR 2000 can be a good solution. There are, however, some conditions where they are not appropriate. To repeat, it seems certain that the owners of some one-design boats will want to test their ability against the obvious competition in other classes, leading to the demand for suitable ratings. New contestants will be found for this and other reasons.

Grand Prix racing is one such example. There are throughout the sport owners who enjoy a contest that includes the technology of their equipment — design, construction, sails, and electronics — and who consider that, for racing at the top level, any subjective element is out of place. For them, it distorts an important objective: the determination of the best boat. When that is the purpose, a good rating rule similar to IMS must be the answer. Rating rules tend to keep yacht designers busy. The ultimate objective, to provide a good race to many differing boats, is hard to meet without looking to known performance for guidance.

There are other cases where the motivation is not so clear, but where subjective elements cause the performance-adjusted handicapping process to fall down. This can happen when races are sailed under conditions that require revised performance standards, because of different sailing weather, such as north or south or east or west coasts, so that a boat with one handicap rating sails in a new area with a new handicap rating. A similar condition exists in many long races when the performance of a fleet or a particular boat has no history. Also, perish the thought, personal judgement or prejudice may result in the award of a debatable rating. Subjectivity can be a misleading influence.

Considering the effect of ratings on race results, whether around the buoys or across the oceans, it should be no surprise that some owners spend incredible sums for the advantage of a few seconds a mile from their ratings, and designers work overtime at their computers searching for rule provisions that may lead to that result. The higher the level of the racing, the more intense are the efforts to gain the advantage of a very few seconds. Often this results in expensive alterations in hull or rig to take advantage of some provision that has had unanticipated effects. Often, too, such provisions by those who have drafted the rule have given openings for new combinations of factors that produce a low rating, and the designer is considered a "rule-beater" (not necessarily a derogatory term) when he makes a useful discovery. Rule management and analysis has interested me from way back because the success of any racing yacht depends on how well it fits the rule.

Reviewing the fundamentals, the flexibility of the IMS has promised to bring corrected times closer, even as the suitability of boats to conditions varies. That is its very *raison d'etre*. But that promise has frequently been turned on its head to become its main fault. To me it does not seem that the objectivity and thoughtfulness the subject deserves have been applied to discussing the pros and cons of this multi-valued VPP-based rule vs. the single-valued rating.

Two facts lie in the background of this discussion of the late 1970s. It had grown clear under IMS that boat types were forming to meet the expected conditions, designed so that their measurements suited expected wind strengths and directions, and further that these types seldom met owners' hopes in terms of suitability for cruising. The existing ability to tune a rule to a boat's performance was not then being employed. Technical studies resulted in the design of an all-condition VPP which was adopted in America as MHS, later to be applied internationally as IMS. We are still debating whether and how to make this work.

The questions that remain regarding the pros and cons of a multi-rating, VPP-based, system against a single-number system seem to me dependent on the intensity of the competition. Surely when competition is keen the multi-rating system spreads the opportunities better among a range of varied designs, while the single number must result in type-forming, with a single type holding the advantage. When uncertain weather or course conditions deter multi-rating, there is the option of the ocean-racing course. Or some average using a rough guess at conditions can be applied giving a better estimate of performance than any existing rule. True, every time a single number is used some boats are helped and some boats are hurt. If this increases the element of luck, is that always bad? I do not hesitate to support that when appropriate, but most of the time a better option remains. One chooses what one wants, but the potential of good racing in a varied fleet has more appeal to some of us than the single-number approach that tends toward questionable type-forming or one-design.

Because I see a system or rule based on a good VPP as ideal, my concern with recent problems may have made me impatient with the lapses I have seen in committee work on the rule. I believe that despite its complexity and expense, sailors (or should I say rulemakers?) had become dissatisfied with single numbers and were ready for the VPP by the late 1970s. It was hoped, particularly by advocates of offshore racing in conservative vessels, that the IMS, in its ability to treat various conditions, would open the door to a wide choice of types. Despite these hopes, acceptance in the form of the IMS has been spotty at best. The number of rated boats has been good in Italy and Holland, and in Grand Prix racing more widely, but has never been popular in England and has declined in the U.S. I have always thought that Solent conditions make it a poor spot for multi-ratings.

To reasonably predict a boat's performance over the full range of conditions requires full information on its geometry — basically, its lines. A single number, needing much less detail, can be grounded on simple measurements. Its existence does not require its use in every race. Yet a single rating, a speed estimate, can always be chosen from a VPP, given an assumption of conditions. But, in addition to more complete measurement, the course and weather conditions must also be known or assumed for the VPP. On the other hand, the single number is necessarily a compromise in the ability to balance different types; it can never be adapted to boat type as it suits course conditions. Neither will the simplicity of the single number eliminate the need for lines unless we are willing to settle for the unhappy bumps and hollows that were a consequence of the IOR Rule.

The large file of measurements to access the lines needed for the VPP makes for expense and hassle in measurement and administration, and this has limited fleets largely to the more refined and expensive boats. New certificates such as IMS Club have already eased that situation. Today, such certificates greatly reduce the cost and difficulty of measurement. But the question persists: is the single number or the VPP-based rule the better choice? If it is true that some boats like certain conditions and others do better when conditions are reversed, while still others are faster upwind than down, and vice-versa, it seems clear that the VPP can provide closer racing, which in turn means better sport. This is what the IMS aims to provide.

It is important to recognize, however, that good local management is the key to good IMS racing. This has been shown by the success of IMS in Italy and Holland.

Present problems are concerned with the VPP as well as the scoring. Although a good start was made with MHS, speed prediction has become increasingly difficult. It is good but not as good as it should be. The VPP is the key to predicting speed from given conditions. In principle it is relatively simple, balancing the driving and resisting forces. After assuming wind conditions, apparent velocity and angle are found for an assumed boat speed in order to give the sail drive. With drive, the assumed speed can be corrected and the sail driving force recomputed for the new speed, in a loop, thus taking steps toward convergence. The elements of hull drag are summed up over the needed speed range and the speed when the drag equals the computed drive is selected. Due to the coupling of forces, the process of optimization is more complex. Because the present VPP has grown like Topsy, still in the computer language Fortran (needed when the program was written more than 20 years ago, but now largely replaced by Basic) it is difficult for many of those interested to read and understand. It has been a plea of mine since I joined the American IMS Committee that this, the body of the rule, should be transparent and easily understood by all committee members and others who are interested. Lip service has been given regularly to the ideal, but it seems farther and farther distant.

I will try to skip detailed criticism in the belief that better days are coming, but I wish to outline some concerns: first an old cry of mine, "Make no allowance for towing the bucket." To minimize type-forming we must predict the best a boat can do, given its proportions and dimensions. Next, the VPP should be made much simpler to use and understand. If the form of the VPP were brought up to date, completely rewritten, each element of drive or drag could be calculated in its own routine or sub-program. Each module could clearly show the way that element was computed, and each could be altered when necessary with predictable results. The overall answer would emerge and the effect of altering any individual routine could be immediately seen.

Further, the underlying data is out of date. The hull drag has been derived from a set of models unlike any boats, old or new, that are racing today, and the method of finding drag by regression has given undue weight to the worst models. In the original MHS the hull drags came from fewer measurements, making them less subject to the manipulation that has necessitated last-minute changes. On the other side of the equation the table of forces delivered by the sails badly needs updating. Sail forces, first brilliantly determined, have been widely studied and now could be greatly improved with new methods.

The objective must be to design a rugged VPP that is resistant to manipulation. The lesson of the CCA Rule should be remembered: type-forming is inevitable, so let's form a type we like by discouraging extremes. The range of acceptable dimensions should be as wide as possible, but raised toward the limits, to minimize departures. The best available data must be used to predict speed, correctly and over a range of types. Individual models have received too much weight. Better models are now being tested. Regression must be a useful guide, but it needs to be thoughtfully applied. And it needs a good data base — one as large and as varied as possible. I believe in severely restricting the number and force of parameters expected to cause drag, as they will lower rating and, if judicially incorporated in a design, can be used to reduce rating more than they hurt performance. For top-level racing, no allowance should be made for less than optimum design, which to me is towing the bucket. Good predictions must assume good designs.

Here we must ask how to treat boats that are not among the best, boats that cannot compete because they have to tow the bucket. Must they join the handicap classes? If it is hard to predict the best accurately, is it not much more difficult to provide for the many factors that reduce performance? Today my thought would be to provide a separate class rule which may be less sophisticated but could be more easily adjusted.

Another possible alternative may be found in club ratings which are available to boats of most production classes. For less-intense racing widened use of low-cost ratings from sistership or club ratings are an alternative. For that purpose a related, variable rating rule known as Americap is being introduced. It uses the simplified PCS method of determining wind strength. The principle is appealing, although I regret some of the circumstances of its beginning. Long association and appreciation tie my loyalty to the ORC, which was not consulted on the American move. That organization warrants full support. Long experience with rating rules has shown me how difficult it is to satisfy conflicting demands. The ORC has also seen the need of a similar rule. I am an Anglophile in appreciation of the British feeling for order and fair play, as well as the British willingness to give offshore rules a good home. In contrast, I share a more American wish to give fair ratings — i.e., a fair chance to win — to wholesome, safe, seagoing types.

Most of today's boats are disappointing to me. That expresses a feeling more than a conviction, though the conviction is that they are uncomfortable and not pretty, while the feeling is that they are less safe than I should prefer. Generally, they are liked by today's sailors. The more extreme types such as the Around Alone singlehanders have been, on the evidence, unsafe. The IMS types and others like them have had a good safety record but have not been tested to a limit, unless you include the Whitbread competitors. They have survived hard driving under extreme conditions, for which the designers deserve more credit than the rule. Under the IMS Rule, rig failures show the need for rig scantlings. The stock boats vary but habitually appear too much like the racers, and are over-crowded with berths and comforts.

A rule that is accurate and robust demands individual and complete measurement. Highly competitive racing under a rating rule offers no alternative. Informal "beer-can" or Wednesday-evening racing can flourish using less formal ratings such as those just discussed, builders' declaration, or some form of self-measurement. The two rules cannot well be combined. Good racing demands that the competitors all share the same attitude toward the competition. The deep pocket or the sailor ready to "do anything to win" does not fit into a fleet whose sailors have a less-intense attitude. Each can enjoy racing against his peers, but not across the line. I am not much concerned with professionalism in that sense; most sailors enjoy competing with the best. Under present rules I would have been a professional, missing some great sailing opportunities. My competitive sailing days are over, but I think I would resent being considered a pro. I don't know just why. I suppose that hints at my feelings. I think good sailors become better sailors competing against the best. I am more concerned about sponsorship, which I think is too often a factor in releasing a sailor from the responsibilities of sportsmanship.

To me, the activities of using and composing rules has become a sort of swamp, but fascinating still. The options and possibilities are enormous. Hope, difficulty, success, and failure have been entwined as long as I have known rules, and history says that the problems and the successes go back and back. That is likely to continue.

ly in 1978 we sold our house in Scarsdale and moved
our partially completed house in Putney, Vermont.
nd this move is the story of a Christmas with our son,
, at his house in Newfane nearby. This was in '72 or
when we — that is Olie and his wife-to-be Carol,
and his then-wife, Nancy, and Susie and I — were
rised to receive gifts from Olie of cross-country skiing
pment, skis, boots and poles. Naturally, we had to try
g and, during following winters, we made good use
e gifts. We particularly enjoyed the days spent on
fane Hill, the original site of the town when height
red some protection from the Indians and before the
roads penetrated the valleys. The white landscape
ently brought us back as did the fun of being with
family. Sometimes we carried a lunch of wine and
se and cookies. They were good days.

On page 228 is a partial view of the Putney house, looking northwest. The house was completed in 1978 by son Sam to plans of mine. The land, at the top of a ridge, slopes both left and right, opening wide on the west to a view of the ski slopes of southern Vermont, Mount Snow, Stratton and Bromley. We looked over rolling hills that might have been ocean waves, constantly enjoying the landscape and the spectacular sunsets.

(Photo: Author's Collection)

Olie was working as a real-estate broker and we asked him to check out land that afforded the views we had enjoyed. The period was inflationary and I thought a modest investment in land was unlikely to go wrong. In a while, he reported that some land on Newfane Hill was available but that it was a long way from power or phone service. This led us to count less on that location, although thoughts of an occasional retreat, not quite so far from the rest of the world, kept recurring. As one thing leads to another Olie came back to us, describing an area with the sort of view that had attracted us, and yet within reach of power. We wound up buying about 40 acres on Putney Mountain, a high wooded ridge, close to Newfane, with long views both east and west.

After a year or so, busy with my work but quiet otherwise, Susie and I began to think about the smallest comfortable shelter. On family visits we looked at examples of local work to learn something about structures and costs and began to discuss possibilities with our carpenter son, Sam. We had grown up in the expanding Scarsdale area where exploring houses under construction was often a weekend pastime and we had a joint interest in new architecture. Our friend, Don deBogdan, architect of two houses we had built, was no longer living, and I started making sketches on my own.

I was bounded by certain principles. We wanted a house easy to build and maintain, small but comfortable for two people, and convenient to expand. We wanted a generally open plan, exposing the view which was generator of the project. We felt the cooking area should receive the morning sun. Our first serious sketches were enclosed by a rectangle which measured 22′ by 35′, the axis roughly north and south with a large chimney about ten feet in from the south wall to partially separate the kitchen and dining areas from the living room. In turn, a 7′-high partition sheltered the bedroom and bathroom areas at the far end. We talked with Sam and settled a few details. We could use a shed roof with the 22′ span. We would build on a concrete slab under a slate floor, with the entire west face, toward a really great view, opened by sliding glass doors. We would heat with a combination of wood and electricity. The chimney opened a fireplace toward the living room and the flue from a wood stove opposite. We all agreed that this was workable and that we would go ahead at a yet-to-be-determined "soon."

As these ideas were developing I was becoming uneasy in the office. The thought of retirement, perhaps vague, was there. Gil Wyland, on whom I counted so much, had not been well and retired to do what work he could at home. A very hard day came for me when I had to discharge the man on whom I counted most after Rod and Gil, because of a continuing personal problem that made it impossible for him to stay on. (I am pleased to say that he is now back at the office.) We had

The Sheffield house, built in the eighteenth century, was our retreat during many happy summers. It was a good summer home, often comfortably occupied by four adults and four boys — our family and that of Susie's brother. Eventually it seemed a good deal to care for, especially in winter, and we moved north to a less-demanding old house in Walpole, New Hampshire, in 1980.

(Photo: Author's Collection)

experienced at least two lawsuits, one settled because of the client's eventual good will, and the other costing our insurance $10,000 for something not of our doing. (Errors and Omissions insurance has since become prohibitively costly.) I was rather frightened by responsibilities not only legal but inherent in sailing. I was also fed up with commuting. Our America's Cup efforts were successful, but those responsible were unwilling to spend on experimental research, and the new offshore racers were winning less frequently. Computers were coming into the office, while I had to spend my time on the phone or writing letters. I became excited when IBM friends let me borrow a computer for a short time at home, but I could not afford to buy it at its cost in the middle of the 1970s. Eventually this all added up to the decision that 50 years was long enough to stay with one thing, and I decided to retire officially on my 70th birthday in 1978. We could sell the house in Scarsdale and live in the family country house in Sheffield, Massachusetts.

As we considered the possibilities, the idea of Vermont had more and more appeal. Both sons were in the area. Susie and I both loved the mountains. I had traveled often to Sugar Hill, New Hampshire, in our courting days, and after marrying in October, 1930, we had gone up to the White Mountains almost every fall. We cheated a little on the exact anniversary date to see the best foliage and often met the snow on the mountain tops around Franconia and further north. I had very similar feelings about the mountains and the sea.

We hated to give up Sheffield, which had become very much a home, but the lovely old house was on a more and more traveled road; and, attractive as it was, the place was right under a high hill, locally Mt. Washington, which insured cool evenings on the hot days of summer but early darkness and cold nights during the winter. With related thoughts getting clearer we studied the expansion of our Putney plans and located an extra bedroom and bath on the northeast corner of our rectangle. So early in 1977 we made arrangements with Sam for him to start building. A driveway to the top and a drilled well were the first steps.

Not surprisingly, the problems of being the architect of a house were not all new to a designer of yachts. In some ways the father/son relationship helped, though maybe not always. Sam has a quick temper, but it quickly passes. He had his heart in the work. I knew that it could be hard to satisfy the builder who might have either too much or too little detail. Invariably the builder wants the plans sooner than they can be done, and if done in good season many changes seem to follow. In the end Sam and I were proud of the house. We moved in, despite Sam, early in the summer of '78 in order to justify the move from New York State to Vermont without a way point in Massachusetts. If much furniture was temporarily stored in the new bedroom that was acceptable. The view was all we had hoped.

The house worked well. As planned, it was comfortable to live in and easy to maintain. The fireplace drew well and the water was easy to drain when we closed in late fall or early winter. Heating arrangements were adequate to warm the house: we had planned the electric heat at about two-thirds the recommended winter capacity and the fireplace and wood stove made up the difference. The first year we stayed well into January. The biggest winter problem was access. A generous neighbor kept the long, steep drive open until we left but said we could not expect it another year, pointing out that he was able to plow his own drive from top down, which was much easier than doing ours in the reverse direction. We had never planned to stay all winter but the view was hard to give up. Testing the new house had been fun.

Our plans were not as firm as they might have been. Sheffield was okay for the winter and we held on, but really expected to find a place in the south to enjoy the deep winter months. In '78 we had Christmas in Putney. In '79 we had moved to

Sheffield after Thanksgiving and returned to Olie's in Newfane for Christmas. In both years we toured the south by car without being seriously attracted anywhere. We agreed that Sheffield would not be a permanent winter solution and decided to look for a winter place close to Putney. We were attracted to the town of Walpole, New Hampshire, and a house we saw there. So when we learned, (a lucky surprise!) the kind of value we had in the Sheffield property, we agreed that the Walpole move would be the right one for us.

To some of our friends this decision to have two homes so close together seemed strange, but we spent a number of happy winters in Walpole, and mud season to late fall in Putney, and had no regrets about the move. The one-hour drive between the two houses made it easy to keep an eye on both, and easy to make the moves in fall and spring. While the climate in Walpole was almost the same as Putney, we enjoyed the changing seasons. The surroundings, town and house, were completely different. Susie truly enjoyed the house. When she first saw it she had said she could immediately place every piece of the Sheffield furniture. The house was built in 1844, Federal-style, for a well-to-do doctor. Since that time plumbing, heating, and electricity had been installed with a good recent kitchen in the original space. The rest of the house was unchanged, including a large stable with two open stalls and a box stall built of chestnut. Neither house was aggressive in its style but the seasonal alteration between the clean, open plan of Putney and the set of boxes, as in Walpole, became a refreshing change. We were also close to good neighbors in both places, but closer in Walpole where we formed good friendships with next-door families.

In Walpole we moved into a lived-in, complete house, changed only by our own things. In Putney almost everything was new. We became busy with planting and gardening, although this was in no way ambitious. While not explicitly Japanese, we both admired that style which seemed directed toward simply doing our best with natural features and making the planting attractive from indoors and developing the surroundings for pleasant views of the house. Wide open for the western view, there was a good deal of shade in the east and we planted some perennials that would do well in the shade. Such as it was, it was very informal, but we enjoyed working at it and were pleased with the results.

I was well-satisfied with the decision to retire, feeling relieved and happy to be free of commuting and the office routine, and I fully enjoyed being in the country. From the house we looked west over the mountains and ski areas, with Mt. Snow almost straight out, Stratton in the middle and Bromley to the right. Our old love, Newfane Hill, was across the valley to the left. The hills between had the shapes of waves at sea and the sunsets were beyond description.

Retirement went well with one exception, which was Susie's concern over my increasing commitment to the computer, a degree of selfishness which I have to admit. Some time after getting over the shock of the IBM price and after leaving the office I learned of a semi-portable Hewlett-Packard machine fitted with its own small monitor and printer at a price that was still steep enough, but which I felt I could afford. It was delivered just before we started on a winter trip south and I took it along. I first had a chance to try it out when we stayed a few days with Susie's sister-in-law in Charlotte, North Carolina. I was hooked and still allow the computer to rule my time.

I hope that my absorption in the computer has not been wasted time. It has made it possible for me to stay active and interested in yacht matters, which I can study now with little competitive bias, and in that respect some ability to use a computer has been beneficial. I go further into this activity in another place, but the other side is that Susie had a different picture of my retirement. This included expectations of my renewed efforts to paint, to spend a lot of time fishing, which I had enjoyed when I could, and probably more varied reading than the technical and computer-oriented fare that had become my staple. I shared these plans in the very beginning, and I think it hurt her more than I realized when she felt that I was in the end hurting myself.

My own efforts with the computer coincided with interest in the MHS Rule for rating offshore sailing boats. This is another story, described in a previous chapter, except as it bears on my activities after moving to the country. Soon after moving I became a member of the MHS technical committee, formed to guide the computer-generated rule which applied a VPP to predict the performance of each individual boat under a wide range of conditions. The Pratt Project at MIT had written the VPP in a more advanced computer language (Fortran) than I could handle, but Patrick Haggerty had arranged for Dr. John Letcher to write a simpler, Basic-language version which, with John's help, I learned to use. This was a great help in considering the workings of the rule, and I have told how I have remained on the committee still working to make IMS — the successor to MHS — a better and fairer way to order boats in a race. I am still behind other committee members with better math understanding, as we constantly move toward more advanced rule applications. I am still trying to understand and review the finer points of rule-making. I am not a quick study and it takes me a lot of time to understand the many aspects of constantly developing rules.

Bearing on this is the story of another America's Cup campaign. Following *Courageous'* America's Cup defense of '77, a match was coming in 1980 and S&S had a new boat to do. Although Bill Langan was now chief designer I think it is fair to say that I stayed very close to the development of this design, which was almost a duplicate of *Courageous*, so that I have willingly accepted *Freedom* as one of my designs. Unfortunately there were minimal funds provided for experiment or

research, so that we simply retested an existing *Courageous* model with some very minor changes, slightly lowering freeboard in exchange for a small penalty in sail area and snubbing the leading edge of the forefoot and keel in the hope of minimizing flow separation and induced drag in the course of tacking. We knew that Dennis Conner, who would be sailing the new boat, was an aggressive sailor who would be likely to tack often in the course of a race. Fortunately, *Freedom* turned out well enough to win in 1980, but this seemed to convince Dennis even further that the way to success lay entirely in handling and sails rather than expensive design studies. To me this is the short answer to why we lost the America's Cup three years later.

It was in the prelude to this campaign that Dennis, extravagantly, but in an otherwise laudable effort to be well-prepared, started sailing a year earlier than had been customary. *Freedom* came out in May of 1979 with *Enterprise* as a very capable trial horse. They worked out together that summer in Newport, and even continued in California during the winter, before they returned thoroughly ready for the Newport trials of 1980. This was a long step in the constant march toward a more expensive America's Cup.

After the trials, *Freedom* was selected as defender. This time the Cup match against Alan Bond's *Australia* was a little closer than it had been since 1970. In two races the winning margin was less than a minute, and in one *Australia* was the winner.

That summer, 1980, was the last during which I spent most of my time with the crew in Newport. I had done this because of the urgency with which I viewed anything that had to do with the America's Cup. I never knew just what my presence contributed, but I was never idle, although a lot of time went into watching either races or tune-up trials. I was listed officially as a crew member and often sailed on one or another of the boats and occasionally steered so as to get to know how well the boat balanced and handled. I think the skipper and manager liked having the designer on the spot. If something broke it was useful to be close enough to find the reason and present a solution for a better fix. Also I was in a position to watch the sails from off the boat and to participate in decisions to order new sails or alter old ones. As in the case of the never-ending yard work, it is hard to say exactly what I did, but I was made welcome and I was glad to be there.

Even so, I felt that there should be a separate and regular designer's representative in the camp to do leg work of a semi-clerical nature. This man was responsible for contacts with the shipyard by preparing and presenting the many lists of required work and for seeing that it was accomplished as needed. He kept a set of plans always available and up-to-date. He kept a record of such tuning activities as mast adjustments in the form of the number of turns taken up or loosened on the rigging rods. I felt entitled to participate in decisions without having to accept responsibility for their execution, which still had to be done systematically. This was a full-time job, ordinarily continued in Newport by a "project engineer" who from the start had been responsiible for keeping the elements in order.

Mentioned elsewhere is my view of the apparent failure of the small models used in most earlier design studies. That failure virtually dictated the use of much larger models, meaning a scale of one-third full-scale length in place of one-thirteenth. As the cost ratio approximated the weight ratio, which was as the cube of the lengths, the numbers indicate a possible increase of 81 times. It was not quite that much, but the cost was suddenly multiplied by a factor of, say, 40, and this meant $25,000 to $1 million for an equivalent schedule of tests. Until the urge to get the Cup back was felt in full force, that equivalence drastically reduced the number of model variations that could be tested. Even a fivefold increase would pay for testing no more than one model. At least one of our earlier small-scale study campaigns used as many as seven models, and with individual modifications, more than 30 different configurations. We had continued testing until we were confident that we had a winner. We were badly fooled just once.

Having become dedicated to holding the Cup, I felt severely restricted in the experimentation that was permissible within budget limits. Unfortunately the need for the larger research budget was swamped by a general feeling that design development had reached a plateau and was unlikely to advance further. This fed a case of self-fulfillment, as the obvious similarity of the new and older boats was coupled with the temporarily proven fact that the American boats could still win. So why pay big bucks to give the designer useless fun? I remember one evening at the New York Yacht Club when the technological guru, Karl Kirkman, warned of the danger of this course, and I tried to speak as a friendly witness. We were not heard until too late.

This was prologue to 1983, when we lost the Cup to the well-backed research supported by Australia's Alan Bond. The summer was not without controversy. Bond's designer was Ben Lexcen, an Australian who was quite legally running model tests in a Dutch towing tank, as Australia had no corresponding facility. In the normal course of reporting and discussing results, consideration was given to the resistance element known as induced drag, which seemed greater than would have been the case had the model shown better ability to support side force. As induced drag is a big part of the drag of aircraft it was agreed to discuss, with an expert in aerodynamics, possible means of reducing that element. An aerodynamicist relates induced drag to aspect ratio, the ratio of wing span to chord, equivalent to the draft-to-length ratio of the keel, which in a yacht hull is very low compared with an airplane wing. This is especially disadvantageous in the limited draft of the International Rule classes, and so an aerodynamicist will be thinking about what might help. The cause of induced drag is the absorption of lifting power by a vortex generated by

differences in pressure between the two surfaces of the wing or keel as they meet and swirl at the tip. With the limited draft of the keel of a Twelve Metre a large proportion of the total lift, here side force, is close to the tip of the keel rather than being spread along the span of an airplane wing, making the induced drag great in proportion to the lift. To visualize this phenomenon is to realize the possibility of reducing drag by impeding the cross flow under the keel. Horizontal surfaces, wings, occur as an answer, and these were found to work when tested.

In such cases very little is free gain, though sometimes advantages can be cumulative. In the case of Lexcen's keel design the wings became added wetted area, increasing friction drag, but if made heavy, as out of lead, the yacht's center of gravity could be lowered, increasing stability and making it possible to reduce length and displacement while winning back sail area. These departures from the stagnant character of the competition were balanced favorably by improving windward performance — when induced drag was important — and by adding sail to overcome the added friction drag of the wings. It is unnecessary to add that this was a winning combination. Dennis Conner's candidate for defense was *Liberty*, a new boat designed by Johan Valentin, another designer somewhat involved in controversy, still to be discussed.

Competing with Dennis, the other competitors for the defense consisted of the Dave Pedrick design *Defender*, and her stablemate *Courageous*, altered under Bill Langan's direction. It was disappointing to me that *Freedom* was no longer eligible as a Twelve Metre. Her freeboard was below new requirements; had she not been altered after her successful defense of the Cup in 1980 her "grandfathered" status would have made her legal. Despite *Australia II*'s wing keel, I felt that *Freedom* could have been a successful defender. As it was, *Courageous* frequently beat *Defender* and gave *Liberty* some good competition; nevertheless, *Liberty* earned the right to defend the Cup.

Alan Bond meanwhile had dominated the challenger trials, easily beating boats from England, France, Canada, and Italy. His *Australia II*'s wing keel was a successful innovation in yacht design and became a pattern for the keels of future Twelves, whose moderate draft made it particularly effective. The wings as hardware and the source of the advice that led to their use caused no little controversy in New York and Newport, which collapsed when it was confirmed that the international measurement body had given advance approval of this feature.

The American, and losing, side of the 1983 Cup summer was one with problems and events that have been reported from many angles. I will try to be brief. I was there, although not as designer. S&S, directed by Bill Langan, was in Dennis' group but as one of two designers, the other being Johan Valentin. Again, Dennis started early. Two boats were built, one to each design, for winter trials in California early in

On the opposite page we see the afternoon when the America's Cup left America. *Liberty*, above, and *Australia II*, are even on the final run in the 7th race, September 26, 1983. *Australia II* pulled ahead at the lee mark and kept *Liberty* covered on the beat to the finish, winning by 41 seconds.

(Photo: Dan Nerney)

1982. Neither was considered good enough. A new boat was accepted as needed for the race year of 1983. Whose design would it be? My story is that after a general discussion the principal characteristics were agreed upon and it was further agreed that, because S&S had on the staff an excellent lines draftsman in the person of Mario Tarabocchia, he would draw lines acceptable to both Johan and Bill Langan of S&S. If they disagreed I was to be the arbitrator with the final word. This was done, and I was told that Johan had visited and approved the lines as drawn. The next day I heard that Johan had disapproved and was to design the new boat. This was obviously a shock and it led to bad feelings. Although I have never had an explanation, I think I may have *the* explanation.

When the new *Liberty* came out and raced with success, it was noted that she floated differently on different race days, and it was eventually learned that the technical powers that be had approved the use of two sets of marks on the hull and rig so that, according to the weather forecast the evening before a race, one of two alternate measurement certificates could be express validated, permitting ballast to be added for strong winds and removed for light weather. Sail area was also adjusted to the altered hull measurements. In one sense the rule of one certificate had not been broken, but this was possible only with a double set of pre-measured marks. I had always assumed that a new measurement required a newly measured hull. I still do.

Dennis had broached this to me some time earlier and I had said it was illegal, understanding and supporting the principle that no boat could have more than one certificate to a given rule at any one time. To use two certificates efficiently the slope of the overhangs must be made so that length and displacement must be coordinated at both levels of flotation. Apparently after learning that I was wrong in the eyes of those responsible, Dennis did not want to let the cat out of the bag. Today I don't know how far this idea was ever carried. It has dropped out of use with the end of new construction of Twelve Metres. But if it were being applied today, and I knew of it, I would go to bat against it in the hope of avoiding chaos.

The final series was still close. Dennis Conner's sailing was excellent, even though his judgement in the final, losing race has been questioned. He won twice when difficulties with steering gear and mast handicapped the faster boat, and a third time on his handling. Meanwhile *Australia II* had taken just one race. Then she won twice, only to see *Liberty*, in the seventh and final race, in the lead running toward the bottom mark. Approaching that mark before the last beat to the finish, *Liberty*'s lead was lost when Dennis let the faster boat split, believing that she was gaining so fast that she would surely pass him. This gamble, though probably necessary, failed. At the lee mark *Australia II* took the lead. Though Dennis seemed to do well on the final beat, overtaking was impossible. The America's Cup was lost.

Challenges came in fast to the Royal Perth Yacht Club in Western Australia.

Fremantle was the designated site of the match and January of 1987 the date. Matching the winner's pattern, preparations were intense and thorough. Tank tests and computer simulations were many and thorough, and were undertaken by challengers representing the U.S.A. (six groups), Great Britain, France, Italy, Canada, New Zealand, and Australia with challenging and defending syndicates.

In most cases, individual designers became groups supported by teams that included specalists in computer studies of hydrodynamics. Costs climbed with little or no restraint. Special emphasis was placed on keel studies and the use of keel wings, which were evaluated by tank and computer in great variety. There was corresponding activity on the waterfront, where the different groups arranged yard support or leased property to build their own facilities for hauling and overhauling at least two boats. These working areas were matched by the renting of properties suitable for the housing and feeding of two crews with their support. Two of the American groups representing the yacht clubs of San Diego and New York were particularly active.

The combined scientific methods applied in the design of these new America's Cup boats suggested a pattern now used widely in high-profile racing yacht design. A design coordinator led a group with expertise in a number of applicable fields which included hull design, model testing, computer simulation, aerodynamics, and game theory. Computer use made it possible to explore a wide range of dimensions and shapes with results that could be predicted by computers and checked by models. Alternatively, models provided anchor points from which the effects of moderate departures could be reliably predicted. Full-scale testing, though limited, gave positive confirmation. The aircraft field had pioneered this approach and it has worked well for yachts. In retrospect the application of game theory supported by weather records made a most important contribution in suggesting dimensions that could handle the varied boats and conditions of the trial races and then win in the final America's Cup series. This gave the designers of *Stars & Stripes* confidence in a big boat, designed for the late stronger winds of Fremantle, yet not too big for the occasional lighter winds more likely in the earlier season eliminations. Dennis Conner had the satisfaction of taking the Cup back to San Diego, U.S.A., when *Stars & Stripes* became a rather easy winner.

S&S did the design for the New York Yacht Club challenger. There was no shortage of funds for a combination of tank-testing and computer simulation on which Karl Kirkman and David Greeley acted as consultants. Three new boats were successively built in Newport of aluminum alloy. Though each of the three was better than her predecessor, even the third, while strongly competitive, was not fast enough to win the challenger spot which went to *Stars & Stripes*, the San Diego boat sailed by Dennis Conner and designed by a strong group that included Brit

Chance, Dave Pedrick, and Bruce Nelson, supported by a number of consultants. The best of the other challengers was from New Zealand. *Kiwi Magic* was the first Twelve-Metre hull built of fiberglass composites.

Without overemphasis I can say that this was a difficult time, both for me and for Bill Langan, who had assumed my former position in charge of design at S&S. I was most interested but without responsibility, and my acquaintance with the new high-tech methods was limited. Yet I was asked by older members of the NYYC to watch and advise. Bill encouraged me to study the data as it emerged from the tank or computer. This material was complete and forecast well the principal parameters influencing performance. The successive hulls were good Twelve-Metre hulls, but there were steering problems with the last and best of them, possibly related to the wide wing keel, and probably also involving the contribution to stability of the wings as well as their size. *America II* may not have been optimum for the strong winds of Fremantle, and a good boat was not good enough to bring the Cup back to New York and Newport.

So ended the era of Twelve Metre ascendance. The class and the rule under which the boats were built had been my comfortable home for more than 50 years.

The next period of America's Cup racing began with more controversy. Even my editor and I cannot agree on the merits of the argument. That started with the fact that a challenger had again won, and this allowed future conditions to remain open. Quite early on, the New York Club had been able to announce that, if their defense was successful, they would accept challenges in the Twelve-Metre Class at a set date. At the same time, they set the policy of accepting the final challenge from an unspecified source determined by competition. The defending Australian club apparently planned this, though the question is moot because they lost. The winners, San Diego, were not in a position to follow this procedure until after the match. So, in the event, there was no early announcement of either class or site. Before such matters had been decided in San Diego, a challenge was made by a small New Zealand club, backed by Michael Fay, no small contender, who had supported the recent strong effort from that country.

The new challenge, in accordance with the America's Cup Deed of Gift which controlled the match conditions, contemplated a boat at the limit of waterline length — 90′. Considering the cost of competing in boats of half that length and the effect on the sport of bringing back such large boats, San Diego was reluctant to accept, and the question of their acceptance of this upsetting challenge was postponed and then went into the courts. The fine points would be better discussed by a lawyer, but the facts are that after considerable time lost in court the period needed for properly mounting a costly defense by San Diego seemed short of that needed to do anything adequate at the same scale.

Arguments are muddied by the building of a boat without the usual restrictions of a rule. It would be a mistake for one lacking legal study to consider that aspect, but one has to ask whether it was sportsmanlike to look for advantage in challenging in a completely unfamiliar type at a size which had been dropped because of its cost? My impression has been negative. Similar thoughts condition the San Diego response. I consider it a case of the pot naming the kettle.

Time would indeed be needed to build a competitive 90-footer. This assumes that the supporting model tests and computer simulations would be needed. If so they would become very time-consuming and should be particularly so when applied to new conditions surrounding a new size without class restrictions. Absence of restrictions offered a quick and economical way out with the decision to build a much smaller but potentially faster catamaran. A design group was assembled, including members with experience in the "Little America's Cup," the traditional international catamaran championship. Two sister 60′ catamarans were built. One with a solid wing sail, sailed by Dennis, raced against the New Zealand 90-footer and won easily. The challenger had already gone to court to question the defender's eligibility, and it was only after the racing that the court upheld the catamaran as a legitimate entry under the America's Cup Deed of Gift, and so confirmed the successful defense of the Cup by San Diego.

The continuous legal activity culminating in a one-sided series was a sad episode in America's Cup history which had, in the recent past, been marked by excellent racing and generally good feeling and stability. The advantages of a stable set of class rules had become clear, but the Twelve-Metre Class seemed outdated. The broader sailing community had seen lighter and faster boats accepted in the offshore classes. A hopeful answer came in the coalescence of an ad-hoc group of designers from the countries that had been active in the recent Cup history. They met first in San Diego with the blessing of the defending club. After a series of meetings, a new formula was published, not entirely unlike that which had applied to the Twelves, but offering freedom to use slightly more length with more sail, more beam, more draft, and much less displacement, constituting a materially faster boat.

I sat with this committee twice when they were meeting in London at the time of the November meetings of the IYRU and the ORC. I took no part in the determination of the rule and was negatively impressed by the decision to permit so-called asymmetrical spinnakers. In earlier days I would have called such a sail a balloon jib; it was set from the masthead to the tack point or spinnaker pole and was required to be shaped with a mid-girth great enough to make it inefficient to windward. It was, and to a degree remains, my fear that the sailmaking community will find out how to make these sails effective close-hauled, defeating the intent that they should be used only downwind. Running and reaching they add sail area —

i.e. power — where it can be carried, making the boats materially faster. Such sails were pioneered in some of the smaller classes, notably the Australian Sydney Harbor 18′ dinghies. On these boats they make possible planing or semi-planing speeds that are out of all proportion to usual size limitation. They have added to the fun and excitement of sailing and I only hope they will not be used effectively to windward as that would mean heavier spars and inclusion in the measured sail area, thus defeating their primary purpose. Despite this negative opinion it seems a fact that one can have no major objection to a clearly stated rule that applies to all concerned. Opposite sides are still drawn up on the subject of the big-boat match. My feeling has been that the letter of the rule took precedence over traditions. It remains difficult to choose.

The new America's Cup Rule worked effectively in its first tests during the 1992 series off San Diego. The best boats were evenly matched in performance and generally similar without being identical in their measurements, though one of the very best of the fleet, the New Zealander, was seen as smaller than the other good boats and came very close to winning. In the use of a new rule the countries and individual designers lost the advantage of long familiarity, as was true with the Twelve-Metre Class, and those groups that were able to make technical studies in depth were evenly matched on the water. Hulls, sails, and keels received intense study and keels were greatly varied. Two movable areas such as rudders were permitted and deep draft was permitted without much penalty. Although some radical forms or arrangements, more or less secret, appeared to work well, the winning boat had the conventional arrangement of deep, high aspect ratio — that is a short, bulbed keel with a separate deep rudder located well aft.

This winner was *America³*, financed, managed, and usually sailed by Bill Koch and designed by a group identified with MIT. She beat Dennis Conner's candidate for the defense in a series of close trials and won over the Italian challenger in the Cup match. An interesting feature of her campaign was the fact, generally understood, that great confidence was placed on hydrodynamic calculations, initially supported by tank-testing but used independently in a late decision regarding final keel design. Her sails also were effectively studied with respect to both shape and material, and an instrumented power boat proved useful in obtaining true wind measurements clear of the influence of the yacht's sails.

Thorough and detailed studies of the local conditions and the application of hydrodynamic study to hull and keel design marked the best in a fleet of good boats all based on similar principles. The 1995 series was sailed under the same measurement rule except for minor points of clarification, and the course was similar but without the Z-shaped reaching legs that had resulted in "follow the leader" sailing rather than the active competition that was continuous on the beats and runs. So the courses were entirely windward and leeward.

The series was easily won by the New Zealand entry *Black Magic*. She had dominated the trials and won easily over the American defender, *Young America*, sailed by Paul Cayard and Dennis Conner, as the result of confusing last-minute negotiations. These seemed a credit to no one although, if Dennis wished to defend once more, he got his wish. Such things have happened before, when, as in this case, the seemingly fastest defense candidate was probably not the best sailed. The Koch boat sailed by a women's crew had an excellent record but lost a critical race to Conner on a fluke. Though I do not know the differences between individual boats, narrow beam seemed to be favored in the San Diego conditions, as well as long length and generous displacement and sail area. What made the New Zealander so good is hard to say, though it could be seen that her sails were very flat and the rig looked rather far aft on the hull. The overall combination was exceptional.

A notable event of the '95 series was the sinking of an Australian boat and considerable wave damage or other structural damage to several others. Whether or not improvements in scantlings are needed is a matter of viewpoint, but there is no doubt that the effort to place all possible weight in the ballast has resulted in carefully designed but fragile hulls.

15

After 1980 the sailing I did was sporadic. Although I was well, age made me feel clumsy on a boat. I remained actively interested in the developing technology of racing-yacht design and followed that activity through membership in several committees on the rules and through such use as I could make of the computer. Still, I was able to spend a little time on the water, mostly at the invitation of owners pleased with older wooden boats that had been meticulously kept or restored. I enjoyed these opportunities a great deal, as well as one or two short cruises with friends.

Although we seem to have returned to the boats, I can say only that many things went on as I lived in retirement. It was during this period, in the early 1980s, that I made a trip to China with a group from the Society of Naval Architects and Marine Engineers. It was a good experience although, due to my concentration on sailing boats, there was not much in the way of common interest between most of the travelers and me. We visited several universities and towing tanks and saw models of river boats, though we assumed there were high-speed naval vessels and probably submarines in the wings. We took turns giving lectures to teachers and students, but I did not feel that there was much interest in my inevitable subject.

In China we traveled by train and plane, both relatively primitive. The planes were not well-instrumented and the pilots were very respectful of the weather, so that our itinerary was twice changed. We were duly impressed by a day at the Great Wall and another visiting historic areas of Beijing. I wished that Xian or the Gorges of the Yangtze had been possible. Though my age was only mid-seventies, I was impressed by the respect of our government-supplied guide for my age, and respect in general for all elderly people. Mainland China was sufficiently interesting in its people and places that when we wound up with two days in Hong Kong they seemed wasted.

I continued the habit of going to London for the annual November meetings of the Offshore Racing Council, where there were many old friends and worthwhile discussions of boats and rating rules. The group had generously made me a Councillor of Honour and Emeritus, and they made me feel very welcome and not the old fogey that I was fast becoming. For several years I did not want to be away from Susie, as she had become ill, but after she went on I attended the meetings. In 1996 I missed the ORC meetings held in Brighton, as I was working on a paper to be presented at the 1997 Chesapeake Sailing Yacht Symposium in Annapolis. I have attended there regularly, meeting friends and keeping up with the technical side of sailing and design. Even though I have many times felt that it was a mistake to be so single-minded, as I fear Susie thought, my computer activity associated with sailing performance has given me an involvement that is lacking in too many retired people, and through common interests this has kept some friendships active which might have faded under other circumstances.

It was in 1985 that Susie told me of a lump in her breast. We talked to our Brattleboro family doctor who sent us to the hospital in Hanover, New Hampshire, about 60 miles north. The usual steps followed, leading to a mastectomy and a hopeful prognosis. It was not something good, but we hoped that the difficulty was over. Maybe it was — almost. I thought with five good years we would be in the clear.

One of our pleasures in Putney was going to the music at Marlboro College.

We enjoyed the music together, but in the summer of 1989 Susie was finding that sitting through a concert was uncomfortable for her and we went less often. As her back grew more painful she went to our doctor in Brattleboro who made tests. He suspected kidneys and made a cat scan and other tests. It was exhaustive in many ways before he said, reluctantly, that it was the cancer back again. Back at Hanover we met the oncologist who was optimistic about the effect of a certain medicine. He visited an office in Brattleboro at intervals and we saw him there, and Susie took the pills. For something like a year she said there was very little change. She made little of it, though we went regularly to see the doctor in Brattleboro.

Always concerned about cancer, I had for years made small contributions to the Memorial Sloan-Kettering Cancer Center in New York, hoping it was right to do something to fight the disease. I wondered whether we should go to see them, but Susie didn't want to do that, and I did not insist. Somehow an active battle was not what either of us wanted, and Hanover had a very good reputation. It was during this time, early in '91, that we realized we could not be entirely passive, that we would have to think ahead. Nancy, our daughter-in-law, though divorced from Sam and remarried to a Dartmouth professor, was still on good terms and friendly. During a visit she remarked "What do you know about Kendal?" We knew little but we checked and what we learned appealed to us both.

Kendal is a retirement community just north of Hanover that had recently been formed by a Quaker organization of Philadelphia and was soon to open. We were pretty easily convinced, by visits and a very good reference by friends in a Philadelphia community operated by the same group, that if we could get in we would be wise to do so. There were good in-house nursing arrangements and good arrangements with the nearby hospital where Susie was already a patient. The costs seemed daunting but we felt we could make it. We were concerned as to whether Susie's health would stand in the way, but it did not. We applied for an apartment and were accepted and given a September date for moving in. All of that went as planned, although it was a wrench to leave the Walpole house with much we could not possibly use in a three-room apartment. We had to accept the fact that Susie was not going to get better and that at Kendal she would have to do no more than she wanted and that she could count on professional care. It meant something, too, that we would be near the boys but in no way dependent on them. I think Susie was glad to realize that I would have a good place to live for as long as I could use it.

While Susie was in the good period after the operation I had my last fling with serious boat racing and it was not an easy one for me. It was even more difficult for Bill Langan who was fully in charge. This was the time of the America's Cup challenge of 1986-87 by the New York Yacht Club, for which S&S had been chosen as the designers with Bill carrying all the weight. I had sold all but a few shares of my

stock in the firm to Bill and Alan Gilbert, the chief engineer, and had no management responsibility, but this did not stand in the way of my great personal interest in
the results of this exciting project. In addition, friends in the yacht club repeatedly
urged me to keep an eye on the progress of the design. I was very uncomfortable at
the prospect of looking over Bill's shoulder. I was conscious of his technical background in the academic side of naval architecture, especially in theoretical fluid
dynamics. I knew this to be far beyond my own, and I felt it to be the path to success. I had brought him into the office with that confidence. On the other hand, he
could not avoid awareness of my long experience, and I'm afraid that he believed, not
entirely without reason, that the sponsors of his work had more confidence in me
than in him.

I became even closer to the work when Bill told me that his wife Candy was
expecting their first child at the time of a so-called World Championship off
Fremantle, Australia, during the year before the Cup races. He hoped I could go
there in his place and I accepted. For this challenge the money tap had been opened
so that Bill and the office had been able to employ the best methods and individual
consultants anywhere available.

In Fremantle I saw that living arrangements and crew routine were familiar from
earlier days. Crew quarters were in one house with kitchen, dining room, and social
room in a new building nearby. There were two crews and two boats in a well-organ-
ized service area that included a sail floor in a shed with room for hull work as well.
Over the slips were lifts for dry-sailing two Twelves. It was very businesslike and
impressive. All the pieces were there but I had to wonder about the whole.

The second of two new Twelves was better than the first, and although she was
well into the upper part of the fleet she did not really look like a winner. Considering
the present and looking to the future, I could see no one who was running the show.
I considered that I was there temporarily, as an observer and advisor with neither the
detailed knowledge of the boat nor the assignment to take charge. The skipper, John
Kolius, handled the boat and the sails well enough, but he felt the undercurrent of
concern and disappointment that was in the air and he was very junior to flag officers
of the NYYC who were on hand. A computer record of the boat's performance was
carefully compiled, and I think this boat was largely written off, though with hope
that the records would help in the design of a third boat, still to be built. It was then
and is now easy to find fault, but the most promising cure looked to me like a complete shakeup which no one was ready to order. The trip was interesting. I was glad
to see the boats and to learn something about Fremantle but I returned in discour-
agement. I felt that the flag officers of the NYYC expected me to turn things around
while I knew that Bill had, in his mind and in his files, two years of background
research and study which was only vaguely familiar to me. I questioned Bill and his

decisions about the final boat, but was not about to tell him what to do. In the end, boat number three was a further improvement, but Dennis Conner's big new boat dominated both the trials and the final match.

This was in 1985. We lived a pleasant, easy life until 1989 when we realized that it would have to change. We had used the car a good deal, always enjoying the country and its excursions, summer and winter. During two summers we shared, for a week or two, a cottage on Caspian Lake with Olie, Carol, and OJ, as our grandson was known. There I sometimes fished with him. During two autumns we made family excursions to Sugar Hill where Susie felt at home after the summers of her 'teens in that area. We regularly went to antique shows in Dorset and Weston and concerts in Brattleboro and Marlboro. I continued with the computer and attended IMS committee meetings, generally in Newport but sometimes farther away, as well as meetings of US Sailing, then USYRU. These were held in various sailing centers.

The move to Kendal was in September, 1991, about two months after it opened. This was certainly a change, but in the circumstances a good one. Our three-room apartment was on the ground floor, reasonably near the dining room. We made our own breakfasts and took lunch and dinner, usually in the dining room, and less often in the cafeteria. We could either take meals as a couple, or be seated with two or more other residents, as we often did, finding our neighbors a very interesting and able group. We found a surprising network of connections with our own friends and acquaintants. For a college drop-out, the population seemed to have a very strong academic flavor: many Dartmouth graduates but even more Harvard alumni, if you count graduate degrees, and many retired physicians. I have come to know them and like them more and more. Of course there are about twice as many women as men.

Susie joined in this life for most of a year, although her breathing became difficult. It grew harder until the time came when she needed a wheelchair carrying oxygen. Then she went to the hospital where fluid was taken from her lungs. Gradually this was needed more frequently and everything she did was harder. About the start of '93 the doctors found the fluid was filling her lungs too quickly to continue the treatment she was receiving and said it would be necessary to scarify the lining of Susie's chest cavity to help in keeping her lungs open. This turned out to be a very difficult and painful operation. It could not be done under a general anesthetic but morphine would make it easier. It became a tough experience for us both. As the procedure was started, the scarifying fluid was injected. Morphine was delivered too, but as the suffering became obvious they found the morphine was not getting through. Correcting this, the dose became an overdose and it was touch and go. I sat with Susie with instructions that she must be kept breathing which she might not do if she went into a sound sleep. I sat there with a machine that timed her breathing. If the count reached six I was worried, and I don't know how many times I said "Susie,

Susie breathe, Susie, wake up." I repeated this over and over, I can't say for how long; but in time, when I suppose the excess morphine had worn off, she was allowed to sleep. I think it would have been better to have let her go then, but at the time my only thought was to keep her breathing.

I stayed with Susie in the hospital. Everybody was concerned, sympathetic, and helpful, but from then on Susie was never alone. Returning home she preferred to stay with me in our apartment, and I was glad that this could be done. Technically the Kendal staff was committed to care for her in the health center but not in our apartment, and the overall nursing and support came through Hospice, although the Kendal nurses and the whole staff were always ready to help. I cannot say enough about the great help of the Hospice group in a strictly physical sense. I don't think either Susie or I could subscribe to their view of dying as a happy extension of life, at least as I have understood it. I believe, and rather hope, it's the end. The support of Hospice nurses and volunteers would have been a great experience if I had not been losing my best friend. She lived with morphine, too little, and the pain was bad, too much, and she couldn't think straight, until June when she went, quietly, as though to sleep. The boys had been with us that day and they came back the next morning. Susie had asked that there should be no service and that her body be cremated. Those minimal arrangements were carried out. Later I scattered the ashes on the Putney hillside.

What I felt at first was mainly relief. Over time I have increasingly missed simple companionship. The Kendal surroundings remained constant. I have remained active and interested in boats and racing. Outside, I picked up old friendships and formed new ones, mostly due to a common interest in sailboat technology. In most cases there have been problems to solve, and the solutions of one have led to solutions for others. One thing leads to another, and as paths cross something new happens. The effort is good for its own sake, let alone for the results.

The International Measurement System (IMS) is a story I have considered elsewhere. It is enough to say now that it was one important project out of perhaps four that kept me interested and busy. Three other projects were more individualized. In these activities the computer has played a big part. I have been slow in learning new things, and I often find this frustrating. I miss a desirable background in math, but it has been the key to participation and communication.

Before talking more of boats I should note my involvement with music. Living at Kendal has increased a long-time enjoyment of music. There is much good music in the area, centered on Dartmouth and performed by both local and visiting individuals and organizations, and there are friends who will go with me to a concert. There is often bus transportation, too. But right at Kendal have been the evenings I have most enjoyed.

At just about the time Kendal opened, the Beveridge Websters moved in. He had taught piano for years at the Juilliard School in New York and was well-known for his recitals. I think he had come reluctantly to Kendal, possibly expecting that it would be a quietly boring way to give up a way of life. But there were residents in Kendal who encouraged him to play, and there were those who arranged to find a really good piano. Beveridge began to play frequently on Saturday evenings and his many short recitals opened my ears and my feelings to piano music. In that I am no technician. I suppose Beveridge, in his eighties, has missed a few notes, but his heart has been connected to his fingers in a way no one could fail to hear. My Saturday nights could not pass without shudders of pleasure and headshaking in disbelief that felt hammers on wire could cause such emotion. I am over and over again mystified by the way surprise becomes inevitability with the touch of a finger. And in a cooler sense it became a new pleasure to realize how, in the piano solo, the structure of the music became increasingly clear and so led to a new understanding of the complexity of the exciting orchestral and choral pieces, heard less often, but still within reach.

Not long ago I had a different sort of fling with music. One day I received in the mail a compact disk with a series of early jazz and blues pieces played by Drake Sparkman's son Bob Sparkman and a young friend of his, Jerry Noble, a pianist. I knew Bob as a very talented clarinetist, though for a living he had handled marine insurance in the S&S office. He had recently retired and was living in the town of Turners Falls. I played the CD and liked it, and when I played it again for a musician friend, a retired pro, she thought it was great. On the strength of our joint opinion I passed it on to the chairman of the committee that arranges entertainment, such as that given by the Websters and others, suggesting that, as Turners Falls was no more than two hours away by car, maybe the duo could give us another good evening. That happened. Everyone who had heard the disk liked it, but none of us realized what they could do in person. The old tunes evidently had great appeal for a nostalgic audience, and the rhythmic energy and spontaneity of the catchy playing brought down the house in applause. My name was made in Kendal just because of my relation to that music, and for several days I passed no one in the hall who did not stop and thank me for a share in finding them.

I have been happy in Kendal, but an occasional change is good too. I like to attend meetings on rating rules and other facets of sailing. I have mentioned enjoying the older boats that have been well-kept or brought back to good condition, and a trip to Italy in the summer of '97 gave me one of the most enjoyable. As a part of my recent Hanover experience while part of an ongoing life, I think often of that visit to the 'thirties and to the boat I knew so well, the boat that carried me so far.

Another good experience involved the schooner *Brilliant*, a 1932 S&S design for which I was responsible, now owned and sailed by Mystic Seaport. It was early in '89 that there was a move to enter her in the CCA's Bermuda Race until the IMS committee ruled that, because the proper rating depended on the prediction of a boat's capability under a broad range of conditions, and because there was little knowledge of the schooner rig, the entry could not be accepted. The performance prediction program, the VPP, contained sail-force coefficients adequate for the sloop rig, and by some extension for cutters, yawls, and ketches, but such data for the very different schooners was lacking. Thus it happened that a Mystic member and volunteer with interests in sailing and aerodynamics, Walt Stubner, decided to try to learn what coefficients might be appropriate for *Brilliant*'s rig. His method was one I had helped Kenneth Davidson to use years before in determining the first applied sail coefficients, named for the small sloop *Gimcrack*. The simple concept was that if the drag of the hull were known, the sail forces would also be known due to the need for balancing forces to exist if the speed was constant. The study has now extended over several years and has become too complex and long to detail here, but my association began with Walt's coming to me for an estimate of *Brilliant*'s hull drag. We, with others engaged in the project, have become firm friends with continuing and constant communication by e-mail. Much of this was the subject of a paper presented to the Chesapeake Sailing Yacht Symposium in January, 1997, in Annapolis.

Tommy Wilder and his wife Adele have done much to keep me happy and busy by our frequent communications and my visits to their very pleasant home in Santa Barbara, California. I first knew Tommy as a CCA measurer in the 1960s and as a dedicated supporter of the USYRU during the early meetings of the Offshore Council in London and Europe. Susie and Adele took to each other and became closer during a wine tour preceding an ORC meeting in La Rochelle, France. This was extended at such times as the Wilders' several visits to Newport during Cup races.

Both as a race participant and as a measurer, Tommy was active in the Transpac Yacht Club, sponsors of racing from the California mainland out to Honolulu. Under successive rating rules the Transpac Race had flourished, partly because of the unique weather conditions on the course, but partly weakened, Tommy believed, because of the growing complication of the rating rules. He was an early computer buff, and our interests continued to keep us corresponding. Tommy, early on, had encouraged me to buy a fax machine, which I first used intensively when I helped him develop scratch sheets intended to make the IMS easier for Transpac competitors to gauge their relative positions in the race to Honolulu.

Complications in racing under the IMS Rule led to consideration of simpler methods, and between us we looked into the pattern of previous races and tested the use of regression by computer on back-checked results. We found the method promising. We both tested the well-known Excel computer program and found the

use of regression easy, although, as we searched for the best combination of parameters, we spent a good deal of time on experimentation. In forming the IMS, regression has been used with model-test results as targets. We had no such data but took the previous race results of selected boats with known dimensions and recorded performance over the course. These were our target points, and over time we thought this method would make for a good set of time allowances. We jointly pressed the Transpac directors to adopt the method for the 1995 race, but the rating committee decided to use the IMS formula with certain modifications. Tommy was more disappointed than I. He felt that it was unwise to use the inexact methods that had to be applied to boats lacking IMS ratings, which were allowed to race, though not eligible for the historically important prizes. As a long-time supporter of IMS I could not feel badly when it was accepted, even in a bastardized form. Checking the results by applying both methods showed close agreement between the two systems.

Soon after settling in Hanover I was told that residents, with the acceptance of the professors involved, could audit classes at Dartmouth. I took advantage of this for two courses in elementary calculus. I had absorbed very little during my time at MIT, but had studied off and on, and this was just one more small but helpful boost in a subject becoming more useful to my computer efforts and their application to increasingly higher-tech methods of yacht design. Whether due to this or something else, I received a phone call one day from a Professor Horst Richter of the Thayer School of Engineering at Dartmouth who explained that he would like to meet me because, although it was not his specialty, as an engineer and a sailor he was giving a course in the mechanics of sailing and maybe I would talk to his students. Though I have never fancied myself as a speaker, I thought this sounded interesting. I wanted to learn more and we agreed to meet. This has led to many happy hours during which we have discussed sailing as theory and practice and the engineering side of yacht design. I have talked to Horst's classes, and so have Walt Stubner and Jim Teeters, a Dartmouth graduate and sometime S&S computer wizard. These classes have normally included members of Dartmouth's sailing team.

Through Horst, and at his prompting, a local producer of flow-simulation software has allowed me to use programs offering sail-force solutions using a different method of determining the coefficients. The method, known as CFD, computational fluid dynamics, is not accepted as fully accurate for sails, making it controversial. I must admit insufficient knowledge of theoretical aerodynamics to consider myself well-informed, but work on the several sail projects has led me to considerable study of the three practical methods of determining sail forces, i.e. full-scale, like *Brilliant* or *Gimcrack*, using a wind tunnel, and CFD. I understand perhaps enough to see both good and bad features in each method, and to search for the path to the best information by study of the results of each. Possibly the best, but by far the most difficult, are really well-instrumented and conducted full-scale sailing trials.

It is true that the best results of CFD are done in three dimensions and depend on the capabilities of very powerful computers, far beyond anything I can afford. But I can do 2-D work and feel that the possibilities of simple visualization can be helpful and that there are certain questions about sail shapes and arrangements that can be usefully compared, especially if one good absolute point is available. Moreover, if given plenty of time, my computer can grind out 3-D results, although these are probably more useful visually than for absolute numbers. Happily, the efforts of Professor Richter in this field have led to contract work to be done by Dartmouth College for which powerful computers will be provided. We are on the way to a better understanding of how CFD can be applied to sail problems. It is good to see how one thing can lead to another and then yet another. At worst it will be a learning experience.

Along with these interests I have been happy in getting to know John Burgess as the organizer and manager of the Landing School of Boat Building and Design. His was another call I received after moving north. He explained that the school gave two courses, one in boatbuilding and one in small-boat design. He asked me to visit the school in Kennebunkport, Maine, and if I would, to talk to the students. We set a time and I have been thankful for the visit. The two courses are divided between about 40 students of all ages, both men and women. They study because of their love of boats and receive good training during a school year of about ten months. John and his wife, Lin, have been very good to me and we have become fast friends.

Because some facets of yacht design have become so technical I was, at first, a little concerned about how far the students could go in a year. I think the school has properly stressed the fact that the graduates were not engineers but that they were qualified in two ways: for entry-level jobs in an office or shop, or to continue a more scientific education.

All this can end only with the question "what is it good for?" and I wonder about the answer. Does better technology add to the sum of pleasure in the world? I have found boats, especially sailboats, a fascinating lifetime study. They have given me a comfortable living, and encouraged many people to get safely out on the water, and to have a good deal of fun. Friends have said they were beautiful. So far, so good. But is a faster or bigger boat any more fun? Is life any better for hundreds of thousands of dollars and hours of testing and calculation? I'm afraid I doubt it. We can't go back, but I'm convinced that knowledge can injure sport. On the surface it's in cost, but when everything can be done with dollars, it's no longer about fun, and participation is limited to the apex.

Personally, I don't care much for the latest racing-sailboat designs, although there can be no doubt that they are fast. The fact that they are less seaworthy simply validates theories of compensation. But as we know more and more, we learn that we have to choose. Racing is the clearest illustration, as the cost for each infinitesimal improvement rises with no end. The game has been spoiled by the very activity that has been my life.

I am not unduly saddened by a natural law. But again I have to ask do we know but not learn? Mine is the twentieth century. It is possible, though most unlikely, that I may reach the twenty-first. If I live so long, I hope more than anything that I don't lose my enjoyment of music. In our increasing ability to know, and perhaps not learn, maybe we are all in a bind between the long and the short term. I have already said that technical activities are combined to satisfy continuing curiosity about what makes sailing boats behave as they do. There are obvious analogies. I still wonder about the value to our world of our studies, but there is no doubt about their value to me.

16

During the 'nineties, sailing for me took a new turn and
made a comeback, and that has been due to the older boats.
My involvement with boats remained after my formal
retirement in 1978, continued through 1980 in active
consulting, and then returned during a period in 1986.
Then I went to Fremantle, Australia, standing in for Bill
Langan whose first child was expected during a Twelve
Metre championship. Separation from the America's Cup
was neither immediate nor complete, but the frequent
opportunities to sail on new boats had been abruptly cut
off, and I was busy ashore. I began the effort to learn the
ways of a computer. Friends asked whether I did not miss
sailing and I replied that I was doing my sailing on a
computer. I enjoyed the country and the activity around
the new house in Putney.

NEW AND OLD

More recently, I have found myself more often on the water. I have liked it personally, and I think it has more positive implications. My new experiences on the water are a result of deepening interest in older boats, especially those that were built of wood. I was first aware of it in California during a visit to Tommy Wilder, maybe in '94. He had arranged a lunch at the Newport Harbor Yacht Club and a number of owners had brought S&S-designed boats in to floats near the club. It was a nice occasion. Most of them were at least 20 years old, and the owners of the still older wooden boats seemed proudest of all to show them to me. I, of course, was happy to sense their appreciation.

Well before that time there were isolated cases of old S&S boats being given new life. *Stormy Weather*, one of my favorites, had been rescued by Paul Applethwaite, and was sailed, even raced, in the Fastnet, at Antigua and elsewhere. Since restoring *Stormy*, Paul has made more than 20 Atlantic crossings. I had also seen *Bolero* undergoing a complete overhaul. *Brilliant* was being beautifully maintained at Mystic Seaport. Good older boats were no longer being left to rot in shipyards or mud berths; rather they were being tracked down by individuals who were prepared to pay, often more than the cost of new building, to make these ghosts live again.

Elizabeth Meyer's restoration of the British America's Cup challenger of 1934 was possibly the most spectacular of these rescues. *Endeavour*, the big J-Boat designed for T.O.M. Sopwith by Charles Nicholson, is a wonderful example of the compatibility of beauty and speed, one of the greatest in all yacht design. She had survived the war, and by the 1980s rested in a mud berth on the Isle of Wight where she had been spotted by a group of young men intent on her restoration. They had moved her to Calshot Spit, a sandy point in the Solent that had been used before the war as a naval seaplane depot. She had been hauled onto the beach and rested in a cradle where their money and determination had run out. Elizabeth then found her and bought her. Applying exceptional management skills, in place of missing shipyard facilities, the deteriorated steel frames and plating were replaced, ballast was restored, and the now-watertight hull was launched and towed to Holland where her full restoration was completed at the yard of Wolter Huisman. There in a good shipyard it took only money, which Elizabeth was lucky to have, but I can't help feeling that she had to have something more important than money to get *Endeavour* off that sand spit and into the water. *Endeavour* has, for several years, been sailed on both coasts, sometimes by her owner, other times by charterers. She has everywhere been admired and has inspired many similar projects, if usually on a smaller scale.

For me the most satisfying and exciting experience has been to see *Dorade* brought back to life. This began with the unexpected travel and excitement of a trip to Italy in the early summer of '97 and the opportunity to see and actually sail *Dorade* reincarnated. I know now that at nearly age 70 she is still in good hands.

It is a nice story. I had seen her once since she left the east coast in 1935. This was about 1979 in San Francisco when she came sailing by the St. Francis Yacht Club where I was having lunch. A friend, Bob Keefe, had set up the meeting. Then, late in May of 1997, I received a phone call from Mitch Neff, in the S&S office, to say that I was going to get an invitation from Italy that he hoped I would accept. It would mean a trip to Italy as the guest of a new owner, Giuseppe Gazzoni, who had bought *Dorade*, badly run down, and arranged for her complete restoration. I duly received the call and needed no persuasion to accept.

I was told that Alitalia would have tickets for me in Boston for the evening flight to Rome on June third. I felt I had a very generous host when I boarded the plane and was met the next morning by Federico Nardi, the proprietor of the shipyard in Porto Santo Stefano and his pretty young office manager, Valeria, who became my chauffeur for the next five days. Valeria admires the older boats, and I have to admit my pleasure in the degree to which she seemed, in our few days, to take a shine to their designer. I am happy to think that the chemistry is good, and I can say that our continued exchanges by mail have given me a lift, but the realities are recognized in the fact that she has a heavy boyfriend in Verona and that I am 92 years old to her 28 and our homes are far apart. Even to say that implies a certain feeling that I hope is not inappropriate. In a report on my life and activity, I feel that Valeria has a place.

The yard was a little more than an hour's drive northwest from Rome on the island of Argentario, where Nardi and his workers have specialized in wooden-yacht restoration. The condition of *Dorade* showed their skill and commitment to perfection. The 1930 boat might have been new, such was the bottle smoothness of her topsides and the shine of her brightwork. The original tiller had replaced the wheel steering installed by a later owner. The interior was back to what it had been in 1930, including some wood lattice I had specified over glass doors in main-cabin lockers. She was up on the ways ready to go overboard the next day.

So it was to a *ristorante* for lunch, then to the attractive Pelicano resort on the Mediterranean side of Argentario for a nap, then back on the road for dinner with Federico, Valeria, and Giles, the English skipper of *Dorade*. Good night all and ready for sleep. The next day *Dorade* was blessed by the priest and baptized by champagne from a bottle broken by owner and designer swinging together, then launched in the rain. It would have taken more than rain to dampen that day. Launching was followed by drinks and hors d'oeuvres, and a ride to a jolly party

Giuseppe Gazzoni and I are shown entering the yard on the day of *Dorade*'s rebirth. I owe Dr. Gazzoni a great debt of gratitude for his readiness to save *Dorade*, as I do also the manager of the yacht yard, Federico Nardi, whose mind and heart are devoted to perfection in the work done by his dedicated crew. (Photo: Valeria Polombo)

at a restaurant high above the yard. Here the meal was the one that would have been served outdoors at the yard. This celebration was primarily for the yard workers and their families, and I think most of the town was there. It was good food and good fun. Following an afternoon rest we had a pleasant, slightly more formal dinner at the summer place of Giuseppe Gazzoni, the owner.

The high point came the next day with a sail under perfect conditions. The sun was out and the breeze light as new sails were bent on and we killed the power that had been added after she left family hands. They let me take the tiller as the breeze grew slowly in the bay east of the island. It was like the 'thirties. What else can I say?

After a great sail I became a sightseer, just happy to be in Italy. After lunch new friends named Corsini showed me their interesting garden of exotic palms. On Saturday we drove up the coast to a big new (to me) marina at Punta Ala and on to Viareggio, where the Italian America's Cup challenge is being prepared. All three boats and their equipment from Bill Koch's powerful America's Cup efforts had been bought by the new challenger, Prada, the firm of Signor Bertelli. Returning south, we stopped again at Punta Ala where we ran into two American designers, Bruce Farr and Doug Peterson, colleagues, friends, and past rivals. Farr had been selected as lead designer of the Young America/NYYC challenge, while Peterson was associated with German Frers in the Prada group. On Sunday the designer-sightseer was glad to absorb another side of Italy, the lovely town of Siena, and then back to Rome and on to Boston on Monday morning. Valeria drove us to Siena and Rome, taking Giles and myself.

I had time to reflect on all the many good people of this recent experience. Signor Gazzoni, the generous owner, Federico who takes so much pride in turning old into new, Valeria, so young and pretty, whose company I so enjoyed. And then, especially, I thought about two more — my brother Rod who had supervised *Dorade*'s building, much still sound after 67 years, and my father, Rod Sr., who had the courage to bet on his two young sons to challenge a successful generation. I reflected, too, that when *Dorade* was designed I had been tested by exactly three boats as hardware — a 21′ one-design class, a Six Metre with some promise but no racing record, and a very simple 30-footer in which we had sailed one race from New London to Gibson Island in Chesapeake Bay. What made that possible? It was luck, pure luck — but not conventional luck. It was luck to have intuition that worked.

I have described my Italian experience in some detail as the high point of the veteran-boat trend as it has affected me. But it has come on as something much wider. Veteran and classic boat rallies have become common in the Mediterranean, and the experience with *Dorade* was renewed when I accepted an invitation to be the guest of the Assonautica Imperia this past September 1998. This was a rally of some 140 older boats, racing in four classes, those of pre-1970 and those more recent but still over a certain age, and those with either jib-headed or gaff rigs. *Dorade* was there with Valeria part of the crew and a frequent dinner companion. I sailed in *Dorade* on three different days in two races which she won easily, even without a generous time allowance resulting from her age. The widespread interest in the S&S boats and the activities of the association of that name made this another exciting time. The constant attention and hospitality of Matteo Salomon and Patrick Mattiessen of the S&S Association, who had set up a large tent with models, photos, and prints of our plans, and the constant requests for autographs added an unexpected dimension to it all. This gathering at Imperia is said to be second in interest and attendance only to the Nioulargue, a similar event held at Nice that includes new boats. There has developed a circuit of older-boat rallies on the Italian, Spanish, and French coasts of the Med.

The recognition signified by the existence of the S&S association is naturally very pleasant and gratifying to me, as have been favorable comments on certain S&S yachts, but when considering the older wooden boats it would be wrong not to recognize the work of two great Scottish designers of the beginning of the twentieth century — William Fife, Jr., and G.L.Watson. Both set patterns for beauty that have truly been for all time and I, in common with other later designers, have paid them the compliment of accepting them as guides to an impossible perfection.

If the appreciation of older boats is better organized in the rallies of the Mediterranean than in any U.S. events, the extension, here and abroad, of racing in the metre classes has still brought out older boats along with new ones. The Six, Eight, and Twelve-Metre Classes are examples. Racing and the construction of new boats has never completely stopped among the Sixes and Eights, although the last Twelves were those of 1986. Now all those classes have divisions for the still older boats, including some with gaff rigs and club topsails, beautiful to see and still fast on the days of light weather. Usually there is a dividing line around 1967, 30-odd years ago, when, among Twelves, *Intrepid* introduced her class to the separated keel and rudder.

Pretty run down after a period of neglect, *Intrepid* was recently rebuilt to her original lines and I sailed her in a fresh and rainy easterly in Long Island Sound. Ashore, later, the rebuilder and designer were guests of the new owner at a dinner that could not have been a greater celebration if *Intrepid* had been new. The older boats have found a number of active centers: Newport for the American Twelves; Rochester, New York and Geneva, Switzerland, for Eight Metres. I think the Sixes are most active in Scandinavia, although there are fleets in the U.S.

Mystic Seaport has contributed significantly to this interest in older boats. The museum's maintainance and constant use of the schooner *Brilliant* has shown many members and visitors the combination of charm and utility possible in early 1930s design and construction. These old boats are safe and practical, too; *Brilliant* has been sailed widely by varied crews of school children and chartering elders, building as by reflection interest in the museum. If *Brilliant* is an example of the best of wooden boatbuilding, she demonstrates well what was possible. Less used, but maintained and exhibited, are the many yachts and commercial vessels shown at Mystic that have encouraged interest in early types. Other marine museums are playing their part in this spreading phenomenon, all combining to contribute to the interest in older boats and the understanding of their capability.

If on a different level for me, a similar movement has developed in the motorboat field. In this country the antique and classic powerboat enthusiasm has been better organized than anything for the sailors. Meetings and rallies are regularly held in freshwater locations such as the Thousand Islands, the Muskoka Lakes in Canada, Lake George and other places in the Adirondacks, the many lakes of Michigan, and Lake Tahoe in the west. Mystic Seaport holds an annual Antique and Classic Boat Show, and a Small Craft Workshop for traditional small boats. Mark Mason, an old-powerboat enthusiast, collector, and restorer, gave me a great day on Lake Winnipesaukee, running in several boats of the late 'twenties and

early 'thirties that I had known when they were being designed or built. That was when I worked at the Nevins yard under their designer, George Crouch. These bright-finished mahogany runabouts, one with a modern engine, were good for speeds up to 70 miles an hour. It was exciting to get out with Mark who knew their handling. They are boats that fully combine beauty and efficiency.

It is intriguing to consider that back in the 1930s I remember yachts that were considered old after 20 years or less. That age might be doubled today without great surprise, while older and often badly deteriorated hulls are now picked up by delighted owners who spend freely to restore them. It is interesting to speculate just why. The best materials were available before the Second World War, and the best yards, among which Nevins stood out, had skilled shipwrights. Now in this age of mass production and synthetic materials, there is reassurance of craftsmanship and value in the older and simpler hulls.

Appreciation of individually done art — drawing, painting, and sculpture — is as old as time. Decorative arts such as fabrics and furniture have a long history; but the high status of other useful objects has come in our lifetime. Interesting to me are cars and boats; but there are collectors and museums of trains and clothes, breadboards and kitchen utensils. Am I right that this is new? And if so, what are the criteria for age and value? The dividing line is less clear than the trend which surely exists.

Beauty is said to be in the eye of the beholder. It is an important but not essential element of the desirable example. I see it as a contrast between few old and many new. To be unique contributes value. Mass production has entered the art museums, but rather as an example of the ironic; the restored boats are mostly one-off, although a good wooden one-design can be highly acceptable — i.e., the Herreshoff New York Thirty *Linet*, restored by Nardi, that received a prize as best restored boat at Imperia. *Dorade* had received the prize in '97. Wood construction is desired, especially if the original was an example of fine workmanship and material. Aluminum alloy is interesting historically, especially if it dates back to the 1950s, the time of wholesale transition from wood. Steel is more acceptable on larger than smaller boats. But metal is hard and lacks the associations and recalled fragrance of wood. Wood's capacity for bending in a fair line is another of its aesthetic values. To be unique is surely part of the charm. Another part is a strong human contribution. With appropriate hand tools and some skill the older boat can be duplicated. I like to think that this also applies to cars. Any part of a Bugatti might be made by a skilled mechanic; given time, that might be true of a Ferrari as well, but a Volkswagen or Ford? No.

If the 1950s mark a steep decline from wood toward aluminum alloy for many of the best custom-built boats, and toward GRP for standardized construction, which then was just beginning to pick up, recent decades have seen wood make a visible return. I think the restored examples, their value in the eyes of some owners, and the opportunity they have given a new generation to appreciate the beauty of wood, have all contributed to a revival of wood boatbuilding, which is a craft and even an art. Younger men, and women too, are taking courses in wood construction from the old-timers and working on new or old designs, as well as restorations. Compared with either metal or GRP, wood's characteristic of bending smoothly and fairly between support points appeals to the eye and aids performance. Not a good conductor of heat or sound, a wooden boat is quiet and insulated from the environment, and it is fragrant, which cannot be said of the plastic resins. Wood needs maintenance, but reacts beautifully to good care. In itself this effort creates a bond to the wood. The renewed appreciation of wood as a material for boats is easy to understand.

I have tried to review this trend as I have seen it grow, and as it has balanced for me a lifelong interest in "new tech." I think appreciation for the traditional and the hand-crafted extends wider than boats and offers a corrective to our times. For my part I have found in it a new source of pleasure and a new reason to go sailing.

CONCLUSION

"Most things have something to do with everything" – Gertrude Stein

S ailing boats have been the center of my life, but by opening other
paths I escaped to a degree from making it only sailing. There were
experiences that resulted from boats and others that just happened.
Most of the travel and many friends were results of sailing experience, but
family and other satisfactions were many. Interest in painting and music,
related in their design aspects; the travel experiences and buildings; architecture, where an afternoon at the Getty in Los Angeles showed again what
architecture can do–these were all constants. The views from the Getty hill-
top were inspiring, and enhanced by the buildings, but were the paintings
put in the shade? I think so. Love of the country and the mountains is the
equal to love of the sea. These gifts have stayed with me.

I have respect for those who practice religion but the words of a church
service make me squirm. But there are times when an experience, the inti-
mate vastness of a cathedral, some view of a landscape, some pattern in
music, some sequence of words in a book, can bring on a feeling of
epiphany. It is Saturday afternoon and I am hearing the "Magic Flute."
That comes close. Though I have not stressed books, I have counted on
reading in many fields, from poetry to the history of science. Books have
been a constant. I have bought and read books from boyhood to the
present. The hardest part of moving to a small apartment has been the loss
of space for books. Old friends have been lost. Libraries I have used very
little, as I like the repeat reference to be handy. Now I read more slowly, but
the things books can do are above value. Yet today it is all so different.

My thinking tends toward design. Though I have always loved paintings,
they remain mysterious. I cannot explain a painting or a landscape as I can
discuss a building or a piece of music, a sculpture or a book. I cannot explain
a progression from the abstract toward the explicit meaning.

I have tried to tell this story as a true history, but I know that no history
is true; it depends on who is telling it, and over the years that who is no
longer the same who. Am I the person who sailed in the Six-Metre Class in
1930? So it is not only sailing that has changed but the yardstick too and the

color of the glasses worn by the recorder. One of the confusions.

To sum up is not easy because I am confused in a confusing world. The conclusions of today could change tomorrow. Complexity, constantly twisting and turning and weaving randomly, patterns without patterns, has grown too fast. Still, of anchors, sailing has been the most secure, and other experiences have made it possible to hang on.

The near sea is a changing, turbulent sea, but the distant sea looks smooth. Life and work find their way across both. Boats and sailing are like that: the details change but the way they move under the wind does not. Acquainted with the sea and boats, I have described how the near view has changed. Maybe the longer view will hold. I hope.

Perhaps the confusion is inevitable because there is so little difference between balance and contrast, contradiction. The beginning and end of a circle. I have observed the growing application of science to my work while becoming convinced that the sport has lost something and offers less enjoyment, less fun. Am I wrong to see this same Ferris wheel motion in the big world? Simultaneously up and down.

I have to accept that my association with boats has been successful. I am told that there has been something unusual about it, and I am asked to tell of exceptional experiences that I don't recall as unusual. All of us weigh events differently. I see an ongoing succession of the lucky and the routine, though it's hard, sometimes, to say which is which. I have tried to describe some events that seemed notable and to express some opinions that have been pro or con. Many looked right at the time but now look wrong. Decisions were pressing and had to be made then, not today. I designed boats because of the joy I had sailing; but I am pragmatic, I say realistic, not romantic. Maybe the old wooden boats are an exception. I believe in the physical laws and the mathematics behind them and am disappointed that I do not know them better. Identical boats sail identically, but recognizing the host of variables that is hard to prove. Good boats result from rational thinking.

Recently there has been concern about professionalism in sailing. Sailing is my first concern, but is there not something incongruous in any sport pursued for money? Confusion describes my thinking about that. We have to agree that it is a fact in today's sailing. It is a source of income to the pros and of interest to us who watch. But is it not the fun that defines it as a sport? The more immediate questions come up in cross-competition, the occasional vs. the constant, and especially when some owners have professional help which others don't want or can't afford. That doesn't appeal to

me, but the owner has a right to learn. That's a conflict between one good
and another. And there is the difficulty of definition. I'd like to think that
the pros are simply those who sail as skipper or crew for prize money or are
paid by an owner to sail or crew his boat. There are fine lines, as between
the designers or sailmakers and the owners, and the lines are exploited. Sadly
that is
another fact.

Other professional sports do not offer good role models.

Sponsorship is another difficult subject. My gut feeling is strongly
negative. But the fox is in the henhouse and evidently there to stay. It is
costly to manage today's racing. The sport has quickly become dependent
on a very degrading practice.

The boats, of course, have changed for the faster but, as sea boats, the
poorer. That negative has to do mainly with comfort and sailing pleasure.
Intelligent use of new materials allows a light hull to be safe in terms of
staying afloat. The extremes are among the racers, and it is only the worst
of them that are literally dangerous: the "around alone" type. It is disappointing that so little of our greatly increased new knowledge has been
applied to all-'round improvement. Comfort at sea is a worthy objective.
Good reinforced GRP construction is now incredibly strong, but beamy,
shallow hull shapes are unkind to their crews at sea.

The trends I have cited have been felt internationally. A boat intended to
meet conditions anywhere in the world must be a good boat. As a long-time
supporter of organized international racing I see it as the best hope for
better boats and better sailing. I hope that through international cooperation
broad solutions may be found and good directions supported. But in this,
again, we have the near and the far. Many of the near details are problems.
It takes thought and responsible consideration to avoid letting local or
short-term concerns stand in the way of broad agreement in matters of
wider policy. That has been a recurrent difficulty. International associating,
battling the urge to split, has meant a lot to me.

Because we went at it hard I am not sure whether or not we sometimes
went too far. I am thinking of the preparations made by the Six-Metre team
that sailed in the Solent in 1932. I have described that, and I could add
similar cases. I have told how hard we worked to prepare and how easily we
won. What are the rational and fair limits to serious preparation? Are there
limits? My broad view has, again, to do with balance. If the contestants have
similar views of the importance of the sport and of winning, and if they are
matched in the degree of effort they are ready to expend, then the match is

fair and good. It's fun to participate. When the competitors have great differences in approach, any contest is less than satisfactory. Or should I say unfair? Today, in the America's Cup, intensity is the norm from start to finish. But the money, demanding sponsorship, puts me off. I wanted to win, always, intensely, and I suppose that is why I often did. And it was intensely good when it happened. But again there was a balance. The will to win helped to offset deficiencies on the technical side, yet that was somehow balanced again by efforts to learn and use what I had.

In all phases of my work I was conscious of the need for balance, and I did my best to find balance in both the long and the short view. Broadly I think I can say that I applied the principles of balance in design, in business and in the pleasures I enjoyed. Since I studied physics in high school I have coupled balance and compensation–disbelief in the free lunch, which to me applies to no end of situations, if not universally. So nothing is expected for nothing, and as in the VPP the forces of drive and drag are balanced. Sometimes after it all works out there is a dividend. Remember and accept the frequent antagonism between good things, multiplicity and good order, cost and return, so many choices. And, happily, the way work and play, when balanced, feed each other.

I come back to the confusion, the contrast, and in the end I feel doubt whether our technological and scientific learning has given us a better sport or a happier world. I fear we have lost. If I am a pessimist on the big issues of our life today, yet I have to reflect on the goodness I have seen in individuals. I see great goodwill every day and kindness beyond description. And I have recalled, in reviewing my own story, the many friends who have helped me on my way. I have lived well with the hope that it is the activity that must count, the process, the doing. The result is only what happens. We press on but we can't control the end. The poet Rilke speaks of "the many-digited sum that solves into zero." Enough said.

INDEX

Page references in *italics* indicate figures or photgraphs. References followed by n indicate notes.